AGEING AND THE MEDIA

International Perspectives

Edited by
Virpi Ylänne

First published in Great Britain in 2022 by

Policy Press, an imprint of
Bristol University Press
University of Bristol
1-9 Old Park Hill
Bristol
BS2 8BB
UK
t: +44 (0)117 374 6645
e: bup-info@bristol.ac.uk

Details of international sales and distribution partners are available at
policy.bristoluniversitypress.co.uk

British Library Cataloguing in Publication Data
A catalogue record for this book is available from the British Library

ISBN 978-1-4473-6203-6 hardcover
ISBN 978-1-4473-6205-0 ePub
ISBN 978-1-4473-6206-7 ePdf

Cover design: Dave Worth
Front cover image: Unsplash / Tim Mossholder
Bristol University Press and Policy Press use environmentally responsible
print partners.
Printed in Great Britain by CPI Group (UK) Ltd, Croydon, CR0 4YY

FSC
www.fsc.org
MIX
Paper from
responsible sources
FSC® C013604

Contents

List of figures and tables

Figures

Tables

Notes on contributors

Doris A. Boateng is a social worker and Senior Lecturer at the Department of Social Work, University of Ghana. She completed a split-site PhD programme in Social Work at the University of Ghana and the University of Manitoba in Canada. She is interested in women's empowerment issues, mental health, gender issues, policy studies and community development. Her current research examines attitudes, experiences and perceptions of Ghanaians toward mental illness, stigma, treatment beliefs, barriers and promoters to access and engagement, and pathways to service utilisation. Her recent publication discusses novel opportunities women in family businesses in Ghana are leveraging to gain economic empowerment.

Gisela G. S. Castro is Full Professor in the Graduate Studies Programme in Communication and Consumption Practices at the Advanced School of Advertising and Marketing (ESPM), São Paulo, Brazil. Her main research areas are ageing and the media, ageing and the entertainment industry, and the shifting portrayals of ageing in the longevity market. She is a licensed psychologist and holds a PhD in Communication and Culture (Federal University of Rio de Janeiro). Her latest books are *Os Velhos na Propaganda: Atualizando o Debate* (Pimenta Cultural, 2018); *Comunicação, Mídia e Envelhecimento no Contemporâneo: Perspectivas Multidisciplinares* (edited with Tania Hoff, Sulina, 2018).

Lucia Cedeira Serantes is Assistant Professor (LDI) at the Faculty of Information and Media Studies, The University of Western Ontario, Canada. Her research focus resides in the interplay between identity, media and social structures to study the complexity of the everyday of reading for pleasure. She has presented her research in library-focused and interdisciplinary conferences and has chapter contributions about comics and reading in the 2nd edition of *Transforming Young Adult Services* (2019), *Reading Still Matters* (2018) and *Young People Reading: Empirical Research Across International Contexts* (2018). She has recently published the book *Young People, Comics, and Reading: Exploring a Complex Reading Experience* (Cambridge University Press, 2019).

Chin-Hui Chen is Associate Professor in the National Pingtung University of Science and Technology, Taiwan. Since graduating from Cardiff University, UK, she has been dedicated to developing gerontological sociolinguistics in Taiwan. Her current research interests focus on communication strategies people employ in social interactions with older people. Her recent publications have discussed such issues in contexts such as young–old first-encounter talk, teacher–student communication in senior education, long-term home care communication and dementia care communication. She has published in journals such as *The International Journal of Aging and Human Development*, *International Journal of Ageing and Later Life* and *International Journal of Society, Culture & Language*.

Christa Lykke Christensen is Associate Professor in Film and Media Studies at the Department of Communication, University of Copenhagen, Denmark. Her research interests include media, ageing and health. She has published on the visual representation of older people and on older people's usage of media regarding health. Her publications can be found, for example, in several issues of *Nordicom Review*, and in an edited book: Christa Lykke Christensen and Anne Jerslev (eds) *Ældre Mennesker i et Mediesamfund* (*Older People in a Media Age*) (Frydenlund Academic, 2017).

Nicole Dalmer is Assistant Professor in the Department of Health, Aging and Society at McMaster University, Ontario, Canada. Nicole's work resides at the intersection of information and care, studying how ageing in place contexts, assumptions surrounding digital literacies and evolving family responsibilities shape who is able and who is expected to be informed in care relationships. Other projects include an international collaboration examining the impact of digital infrastructures on feelings of connectedness in later life and an investigation of the role that public library branches play in mitigating older adults' experiences of social isolation. She has published in *Ageing & Society*, *Journal of Aging Studies*, *Dementia* and *Library and Information Science Research*.

Chris Gilleard is Honorary Associate Professor in the Division of Psychiatry at University College London, UK. He has co-authored a number of books with Paul Higgs including *Cultures of Ageing* (2000); *Contexts of Ageing* (2005); *Ageing, Corporeality and Embodiment* (2013); and *Social Divisions in Later Life* (2020). He has published widely on the social and historical aspects of ageing and old age. He is a Fellow of the Academy of Social Sciences.

Jeff Hearn is Senior Professor in Human Geography, formerly Gender Studies, at Örebro University, Sweden; Professor Emeritus in the Hanken School of Economics, Finland; Professor of Sociology at the University of Huddersfield, UK; and co-managing editor of Routledge Advances in Feminist Studies and Intersectionality. His recent books include *Unsustainable Institutions of Men*, co-edited with Ernesto Vasquez del Aguila and Marina Hughson (Routledge, 2019); *Age at Work*, with Wendy Parkin (Sage, 2021); *Knowledge, Power and Young Sexualities*, with Tamara Shefer; and *Digital Gender-Sexual Violations*, with Matthew Hall and Ruth Lewis (both

Routledge, 2022). Hearn is a co-researcher in the MASCAGE project (2019–22).

Paul Higgs is Professor of the Sociology of Ageing in the Faculty of Brain Sciences at University College London, UK. Higgs edits the journal *Social Theory and Health* and has published widely in social gerontology and medical sociology. He has been involved in researching the social effects of dementia through two UK government funded projects, MARQUE and PRIDE, and is currently involved in project APPLE-tree. He is also a collaborator on the EU-funded INDUCT and DISTINCT international training networks, examining the role of technology in dementia. He is a Fellow of both the UK Academy of Social Sciences and the Gerontological Society of America.

Yan-Hua Huang is a postgraduate, affiliated with the National Pingtung University of Science and Technology, Taiwan, working with Dr Chin-Hui Chen as a research assistant, for her research on dementia care communication and the media representation of older people with dementia.

Laura Hurd is Professor of Sociology in the School of Kinesiology at the University of British Columbia in Vancouver, Canada. She has published widely in the areas of ageing, the body and social inclusion/exclusion in journals such as *Ageing and Society*, *Journal of Aging Studies*, *Women and Aging*, *Men and Masculinities*, *Qualitative Health Research*, *Canadian Journal on Aging*, *Health: An Interdisciplinary Journal for the Social Study of Health, Illness and Medicine* and *Sociology of Health and Illness*. Her book, *Facing Age: Women Growing Older in Anti-aging Culture*, was published by Rowman & Littlefield in 2011.

Loredana Ivan is Associate Professor in the Communication Department at the National University of Political Studies and Public Administration, Bucharest, Romania. She has a PhD in Sociology and a postdoctorate in Social Psychology and is the Chair of the European Network of Aging Studies. Her areas of research interest include interpersonal communication mediated by technology, fake news and generations, and family communication. She has led special issues on ageing and communication technology ('Fighting Fake News: A Generational Approach', *Societies*, 2021; 'Ageing and Interpersonal Communication', *Societies*, 2020; and 'Ageing and Digital Communication', *ESSACHESS – Journal for Communication Studies*). She is the author and co-author of several book chapters that draw on ageism and digital communication.

Eugène Loos is Associate Professor at the Utrecht University School of Governance, the Netherlands, and a member of the Research School NIG

(Netherlands Institute of Government). He researches the (ir)relevance of age and life stage for digital information search behaviour, the perception of the reliability of digital information, and the identification with images in digital information sources. His publications include *Generational Use of New Media* (Ashgate, 2012, co-edited with Haddon and Mante-Meijer), *New Media Technologies and User Empowerment* (Peter Lang, 2011, co-edited with Pierson and Mante-Meijer) and *The Social Dynamics of Information and Communication Technology* (Ashgate, 2008, co-edited with Haddon and Mante-Meijer), and other refereed (inter)national publications.

Karin Lövgren is Lecturer and Researcher at Gävle University, Sweden. Lövgren's research interests are in ageing, gender, media and popular culture. She has published in the *Journal of Women & Aging*, *Kulturella Perspektiv* (Cultural Perspectives) and *Äldre I Centrum* (Elderly in Focus), and contributed to several anthologies: *Representing Ageing: Images and Identities* (Ylänne, 2012), *New Perspectives on Consumer Culture Theory and Research* (Sedáková and Zahrádka, 2012) and *The Ages of Life: Living and Aging in Conflict?* (Kriebernegg and Maierhofer, 2013), as well as edited and contributed to *Ageing, Culture and Identity* (2015). She has published extensively in Swedish. Lövgren is a co-researcher in the MASCAGE project (2019–2022).

Raveena Mahal, MA, is a qualitative sociological researcher in the School of Kinesiology at the University of British Columbia, in Vancouver, Canada. Her primary research areas include the sociology of ageing, gender, sexualities, social inequalities and popular media. Recent work has examined the body image perceptions of older Canadian men, as well as media representations of older LGBTQ+ adults, and has been published in the journals *Men and Masculinities* and *Journal of Aging Studies*.

Barbara Ratzenböck is a sociologist and Senior Scientist at the Center for Inter-American Studies, University of Graz, Austria. Her research focuses on digitalisation, gender and generations. She serves as dataset coordinator of the Austrian survey of the ACT Cross-national Longitudinal Study: Older Audiences in the Digital Media Environment (https://actproject.ca/act/longitudinal-study/). She has published in *Nordicom Review* and the *Romanian Journal of Communication and Public Relations*, and in edited volumes, including in *Human Aspects of IT for the Aged Population: ITAP 2017*, edited by Zhou and Salvendy (Springer), and co-edited, with Roberta Maierhofer and Ulla Kriebernegg, *Alive and Kicking at All Ages: Cultural Constructions of Health and Life Course Identity* (Transcript, 2014).

Linn Sandberg is Associate Professor of Gender Studies at Södertörn University, Sweden, and the Associate Editor of the *International Journal of Ageing and Later Life*. Sandberg's research interests are in the field of ageing, gender, sexuality and embodiment, and more recently dementia. Her work on ageing and masculinity has been published in journals such as *Sexualities* and *Men and Masculinities* and she has authored a chapter in *Ageing in Everyday Life: Materialities and Embodiments* (Katz, 2018). Sandberg is one of the founders of the Critical Dementia Network, co-managing editor of the book series *Critical Dementia Studies*, published by Routledge, and the principal investigator in the Swedish team of the European research consortium MASCAGE (2019–2022).

Dana Sawchuk is Professor of Sociology at Wilfrid Laurier University in Waterloo, Canada. In addition to studying older adults and the print media, she is also interested in religion and ageing, activism and ageing, and job loss among older workers. Her work includes publications in *Ageing & Society*, *Journal of Aging Studies*, *Journal of Religion, Spirituality & Aging*, *Journal of Women & Aging* and *Gerontology & Geriatrics Education*. She is currently writing a book on neoliberalism and unemployment among older workers in the aftermath of the Great Recession in the US.

Maria Sourbati is Senior Lecturer at the University of Brighton, UK. Her current research explores the social implications of emerging technologies, with a focus on mobility, age and data. Sourbati's areas of expertise include communications and social policy, new media and older people, digital media, smart mobility and age relations. In these areas she has led qualitative research, worked on a range of projects as part of interdisciplinary teams and published in numerous top-ranked peer-reviewed journals including *New Media & Society*, *The Information Society*, *Media, Culture & Society* and *International Journal of Environmental Research and Public Health*.

Monika Wilińska is Senior Associate Professor in Welfare and Social Sciences at Jönköping University, Sweden. In her research, Monika explores the processes and practices of inequality (re)production with a particular focus on the intersecting orders of age and gender. She has published widely on the construction and relevance of gendered age in media, working life and welfare institutions in journals such as *Current Sociology*, *Journal of Family Issues*, *Journal of Women and Aging*, *Journal of Aging Studies*, *International Journal of Ageing and Later Life*, *Sociology* and *Work, Employment and Society*.

Wenqian Xu is a consultant for partnership and advocacy within the Division of Healthy Environments and Populations (DHP) at the World Health Organization Regional Office for the Western Pacific. He leads regional level advocacy for the actions proposed in the Regional Action Plan on Healthy Ageing. He also works on building partnerships with key stakeholders, opinion leaders and technical expert groups. He obtained his PhD in Ageing and Social Change at Linköping University, Sweden.

Virpi Ylänne is Senior Lecturer in Language and Communication at Cardiff University, Wales, UK. She has published widely on media representations of older adults, and ageing and identity in journals including *Discourse & Communication*, *Journal of Aging Studies*, *International Journal of Aging and Human Development*, *International Journal of Ageing and Later Life* (where she is also a member of the Editorial Board) and *Text & Talk*. She is the editor of the collection *Representing Ageing: Images and Identities* (Palgrave Macmillan, 2012).

Acknowledgements

This book project has been, for me, intellectually and professionally very fulfilling. I have been fortunate to work with a wonderful team of contributors who have been most respectful of deadlines and editorial suggestions along the way. I would like to thank you all. Many contributors also reviewed others' draft chapters, which is gratefully acknowledged, as is also the reviewing by Kirsi Lumme-Sandt of Tampere University, Finland, as well as the anonymous reviewers for their useful comments on the original proposal and the draft typescript. I am indebted to the series editors, in particular, Toni Calasanti, as well as Thomas Scharf and Chris Phillipson, for their interest and constructive feedback during the preparation of the collection. I would like to thank Laura Vickers-Rendall, Zoë Forbes, Caroline Astley and others at Policy Press for their efficiency and dedication during the publication and production process. DaneAge Association (Denmark), Norrköping municipality (Sweden), Mediatoon licensing (France) and Oni-Lion Forge Publishing (US) are thanked for copyright permissions to publish visual images. I would like to thank my department, the Cardiff School of English, Communication and Philosophy at Cardiff University, Wales, UK, for granting me one semester's research leave, which enabled me to focus on various editorial tasks for this book. And last, but not least, as always, I am indebted to my soon-to-be husband Chris and my daughter Emma for their love, support and encouragement.

Series editors' preface

As global ageing and the numbers of older people continue to expand, academics, policy makers and health and social care professionals around the world must address the concerns that emerge as a result. Ageing in a Global Context is a book series, published by Policy Press in association with the British Society of Gerontology, that seeks to influence and transform debates in this fast-moving field of research and policy. First, the series publishes books which rethink key questions shaping debates in the study of ageing. This has become especially important given the restructuring of welfare states, alongside the complex nature of population change, both of which open up the need to explore themes beyond traditional perspectives in social gerontology. Second, the series represents a response to the impact of globalisation and related processes, which are contributing to the erosion of national boundaries that originally framed research on ageing. From this has come the emergence of issues explored in various contributions to the series to date: the impact of transnational migration; growing ethnic and cultural diversity; new forms of inequality; and explorations of ageing in different environmental contexts. Third, a key concern of the series is the interdisciplinary connections within social gerontology. Contributions to the series provide a critical assessment of the disciplinary boundaries and territories that influence later life, thereby creating new perspectives and approaches relevant to global ageing in the 21st century.

Against this backdrop, we are pleased to be able to include in this series a book that critically examines media representations of older people in different countries, both positive and negative, as well as older people's responses and uses of media. The editor, Virpi Ylänne, has brought together analyses of a range of mass expression on such contemporary concerns as the pandemic, dementia and mental health, that also consider how inequalities might shape these. The various chapters herein reveal the power of media to reinforce or to challenge the ageism prevalent in depictions of older people as an homogenous group (despite differences emerging from such statuses as gender or sexual orientation), who are vulnerable or victims on the one hand and exceptions to assumed decline, and who should be admired, on the other. As well, authors examine how older people in various countries themselves respond to their representations and also make use of media. Taken together, this book contributes to our understanding both of older people as objects and as subjects, as diverse populations who can and do respond to media representations and their potential to challenge these. As such, it will be an important text for scholars and practitioners who seek to understand the complexities of the use of media and address the challenges older people face in a context of global ageing.

Chris Phillipson (University of Manchester, UK)
Toni Calasanti (Virginia Tech, USA)
Thomas Scharf (University of Newcastle, UK)

Introduction: Ageing in/and the media

Virpi Ylänne

Introduction

The media play a central role in the production of meaning in modern society. The relevance of the media to age studies has grown, with an increased cultural dimension to the analysis of ageing and later life (Gullette, 2004; Twigg and Martin, 2015). Media texts and images are produced and read against the concurrent social, cultural, political and economic background and their composition entails the selection of language and images that symbolise a social 'reality'. Media texts and images are therefore not simply reflective of societal and cultural ideologies – for example about ageing – but instead are both socially shaped while also simultaneously constructing social meanings (Fairclough and Wodak, 1997). The audience plays an active role in interpreting media messages and in selecting what it consumes and, more recently, media users have been able to create media content themselves, too. The media shape public attitudes via stereotyping and the framing of content in particular ways. Studying media portrayals of older people and ageing can therefore reveal current age stereotypes and help us understand ageism in its many forms (Phelan, 2018; Markov and Yoon, 2021).

How might a focus on the media inform social, cultural and critical gerontology? Understanding that 'ageism refers to the stereotypes (how we think), prejudice (how we feel) and discrimination (how we act) directed towards people on the basis of their age' and that it can be institutional, interpersonal or self-directed (WHO, 2021), also relates to media content and media practices. The identification and description of ageism and age stereotypes and resistance to them can benefit from an examination of portrayals of ageing and older age in the media. This can give us access to the predominant discursive and visual symbols of old age that circulate in society. Media content contributes to how we think about ageing, how we feel about ageing and what actions we take regarding ageing, both as individuals and as society. The decisions made by media producers have the power to reinforce or challenge ageist attitudes. Therefore, age scholars can play an important role in the critical examination of media practices, and their research can inform those practices in turn. This collection aims to make a contribution to this endeavour.

Ageism intersects with other inequalities. 'The concept of intersectionality illuminates the complex ways in which people's experiences over the lifecourse and in old age emerge from the intertwining of their various categorical memberships within systems of inequalities' (Calasanti and Giles, 2018, p 70). Such memberships might reside in gender or sexual identities, for example. The media play a prominent part in promoting hegemonic models about 'appropriate' ways to age, typically tied up with gendered, heteronormative cultural scripts. They may thus sustain ageism by institutional practices that maintain inequalities (Calasanti and King, 2015, p 193). Similarly, mainstream media and promotional media, such as advertising, for example, might primarily target more privileged and more affluent demographics and therefore ageing audiences and consumers from higher social classes might find it easier to identify with the images and the rhetoric therein, highlighting the role of class in (media) consumption, intersecting with ageism. In turn, more economically disadvantaged as well as Black and minority ethnic populations may find it much harder to 'see themselves' in the media, and this is particularly the case for older adults.

This volume will cover intersections, for example between sexuality and ageing, and gender and ageing, in many of the chapters. Questions about how sexually diverse and gender minority older adults feature in the media are addressed by analysing coverage in both news and magazines, as well as in fictional contexts, extending the focus to hitherto underexplored genres such as graphic novels. The connections between gendered mental health and ageing are addressed and the role of the media in both exposing prejudices and affirming them is discussed, linked with the social status of older women. Also featured is how ageing masculinities and femininities are negotiated by individuals (as media consumers and users) and in media texts and imagery. To address ageism in the media, several chapters focus on older adults as a social group, whether in the context of marketing, or in contexts of health, illness or social care. Potentially ageist discourse and visual ageism are explored from linguistic and semiotic perspectives, and the cultural and media framing of later life more generally is theorised. Of note are also empirical observations about how older adults and ageing are variously invisible in the media. In sum, the book covers topics of relevance to social, cultural and critical gerontological concerns in media contexts.

This collection draws together research from various parts of the globe, ranging from Northern Europe (Denmark, Sweden, the United Kingdom [UK] and the Netherlands) and North America (Canada) to South America (Brazil), Asia (Taiwan) and Africa/the Global South (Ghana). One of the aims was to cover regions under-represented in age scholarship published in English to date. While the media have a huge impact on globalisation via the transmission of cultural products across borders, they influentially contribute to questions about identity and cultural norms, including those relating to ageing. The coverage here, however, tends to focus on more localised data in national media, now accessible much more widely than before, and this affords a close examination of ageism in diverse parts of the world. The chapters investigate the relationship between the media and later life by focusing on media texts and images of older adults, media framing of later life and how older adults relate to and use various media.

As an introduction to the coverage in the subsequent chapters, we start with a brief introduction to ageing in the media as a precursor to the themes and reviews of the literature that will be vastly expanded on in the chapters that follow. The key themes and questions addressed in the book are introduced and, lastly, a short synopsis of all the chapters is presented.

Ageing in the media

The media are a resource to model phenomena such as ageing, as proposed by social cognitive theory (Bandura, 2009) and, with reduced intergenerational contact, they remain an important source of information about ageing and older age. Those older adults and others who are heavy consumers of media are more likely to associate media representations with reality and internalise ageist messages, according to cultivation theory (Gerbner et al, 2002). The role and degree of influence of social groups are reflected in their presence (or absence) in the media, according to vitality theory (Zhang et al, 2006; Olsen and Scott, 2021), for the media reproduce societal power structures. The under-representation of older adults in the media has been reported across the globe. Under-representation is manifested, for example, by the representation of older adults in limited contexts and in visually narrow ways. This is typical, for example, in advertising, where food, pharmaceuticals, health aids and financial/insurance products and services are the categories of product where adverts most often use older models, in both Western and Asian contexts (Prieler, 2012; Chen, 2015; Ylänne, 2021). 'Third age' rhetoric (Laslett, 1996) and imagery are visible in advertising and in publications directed mainly at affluent older consumers (Williams et al, 2010; Lumme-Sandt, 2011). Appearing, on the surface, to frame later life with positive qualities, this discourse links with neoliberal ideas of self-responsibility for one's ageing, promoting an active lifestyle in later life and subscribing to a 'successful ageing' ideology (Timonen, 2016). However, this type of portrayal has been criticised for homogenising later life (Pickard, 2019) and typically offers, for people other than celebrities (see Marshall and Rahman, 2015), an unrealistic and unattainable model for ageing. Several of the chapters in this volume will critically examine such representations.

In contrast with active third-age representations, older adults also frequently appear in the media as vulnerable, passive and dependent. This is particularly the case in news and newspaper discourse (Fealey et al, 2012), where in recent decades a 'burden discourse' and an 'apocalyptic discourse' have dominated (see, for example, Rozanova, 2010), presenting growing older populations and older adults' health and social care needs as a drain on resources. These discourses will be discussed in this book. However, the apparent 'positive' images in advertising, set against negative depictions in news reports, arguably 'simplif[ies] the ... representation of older people as being either positive or negative' (Xu, 2021, p 23). We will also critically explore such dichotomies.

Age stereotypes in the media are often conflated with gender stereotypes. For example, in (Western) film, despite a growing presence of older adults as main characters (Swinnen, 2015), different challenges for ageing women and men appear, emphasising the ageing feminine/masculine binary. And 'successful ageing' is typically linked with heterosexual coupling. Furthermore, older main characters tend to conform to a limited range of ethnicities (perpetuating further types of intersecting inequalities), body shapes and roles, and the films themselves are limited to a range of genres (Dolan, 2017). Older adults identifying with minority gender and sexual orientations remain largely absent from mainstream media and are under-researched in media contexts.

In social media contexts, researchers have looked at user engagement with current topics relating to ageing and age relations, and how content, for example on Twitter, may perpetuate or challenge ageist discourses (see, for example, Makita et al, 2021; Skipper and Rose, 2021; and also coverage under the hashtag #NoMoreWrinklyHands that has attacked the frequent representation of older adults via the symbols of disembodied old hands in health and social care contexts, since at least 2018). National and international collaborations are emerging examining ageing and the use of technologies, such as smartphones (see, for example, Garvey and Miller, 2021; Walton, 2021). There is coverage in this book, too, of digital communication on websites and social media sites, and older adults' use of communication technologies. Space is also devoted to discussions of how older adults interact with and receive media texts and imagery, including that of older age, and how they position themselves as older audiences. This potentially links with internalised and/or self-directed ageism and the reflective and active identification work of older adults. The media are part of the daily milieu of audiences of all ages, but some older adults might still feel variously excluded from, or that their interests and concerns are ignored by, the media.

Key themes of the book

The contributors to this collection work in fields ranging from sociology, information science, communication, gender studies, sociolinguistics and discourse studies, to film and media studies, marketing, cultural studies, health and welfare, and digital humanities, but are united in their endeavour here to critically examine the relationships between the media and ageing, thus contributing to critical age studies and cultural gerontology from an interdisciplinary perspective. The authors work in various geographical locations, too, and thus provide us with access to data from different parts of the world. The main focus of this book is not primarily on the workings of the media or media technologies per se. Instead, we investigate ageing and later life as represented in various media and as something that older adults (and others) are surrounded by, influenced by and interact with in their everyday lives.

Some of the central themes and questions that are explored are:

- How do older adults feature and how are they represented in the media in different cultural contexts?
- What visual, semiotic and discursive strategies are employed in these representations?
- How do particular cultural/economic/demographic contexts structure and give meaning to ageing in media texts and images?
- What discourses of ageing (potentially perpetuating ageism and other forms of marginalisation) are reflected and reproduced in the media?
- What is the role of older adults in the mediascape?
- How do older adults relate to media representations of ageing and older age?

These themes are addressed empirically and theoretically in media contexts that cover countries in Northern Europe, North America (Canada), South America (Brazil), Africa/the Global South (Ghana) and Asia (Taiwan), as previously mentioned. In line with the aims of the book series, we also recognise the impact of globalisation in increasingly minimising national boundaries, in this case in the media and how they deal with aspects of ageing and later life.

Overview of chapters

This collection starts in Part I, 'Framing and constructing ageing in media reporting', with chapters that discuss the representation of aspects of ageing and later life in newspapers, magazines and other media. They critically explore ways in which different media portray ageing individuals, such as older women, older adults with dementia, or older lesbian, gay, bisexual, transgender and other minority sexuality (LGBTQ+) adults, as well as older adults as a social group, such as how they are written about in the context of the COVID-19 pandemic. In Part II, 'Imagined ageing in promotional and fictional contexts', the focus is on textual and visual representations that are produced to attract consumers or to imagine alternative versions of ageing. They thus look at the role of the media in influencing our orientation to ageing, or in inviting us to imagine and aspire to a different kind of later life. These imaginings are, nevertheless, typically products of discourses of acceptable ageing, although these can be questioned, for example in fiction. In Part III, 'Older adults' interaction with the media and media technologies', the chapters examine how older adults interact with different media, giving voice to their age identification, their appraisal of media representations and their relationship with the media. They cover audience research, which is an important area of media research. In sum, the 'story' of the volume develops from 'reporting on' to 'reimagining' to 'reflecting on' ageing in the media across 11 chapters, followed by a Conclusion.

In the first chapter following this introduction (Chapter 2), Paul Higgs and Chris Gilleard provide a theoretically oriented critical discussion of the contrast between the social and cultural imaginaries of the 'third' age and the 'fourth' age. These refer to the 'baby boomer' generation, seen as keen on 'continuing style' and resistant to age, and a vulnerable, frail and steadily growing demographic, respectively. These notions shape and structure much current conceptualisation and media coverage of older age, expanded in many later chapters. Higgs and Gilleard also argue that the distinction has particular relevance in the context of the recent COVID-19 pandemic in media discussions about the interests of different generations. This latter theme is further addressed in Chapter 3 by Virpi Ylänne, who examines UK newspaper coverage of older adults in the first four months of the pandemic. She demonstrates the discursive and linguistic strategies used in the othering of older people and their positioning in the texts from a critical discourse analysis and thematic analysis perspective. The newspaper articles are found to continue the trend noted in previous research of representing older adults as a homogeneous group, foregrounding their vulnerability, passivity and dependency on others, or, at times, their exceptional status, illustrated via a more language-based focus.

In Chapter 4, Monika Wilińska and Doris Boateng discuss the representation of older women with mental health problems in Ghanaian media. These women are often called 'witches', which influences their objectification as targets of abuse, neglect and violence. Their depiction as users of witchcraft both reflects and reinforces cultural stereotypes and prejudices regarding gender, ageing and mental health, but also relates to media logics. On the other hand, changing media practices and the role of social media have had an important role in highlighting and potentially improving the treatment of the so-called witches in Ghana.

Chin-Hui Chen and Yan-Hua Huang (Chapter 5) focus on the coverage of people with dementia in Taiwanese news discourse. Adopting critical discourse analysis, the authors exemplify what actions older adults living with dementia are associated with, the social relationships they are depicted as having, how they are socially categorised and how they are labelled and identified. A micro-analysis of the linguistic strategies used in Taiwanese news discourse reveals an overwhelmingly derogatory representation of this social group, for example by foregrounding their status as victims, their vulnerability, the concern they cause other people and, in essence, their agedness. Here we see a prime example of the concept of the 'fourth age' framing the discourse, and it is likely that people living with dementia are represented in similar ways in other cultural contexts, too, reflecting and in turn contributing to a fear of old age and dementia.

In Chapter 6, Laura Hurd and Raveena Mahal turn to the representation in Canadian newspapers and magazines of other minority older populations, namely LGBTQ+ communities. Their investigation using critical discourse analysis reveals how older LGBTQ+ individuals' identities, experiences and social statuses are discursively constructed as invisible, as victims and as extraordinary. Invisibility is manifest in under-representation and misrepresentation, but also in the narrow depictions and discursive silencing of the people in the texts. The protagonists feature as victims of ongoing and historical discrimination and exclusion. But some are also depicted as extraordinary role models, activists and pioneers. It appears that media coverage of older sexual and gender minorities at times 'sanitises' their experiences for the readership at large and there is a need for greater media attention to be paid to the diversity of experience among older LGBTQ+ adults.

Part II starts with Gisela Castro's discussion in Chapter 7 of ageism and the promotion of 'agelessness' in Brazilian advertising. By offering case studies of multimodal adverts for different products, Castro demonstrates how negative assumptions about ageing still inform Brazilian media. This is the case in a changing demographic context that is not very different from that in many other regions, but which has undergone rapid change very recently. The 'successful ageing' discourse underpinning much advertising content in Brazil is discussed and exemplified, as is the transformation of older age into a segment of the consumer market.

This is followed by Chapter 8, authored by an international group: Eugène Loos, Loredana Ivan, Maria Sourbati, Wenqian Xu, Christa Lykke Christensen and Virpi Ylänne. Their focus is on public organisations' digital communication, such as on websites and social media pages, and their visual representation of older adults. Drawing on the concept of 'visual ageism', they show which connotations of the visual signs predominate in the data. The use of signifiers connoting health and activity on the one hand, and those connoting physical incapacity and vulnerability, on the other, enhance the risk of misrepresentation in the sites examined. However, it is pointed out that the analysis of 'visual ageism' is as complex as any analysis of 'ageism', and the specific context of the organisation and the distribution and consumption of the images needs to be considered.

In Chapter 9, Nicole Dalmer and Lucia Cedeira Serantes highlight how a selection of comics and graphic novels, originally published in various countries, construct versions of older age, older adults and lifestyles. The recently increased popularity of comics and graphic novels justifies an examination of the role of older adults therein. The stories feature the fictional everyday life of a range of older protagonists, as well as an alternative reality plot. The texts and images have the potential to disrupt conventional understandings and stereotypes of ageing and later life and provide new models of ageing for their readers. The authors propose that these liminal texts interrogate and challenge the narrow binaries of success and failure in dominant successful ageing discourse and offer a space to queer ageing futures, too.

In Part III, the chapters turn to older adults' interaction and relationship with the media. In Chapter 10, Karin Lövgren, Linn Sandberg, and Jeff Hearn investigate old(er) Swedish men's reactions to adverts depicting older men, as discussed in focus groups. This gives access to the men's orientations to masculinity (or masculinities) and ageing and shows the potential role of the media both in shaping people's gender and age identifications, but also as a research tool for studying how these are articulated. The relative absence of older men in advertising means that ageing men have few available images against which to reflect themselves. The Swedish men are also seen to resist the representations that are available, suggesting that they are unrealistic. On the other hand, the widespread invisibility also affords a certain freedom for older men from being disregarded as 'old'.

Next, Chapter 11 focuses on older Canadian women. Dana Sawchuk reports on her interview study on how older women relate to and read women's magazines. As readers of magazines not explicitly targeting their age group, the women express a lifecourse-based rationale for finding meaning in the magazines for themselves. They display agency and control as readers and challenge a narrow age-based concept of a target audience. This is an important finding considering that various media increasingly specifically target older cohorts. Also, it is a welcome reminder to scholars of ageing and the media of the dangers of narrowly focusing on age-targeted media, and that media consumption interacts with various social, familial and other factors besides age.

Finally, in Chapter 12, Barbara Ratzenböck discusses older Austrian women's use of information and communication technologies (ICTs), as reported in interviews and an online survey. The women's use of ICTs in their daily life emerges as highly gendered and as revolving around a 'double logic of care'. They engage with ICTs to care for others in various ways, or, alternatively, report being too busy caring for others to have time for ICTs.

Traditional gender roles are thus linked with the women's use of new media technologies, although for some women these are a backdrop from which they report to deviate. This is yet another example of the lens provided by ageing and media research on wider societal stereotypes and expectations about ageing, but also on other aspects of identity, such as gender.

Chapter 13 is the conclusion to the volume, bringing together the main arguments and themes from the preceding chapters. It also considers how the specific context and workings of the media need to be taken into account in any appraisal of ageing in the media, as well as the relevance of the media to age scholars going forward.

References

Bandura, A. (2009) 'Social cognitive theory of mass communication', in J. Bryant and M.B. Oliver (eds) *Media Effects: Advances in Theory and Research*, New York, NY: Routledge, pp 94–124.

Calasanti, T. and Giles, S. (2018) 'The challenge of intersectionality', *Generations: Journal of the American Society on Aging*, 41(4): 69–74.

Calasanti, T. and King, N. (2015) 'Intersectionality and age', in J. Twigg and W. Martin (eds) *Routledge Handbook of Cultural Gerontology*, Abingdon: Routledge, pp 193–200.

Chen, C.-H. (2015) 'Advertising representations of older people in the United Kingdom and Taiwan: a comparative analysis', *The International Journal of Aging and Human Development*, 80(2): 140–83.

Dolan, J. (2017) *Contemporary Cinema and 'Old Age': Gender and the Silvering of Stardom*, Basingstoke: Palgrave Macmillan.

Fairclough, N. and Wodak, R. (1997) 'Critical discourse analysis', in T.A. van Dijk (ed) *Discourse as Social Interaction*, London: Sage, pp 258–84.

Fealey, G., McNamara, M., Pearl Treacy, M. and Lyons, I. (2012) 'Constructing ageing and age identity: a case study of newspaper discourses', *Ageing and Society*, 32: 85–102.

Garvey, P. and Miller, D. (2021) *Ageing with Smartphones in Ireland: When Life Becomes Craft*, London: UCL Press.

Gerbner, G., Gross, L., Morgan, M., Signorielli, N. and Shanahan, J. (2002) 'Growing up with television: cultivation processes', in B. Jennings and D. Zillmann (eds) *Media Effects: Advances in Theory and Research*, Mahwah, NJ: Lawrence Erlbaum Associates, pp 43–68.

Gullette, M.M. (2004) *Aged by Culture*, Chicago, IL and London: The University of Chicago Press.

Laslett, P. (1996, 2nd ed) *A Fresh Map of Life: The Emergence of the Third Age*, Basingstoke: Palgrave Macmillan.

Lumme-Sandt, K. (2011) 'Images of aging in a 50+ magazine', *Journal of Aging Studies*, 25(1): 45–51.

Makita, M., Mas-Bleda, A., Stuart, E. and Thelwall, M. (2021) 'Ageing, old age and older adults: a social media analysis of dominant topics and discourses', *Ageing & Society*, 41: 247–72.

Markov, C. and Yoon, Y. (2021) 'Diversity and age stereotypes in portrayals of older adults in popular American prime time television series', *Ageing & Society*, 41: 2747–67.

Marshall, B.L. and Rahman, M. (2015) 'Celebrity, ageing and the construction of "third age" identities', *International Journal of Cultural Studies*, 18(6): 577–93.

Olsen, D. and Scott, C. (2021) 'Golden years, wise mentors and old fools: an updated typology of older characters in British TV advertising', *The Journal of Aging and Social Change*, 11(2): 83–94.

Phelan, A. (2018) 'Researching ageism through discourse', in L. Ayalon and C. Tesch-Römer (eds) *Contemporary Perspectives on Ageism: International Perspectives on Ageing*, Cham: Springer, pp 549–64.

Pickard, S. (2019) 'Age war as the new class war? Contemporary representations of intergenerational inequity', *Journal of Social Policy*, 48(2): 369–86.

Prieler, M. (2012) 'Social groups in South Korean television advertising: foreigners and older people', *Keio Communication Review*, 34: 57–78.

Rozanova, J. (2010) 'Discourse of successful ageing in The Globe and Mail: insights from critical gerontology', *Journal of Aging Studies*, 24: 213–22.

Skipper, A.D. and Rose, D.J. (2021) '#BoomerRemover: COVID-19, ageism, and the intergenerational twitter response', *Journal of Aging Studies*, 57: 100929.

Swinnen, A. (2015) 'Ageing in film', in J. Twigg and W. Martin (eds) *Routledge Handbook of Cultural Gerontology*, Abingdon: Routledge, pp 69–76.

Timonen, V. (2016) *Beyond Successful and Active Ageing: A Theory of Model Ageing*, Bristol: Policy Press.

Twigg, J. and Martin, W. (2015) 'The field of cultural gerontology: an introduction', in J. Twigg and W. Martin (eds) *Routledge Handbook of Cultural Gerontology*, London: Routledge, pp 1–15.

Walton, S. (2021) *Ageing with Smartphones in Urban Italy: Care and Community in Milan and Beyond* , London: UCL Press.

WHO (World Health Organization) (2021) *Global Report on Ageism*, Geneva: WHO.

Williams, A., Wadleigh, P.M. and Ylänne, V. (2010) 'Images of older people in UK magazine advertising: toward a typology', *International Journal of Aging and Human Development*, 71(2): 83–114.

Xu, W. (2021) *Ageism in the Media: Online Representations of Older People*, Linköping, Sweden: Linköping University.

Ylänne, V. (2021) 'UK magazine advertising portrayals of older adults: a longitudinal, content analytic and a social semiotic lens', *International Journal of Ageing and Later Life*, 15(1): 7–38.

Zhang, Y.B., Harwood, J., Williams, A., Ylänne-McEwen, V., Wadleigh, P.M. and Thimm, C. (2006) 'Older adults in advertising: multi-national perspectives', *Journal of Language and Social Psychology*, 25(3): 264–82.

.

PART I

Framing and constructing ageing in media reporting

2

'Apocalyptic demography' versus the 'reckless generation': framing the third and fourth ages in the media

Paul Higgs and Chris Gilleard

Introduction

This chapter explores the bifurcation of UK media discourse and imagery in the representation of later life, especially the contrast between the social and cultural imaginaries of the 'third' and the 'fourth' age (Gilleard and Higgs, 2014; Higgs and Gilleard, 2015a). Evident for some years now, this bifurcation has become more salient in the context of the COVID-19 pandemic, where the treatment of older people has been one of the most visible aspects of the entire crisis (Fletcher, 2021). The contradictory framing of later life represented by a 'third' versus a 'fourth' age imaginary reflects the fracturing of old age as a social category in contemporary society. At their extremes, these two imaginaries pivot between the expressed fear of growing dependency and an incipient social death associated with an 'apocalyptic demography' of excess agedness (Gee and Gutman, 2000), and the anger expressed by the pejoratively termed generation of 'OK boomers' who are judged to have benefited from a disproportionate degree of assets along with an increased means to capitalise on them.

The imaginary of the fourth age has its roots in pre-modern social life when old age was seen as the site of physical illness and financial impoverishment. Formulations of the third age, by contrast, are more recent and have associated it with the ageing of a particular generation – the baby-boomer cohorts – and their active engagement with a consumerist culture. These two contrasting discourses have been set in relief by the increasing deployment of demographic data within the public sphere (Hacking, 2015). Metaphors of ecological disaster and images of the accumulation of needy old bodies are used to project the requirement for urgent policy change (Mander, 2014). At the same time, these media discourses of physical dependency, mental decline and health vulnerability alternate with those concerning 'boomer' ageing that project an image of later life as 'fit, fashionable, functional and flexible' (Marshall and Rahman, 2015, p 577). Within the UK, neither mode dominates the media; rather, they exist as parallel discourses, as if unconnected to each other, reflecting the Janus-like approach to later life evident in many contemporary Western societies. The emergence of the COVID-19 pandemic has given a new slant to this double coding of later life, yielding calls for cost–benefit analyses regarding the trade-off between the economy and health, and between the interests of different generations (*The Economist*, 2020). Questions are raised about whether older people should be understood as a vulnerable group who must be defended against the pandemic, or whether they are an excessively supported segment of the population whose constant demands risk exhausting the economy and society. To address these matters, we begin by outlining what we mean by framing this media debate as a conflict between 'third age' versus 'fourth age' imaginaries.[1]

Third age/fourth age

The distinction between a flourishing and a frail old age is not new. Such a division has existed as long as attempts have been made to represent the stages of life (Burrow, 1986). What is distinct about its framing in contemporary Western society is its connection to the economy, to markets and to the state. There are many different debates about the make-up of the third age, understood as either a 'stage' of life (the young old) or as the later life of a distinct cohort (the baby-boom generation). In a number of publications, we have argued in favour of the latter position, contending that the third age can be best understood in Bourdieusian terms as a distinct 'generational field' formed by the increasing affluence of post-war Western society (Gilleard and Higgs, 2011). This generational field is in large part defined by the historical diffusion of a consumerist habitus that has steadily extended across the lifecourses of both those growing up and those growing old during this period (Gilleard and Higgs, 2005, 2011).

Part of the cultural ethos of this generational field is a resistance to all that is perceived to be 'old'. The ageing of post-war youth culture has not seen the abandonment of youthful concerns, so much as their continuing modification and elaboration, first in mid-life and now in later life. It is, in a sense, a generation ageing differently, ageing without becoming seen to be or thought to be either 'old' or 'old-fashioned'. These aspirations have been, to use a term developed by Louis Althusser (1971), 'interpellated' by a consumerist lifestyle and a retail economy marketing products and services that project 'continuing style' – in the form of cosmetics, diet, fashion, fitness regimes and/or leisure activities – combined with a general resistance to age (Gilleard and Higgs, 2014). Connected to this, a new genre of films, magazines and television programmes has emerged, incorporating many of the ideals of 'boomer hood' and 'successful' ageing (King, 2014).

At the same time, a counter-critique of 'third-ageism' has developed, expressed in the academic world by the development of an explicitly 'anti' anti-ageing approach (Vincent, 2009). Such critiques of the third age have tended to focus on its location within a particular cohort or generation, the baby boomers, addressing two related issues, that of an assumed generational inequity and rampant consumerism (Higgs and Gilleard, 2015b). While anti anti-ageing discourse and imagery are rarely present in the media that is directed towards older people as consumers, it is often found in academic journals as well as in some of the opinion and editorial pieces ('op-eds') in the broadsheet media and popular sociology books. Here, the boomers are seen not as individual pioneers of new later lifestyles but as the collective representatives of a selfish, reckless, 'me' generation (Paxman, 2011; McInnes, 2016; Cooper, 2021). This negative projection has recently mutated into the meme 'OK boomer', which has been amplified by younger users of social media to identify older cohorts as both selfish and socially dominant (Meisner, 2020) and COVID-19 as a 'boomer remover' (Lichtenstein, 2021).

The fourth age, by contrast, is realised in discourses framed around older people as 'third person' persons, those irredeemably 'othered' by their age, who have failed to stay fit, fashionable and functional. Realised neither by lifestyle nor through identity, the fourth age functions as an intransigent social imaginary – whose imagery grows more powerful as the aspirational cultures of the third age wax larger. In many ways it forms the antithesis of the third age, rendering later life 'bound in a binary discourse as either decline or success' (Sandberg, 2013, p 13). But unlike the practices and discourses enacted by the participant consumers of the third age, the fourth age is a discourse shaped by others; a discourse about others realised through the dividing practices of social welfare and the expressed anxieties that readily spill over into the media. In contrast to the third age, the fourth age represents not diversity but uniformity: a sad uniformity culminating in abject frailty (Higgs and Gilleard, 2014). This contrast has already been evidenced in empirical research on the images of older people in the media where a number of different clusters defining potential third-age participants have been observed, in contrast to the unitary portrayal of a fourth age construed only through frailty and vulnerability (Williams et al, 2010).

The fourth age and apocalyptic demography

Discourses derived from demography and epidemiology perform an influential role in framing social and health policies; activating 'health promotion' strategies by implying or actively articulating the 'negative' social imaginary of the fourth age; and alerting the public to the dangers of ageing, at an individual and societal level (Higgs and Gilleard, 2015a, 2017). Unlike other 'folk devils' besetting modern societies, the threat represented by 'the old' does not stem from their capacity to be actively dangerous elements in society. Instead, it centres on their unlimited neediness that threatens to overwhelm the nation state's limited capacity to handle these claims. Unsurprising, then, that the analogies and metaphors most often used in relation to this danger are those of ecological disaster, with constant reference in the media to rising tides, 'agequakes' and 'silver' tsunamis (Robertson, 1997; Laureys, 2009; Saharia, 2014; Zeilig, 2014; Calasanti, 2020). In the COVID-19 pandemic this framing was dominated by accounts of residents of nursing homes being abandoned to the full ravages of the virus (Sepulveda et al, 2020; see also Chapter 3). In the UK, the fear of the National Health Service being overwhelmed led to older hospital patients being discharged to nursing homes without being tested for the virus (Lacobucci, 2020). In Sweden, a focus on giving citizens personal responsibility for taking precautions rather than implementing a mandatory lockdown contributed to COVID-19 going into facilities for older people through care workers mingling with the population at large (Orange, 2020). In Spain, the spread of the pandemic was so fast that many nursing home residents were abandoned by their carers; later, they were found dead by army units sent out to discover what had happened to them (Minder and Peltier, 2020). It is therefore something of a paradox that as this form of 'fourth ageism' (Higgs and Gilleard, 2021) became more widely known, 'the moral imperative to care' kicked in to a greater degree, so much so that some commentators have raised the criticism of 'caremongering' as being a form of compassionate ageism (Vervaecke and Meisner, 2020).

Demography and epidemiology have been combined to render 'apocalyptic' this ageing of already aged societies. The COVID-19 pandemic may seem to challenge some of the assumptions of the demographic and epidemiological transition, but the underlying notion remains, that disease has ceased to be deadly for children and the young, and now frames the backdrop for old age, for 'real' old age, for the fourth age. The discourses of apocalyptic demography assume that medical, health and social costs will increase to previously unexperienced, unsustainable levels (Amalberti et al, 2016). The rise in the age of the older population has certainly led to a concomitant increase in chronic disease; the incidence – as well as the prevalence – of multi-morbidity, however defined, rises steeply with age (Formiga et al, 2013; St Sauver et al, 2015). Whether this is an inevitable, intrinsic and universal feature of living longer can be challenged. One of the largest surveys of the oldest old conducted in mainland China, for example, observed that the prevalence of chronic disease in fact *declined* after age 80, with fewer nonagenarians and centenarians suffering from chronic diseases compared with their younger, octogenarian peers (Dupre et al, 2008). What these and other related studies suggest is that living through 'the oldest ages' may not lead to progressively greater levels of disability and dependency. Such views, however, rarely feature in the mass media, which remain dominated by a narrative of increasing ageing as a 'growing pandemic' (Martin et al, 2009) or, in the context of COVID-19, a threat to public health (Zhang and Liu, 2021). Real old age – the fourth age – is invariably portrayed as disastrous both for individuals and for the wider society.

'Generation reckless': baby boomers as a social problem

An alternative rendering of later life can be seen in the media discourses surrounding the ageing of the post-war cohorts, the so-called 'baby boomer' generation. An example of their representation and the formulation of the difficulties that they create has been provided by the UK political commentator and one-time collaborator of Anthony Giddens, Will Hutton (2010), who writes:

> The baby boomers. Born between 1945 and 1955, they are busy ignoring the biblical calculus that a man's span is three score years and 10. Having enjoyed a life of free love, free school meals, free universities, defined benefit pensions, mainly full employment and a 40-year-long housing boom, they are bequeathing their children sky-high house prices, debts and shrivelled pensions. A 60-year-old in 2010 is a very privileged and lucky human being – an object of resentment as much as admiration.

The designation *baby boomer* was initially used in the United States (US) to describe the large 20-year birth cohort born between the mid-1940s and the early 1960s (Russell, 1982; Light, 1988). It has grown to cover all those reaching retirement age in the second and third decades of the 21st century (Dytchwald, 1999). In part this reflects the powerful cultural and social effects that this generation has had as it has moved through the lifecourse. In previous work (Gilleard and Higgs, 2005), we have pointed to the significance of the 'generational schism' that occurred between those who were young during the 'long' 1960s, and those members of the population who were already grown up and were growing older during this period. Writings of the time stressed the problems of this generational split and the conflict of value systems (Marwick, 2001). In recent times, the baby-boom cohorts have been seen again as problematic not so much for their size or rebelliousness, but for their expectations and influence. As Hutton alluded to in the earlier quote, they have become stereotyped as a particularly favoured group whose retirement would not only rewrite the rules for old age but also bring about renewed generational conflict.

Outside of North America and the UK, the demographic nature of the baby boomers has been less salient, mainly because different European nations have had different experiences of the post–Second World War period. In Finland, for example, the post-war baby boom only lasted for about three years (Suokannas, 2005; Karisto, 2007); in Eastern Europe, the post-war period saw a decline in fertility, which continued all through the 1950s (Therborn, 1995, p 37); the same was true in Italy (Livi Bacci, 1967); while in Germany, the post-war baby boom was a feature of the 1960s. In France, and in the UK, there were two quite separate booms, the first occurring between 1945 and 1950 and the second between 1960 and 1965 (Evandrou and Falkingham, 2000; Chauvel, 2002). Hence, it is only in the last decade that the ageing of the baby boomers has become a trope deployed in the media of European nations (Lundgren and Ljuslinder, 2011), in part the consequence of the internationalisation of US debates on generational equity and generational accounting, but also a consequence of population ageing in parts of the European Union (Boersch-Supan et al, 2011).

Intergenerational considerations consequently have become influential in debates on welfare reform across many of the world's developed economies. Intergenerational inequalities were identified as a significant threat to the future of welfare; a threat flowing from the realisation that existing pension entitlements were seemingly providing financial security in retirement at the expense of other groups in society who were identified as having greater needs (Myles, 2002). This perceived threat has since become the source for media attacks on the members of post-war cohorts who are projected to be putting their interests and dispositions ahead of those of the rest of the population, particularly the young. It is in this context that the term 'baby boomers' has achieved a wider currency. This is evident in a number of well-received books that lambasted the baby-boom generation, their titles giving a fair impression of their general tone: *What Did the Baby Boomers Ever Do for Us?* (Beckett, 2010); *Jilted Generation: How Britain Bankrupted Its Youth* (Howker and Malik, 2010); *The Pinch: How the Baby Boomers Took Their Children's Future – And Why They Should Give It Back* (Willetts, 2010); and *The Baby Boom: How It Got That Way (And It Wasn't My Fault) (And I'll Never Do It Again)* (O'Rourke, 2013).[2]

In these works, as well as their accompanying amplification in the mass media, the moral stature, character and upbringing of the baby boomers are critically questioned.[3] There is often an explicit message that collectively these cohorts are taking more from society than they are prepared to give back. These baby boomers (whose generational identity is stressed more than their chronological age) have been projected as engaging in a form of moral recklessness, destroying the inheritance that their own parents had worked so hard to bestow on them (Beckett, 2010, p xii). In the parlance of the 2020s, these are the 'OK boomers', a term coined to reflect this combination of privilege and lack of concern for other generations (Meisner, 2020).

Bristow (2015, p 86) has outlined some of the ways in which the baby-boomer generation has been constructed as a problem in the British media. The cultural script of the baby-boomer problem, she argues, consists of five influential categories: the 'lucky' generation; the 'affluent' generation; the 'large' generation; the 'selfish' generation; and the 'reckless' generation. She draws particular attention to the portrayal of a 'reckless generation', who are seen to be focused on the present to the detriment of longer-term issues. To the charge that the baby boomers have 'dispossessed' younger generations and squandered their parents' legacy are added accusations that they have 'infantilised' society and subjected it to a valorisation of 'experimentation' as an end in itself. Infantilisation, Bristow contends, has meant that young people are now unable to achieve what were once seen as adult goals, such as having a stable job or family life, or indeed owning their own home. As she points out, such critical representation of the baby boomers 'expresses both a concern about the Sixties' assault on tradition, and a concern about the quest implied in that assault, for seeking out new knowledge and experimenting with the social order' (Bristow, 2015, p 104). Many of the 'virtues' associated with baby boomers have been turned into 'vices': ambition has become greed; affluence, wastefulness; being youthful, being infantile; being self-actualised, being self-obsessed; being leisure loving, being lazy; and being individualistic, being selfish (Bristow, 2015, p 106).

Many of these dispositions are evident in a series of interviews with UK baby boomers, conducted by Naomi Woodspring (Woodspring, 2016). These interviews illustrate both the desire to be different and the importance attached by boomers to enjoyment. One of the respondents put it like this: 'You see, having fun is part of the picture as something that's on the table, that's open to you because you're more open minded' (Woodspring, 2016, p 111). The baby-boom cohorts are praised for their concern with fitness and health, and simultaneously castigated for it (Mendes, 2013; Timonen, 2016). Part of the criticism is that in focusing on these new 'technologies of the self', an invidious distinction is made between those who are able to participate in these fields, and those who are excluded from being able to do so (Jones and Higgs, 2010). In a study of UK baby boomers' sense of generational identity, Leach and colleagues (2013) found that while there was evidence for baby boomers' engagement with consumption as an end in itself, this was tempered with other, more ethical considerations:

This notion of an ethic of consuming that is generationally specific is strong in the accounts of baby boomers' sense of themselves, yet it demonstrates a bridging between two different consumer ethics which address the passage of time in different ways. The 'make do and mend' and 'ageing' ethic, in which time is extended by making good and through carefully researched rational choices; and the speeding up of time or 'youthful' ethic through the adoption of credit, the need for novelty, and 'early adoption' of consumer goods. (Leach et al, 2013, p 114)

As part of the 'critique' of baby boomerism, the cultural distinction sought by members of the baby-boom cohorts is represented not as a sign of their 'successfully' resisting age but as the demonstration of their failure to accept the realities of decline and their common location as 'old people'. This theme has been picked up by those trying to engage with the more individualised spirituality associated with the post-1960s' generational habitus. Theologians such as Elizabeth MacKinlay (2014), for example, advocate self-transcendence and transformation as important strategies to deal with extended lifespans and the limitations of old age. As she writes: 'There are many things to learn about the process of ageing and how we might best approach this, and the big choices are either to join the anti-ageing lobby or to embrace our ageing' (MacKinlay, 2014, p 120). It is clear that MacKinlay favours the latter; one that prioritises forgiveness and gratitude as ways of moving to what she describes as 'other centredness'.

COVID-19 and the confounding discourses of later life

As we hope to have shown, the discourses connected to the third age differ substantially from those concerned with the fourth-age imaginary. These have become particularly exposed in the context of the COVID-19 pandemic, although they are seldom commented on (Verbruggen et al, 2020, p 230). While the themes of *apocalyptic demography* and of the *reckless generation* are generally kept separate, sometimes they are brought together as alternate sides of the same coin – of age as a new emerging source of conflict and threat to the social order – criticised for its agedness on the one hand, and for its rejection of agedness on the other. In relation to the COVID-19 pandemic, however, the overarching image has been that of the fourth age – with deaths among frail nursing-home residents accounting for almost half of all reported deaths in many countries (Thompson et al, 2020). This notion of age vulnerability is not just confined to Europe and North America. In their study of COVID-19 media coverage in China, Zhang and Liu (2021) pointed out how the media there have presented the whole of the older population as a homogenised, passive and vulnerable group. One consequence has been that many older people, certainly in countries such as the UK, have protested against the over-generalised view of agedness introduced by the pandemic, as well as the government's use of chronology in targeting those expected to self-isolate.[4] Older people have written to the press both in support of and in opposition to this age targeting, some describing these policies as being inherently 'ageist', insisting instead that they are as fit and robust as many younger people, while others have argued for the necessity of such 'benign' ageism. Many commentators (including gerontologists) have ignored the implicit 'othering' that lies behind the 'young old' complaining about being categorised alongside those who are truly 'old'. It is clear that many of those most actively participating in the third age both recognise and resent the chronological corralling of later life back into a framework of need and dependency that many thought they had escaped.

Accepting that many of the 'oldest old' are vulnerable, while denying that old age has any inherent connection with disease or decline, poses a dilemma both for older people themselves and for gerontology (Fletcher, 2021). On the one hand, there is justifiable anger at the 'ageist' neglect shown towards residents and staff in long-term care facilities; on the other, accusations of ageism are directed at the use of age as a criterion for mandatory 'shielding' – effectively restricting access to the everyday practices of shopping, visiting friends and family, and the various pleasures of being among people, to those judged not yet 'old'. The two US presidential candidates in the 2020 election exemplified many of these contradictions in their use of the mass media. One, the arch-libertarian, projected his freedom to do as he liked, including not identifying as 'old and vulnerable', feeling at liberty to run the risk of infection; the other, more conservative, projected the need to display caution without at the same time drawing attention to his own age-related vulnerability. While both, in different ways, demonstrated the kinds of power attached to the third age, it was their political power, not their age, which ensured this realisation of third-age culture. For those with more limited assets and capital, given the turn in circumstances as has been brought about by COVID-19, the social category of a homogenising agedness can quickly be brought back into play. At the same time, while the residents of the nursing homes remain invisible figures lost in the calculation of the costs to the nation of the pandemic, the two septuagenarian politicians competed in their claims to restore to health the sick body of the state.

Conclusion

Our intention in writing this chapter has been to draw attention to a dichotomy underlying media discourses of ageing in contemporary Western society. These discourses run in parallel as ways of situating the changes to old age that have emerged over the past 30 years. Discourses reflecting the cultures of the third age are imbricated in various forms of mass media through their connections to the generation habitus of the baby-boom cohorts. Given the valorisation of agency and choice in these discourses, it is not surprising that the third age is thoroughly mediatised, as a cultural imaginary reflecting the various constructions of 'ageless ageing' (see also Chapter 7). This is not without consequences, as we have shown in the rise of the criticisms directed at both the imaginary and the 'OK boomers' themselves.

While the fourth age also operates as a discursive trope within the media, it is one put at a distance from everyday desires and experience. Its focus is on feared futures and an imaginary otherness that maintains its irreconcilable distance from any mediatised subjectivity. The fourth age is no place for desiring subjects. Some commentators argue that the principal difference between the third and fourth ages lies in the negative attributes that are given to the fourth age by society and the mass media. We would disagree with this assessment by pointing out that the two discourses are constituted by quite different processes; one being agentic and aspirational, while the other is ascribing and threatening. Trying to overwrite one discourse with the techniques of the other misses the point that ageing and old age are neither simply discursive nor performative.

Media accounts of the COVID-19 pandemic and the various nation states' responses to it might seem to have erased the distinction between the third age and the fourth, focusing so much on the common vulnerabilities of agedness and its equivalence with disease. At the same time, a resistance to such homogenisation has also been evident, if not so widely reported, both by older people and by organisations representing older people. This, we suggest, testifies to the continuing struggle over the symbolic space that is later life. While the material differences supporting this symbolic distinction are matters of degree and dimensionality, the symbolic struggles evident in the media and in the mediatisation of later life tend towards a simplified binary contest, between those who are 'really' and those who are 'not really' old. The absoluteness of the former and the contingency of the latter will remain, long after COVID-19 has become a collective, if fractious, memory.

Notes

[1] Describing this as a contrast between two imaginaries is our preferred formulation, but it could equally be treated as a contrast between two dominant *frames* employed by the media. Our preference reflects our desire to extend the analysis to social contexts beyond media texts and imagery.

[2] These books were reviewed and discussed across the media in numerous articles and op-ed pieces; so much so that they have produced their own complement of book-length reposts such as Jane Bristow's *Stop Mugging Grandma* (Bristow, 2019).

[3] British broadsheet newspapers have been influential in developing this trope. See, for example: Nick Cohen, 'Let the children pay', *The Observer*, 19 August 2005; Richard Edwards, 'Baby boom generation have failed their children', *Daily Telegraph*, 18 January 2010; Paul Vallely, 'Will the baby boomers bankrupt Britain?', *The Independent*, 5 April 2010; Madeleine Bunting, 'Generational warriors have a point but go easy on the old', *The Guardian*, 22 August 2010; Robert Colvile, 'The boomers' bonanza has left precious little for the rest of

us', *Daily Telegraph*, 1 September 2010; and Philip Inman, 'Baby boomers must do their bit for Britain's economy', *The Guardian*, 5 January 2011. This theme is continuing a decade later. See, for instance, Yvonne Roberts, 'Millennials are struggling. Is it the fault of the baby boomers?', *The Observer*, 29 April 2018; and Alexis Self, 'Forget pensions – why Britain's millennials are preparing for social collapse', *Prospect*, 28 March 2021.

[4] A flavour of this protest is illustrated in a letter to *The Guardian*, 29 April 2020. Its author, Hella Pick, wrote: 'I live on my own. For me, the imposition of self-isolation for any length of time – in plain words, being caged in – would be tantamount to a living death. That is why I applaud and join the growing number of people who are protesting against moves to separate the over-70s from their families and fellow citizens, and why I hope that many more will make themselves heard, and if necessary join in seeking legal action to restrain the authorities.' More recently, a theatre group based in Cardiff, Wales, has put on a drama illustrating the same point – namely that '[w]e don't want to portray ourselves as victims or as being vanquished' (Clare Horton, *The Guardian*, 15 December 2020).

References

Althusser, L. (1971) 'Ideology and ideological state apparatuses' (B. Brewster, trans.), *Lenin and Philosophy and Other Essays*, New York, NY: Monthly Review Press, pp 85–126.

Amalberti, R., Nicklin, W. and Braithwaite, J. (2016) 'Preparing national health systems to cope with the impending tsunami of ageing and its associated complexities: towards more sustainable health care', *International Journal for Quality in Health Care*, 28(3): 412–14.

Bacci, M.L. (1967) 'Modernization and tradition in the recent history of Italian fertility', *Demography*, 4(2): 657–72.

Beckett, F. (2010) *What Did the Baby Boomers Ever Do for Us?*, London: Biteback Publishing.

Boersch-Supan, A., Heller, G. and Reil-Held, A. (2011) 'Is intergenerational cohesion falling apart in old Europe?', *Public Policy and Aging Report*, 21(4): 17–21.

Bristow, J. (2015) *Baby Boomers and Generational Conflict*, London: Palgrave Macmillan.

Bristow, J. (2019) *Stop Mugging Grandma*, New Haven, CT: Yale University Press.

Burrow, R. (1986) *The Ages of Man*, Oxford: Clarendon Press.

Calasanti, T. (2020) 'Brown slime, the silver tsunami, and apocalyptic demography: the importance of ageism and age relations', *Social Currents*, 7(3): 195–211.

Chauvel, L. (2002) *Le Destin des Générations* (2nd edn), Paris: PUF.

Cooper, M. (2021) 'A burden on future generations? How we learned to hate deficits and blame the baby boomers', *The Sociological Review*, 69(4): 743–58.

Dupre, M.E., Liu, G. and Gu, D. (2008) 'Predictors of longevity: evidence from the oldest old in China', *American Journal of Public Health*, 98(7): 1203–8.

Dychtwald, K. (1999) *Age Power: How the 21st Century Will be Ruled by the New Old*, New York, NY: Tarcher.

The Economist (2020) 'COVID-19 presents stark choices between life, death and the economy', *The Economist*, 4 April.

Evandrou, M. and Falkingham, J. (2000) 'Looking back to look forward: lessons from four birth cohorts for ageing in the 21st century', *Population Trends*, 99: 27–36.

Fletcher, J.R. (2021) 'Chronological quarantine and ageism: COVID-19 and gerontology's relationship with age categorisation', *Ageing and Society*, 41(3): 479–92.

Formiga, F., Ferrer, A., Sanz, H., Marengoni, A., Alburquerque, J. and Pujol, R. (2013) 'Patterns of comorbidity and multimorbidity in the oldest old: the Octabaix Study', *European Journal of Internal Medicine*, 24(1): 40–4.

Gee, E. and Gutman, G. (2000) *The Overselling of Population Ageing: Apocalyptic Demography, Intergenerational Challenges, and Social Policy*, Oxford: Oxford University Press.

Gilleard, C. and Higgs, P. (2005) *Contexts of Ageing: Class, Cohort and Community*, Cambridge: Polity Press.

Gilleard, C. and Higgs, P. (2011) 'The third age as a cultural field', in D.C. Carr and K. Komp (eds) *Gerontology in the Era of the Third Age: Implications and Next Steps*, New York, NY: Springer Publishing, pp 33–49.

Gilleard, C. and Higgs, P. (2014) *Ageing, Corporeality and Embodiment*, London: Anthem.

Hacking, I. (2015) 'Biopower and the avalanche of printed numbers', in V. Cisney and N. Morar (eds) *Biopower: Foucault and Beyond*, Chicago, IL: University of Chicago Press, pp 65–81.

Higgs, P. and Gilleard, C. (2014) 'Frailty, abjection and the "othering" of the fourth age', *Health Sociology Review*, 23(1): 10–19.

Higgs, P. and Gilleard, C. (2015a) *Rethinking Old Age: Theorising the Fourth Age*, London: Palgrave Macmillan.

Higgs, P. and Gilleard, C. (2015b) 'Generational justice, generational habitus and the "problem" of the baby boomers', in C. Torp (ed) *Challenges of Aging*, Basingstoke: Palgrave Macmillan, pp 251–63.

Higgs, P. and Gilleard, C. (2017) 'Ageing, dementia and the social mind: past, present and future perspectives,' *Sociology of Health & Illness*, 39(2): 175–81.

Higgs, P. and Gilleard, C. (2021) 'Fourth ageism: real and imaginary old age', *Societies*, 11(1): 12.

Howker, E. and Malik, S. (2010) *Jilted Generation: How Britain Bankrupted its Youth*, London: Icon Books.

Hutton, W. (2010) 'The baby boomers and the price of personal freedom', *The Observer*, 22 August.

Jones, I.R. and Higgs, P.F. (2010) 'The natural, the normal and the normative: contested terrains in ageing and old age', *Social Science & Medicine*, 71(8): 1513–19.

Karisto, A. (2007) 'Finnish baby boomers and the emergence of the third age', *International Journal of Ageing and Later Life*, 2(2): 91–108.

King, R. (2014) 'Chilling to the big chill: representations of boomers in movies', in B. Cogan and T. Gencarelli (eds) *Baby Boomers and Popular Culture: An Inquiry into America's Most Powerful Generation*, Santa Barbara, CA: Praeger, pp 135–46.

Lacobucci, G. (2020) 'COVID-19: lack of testing led to patients being discharged to care homes with virus, say auditors', *British Medical Journal*, 369: m2375.

Laureys, G. (2009) 'A tsunami of good wishes: on the metaphorical use of meteorological expressions', in S. Slembrouck, M. Taverniers and M. van Herreweghe (eds) *From Will to Well: Studies in Linguistics, Offered to Anne-Marie Simon-Vandenbergen*, London: Academic Press, pp 305–12.

Leach, R., Phillipson, C., Biggs, S. and Money, A. (2013) 'Baby boomers, consumption and social change: the bridging generation?', *International Review of Sociology*, 23(1): 104–22.

Lichtenstein, B. (2021) 'From "coffin dodger" to "boomer remover": outbreaks of ageism in three countries with divergent approaches to coronavirus control', *The Journals of Gerontology: Series B*, 76(4): e206–e212.

Light, B. (1988) *Baby Boomers*, New York, NY: Norton.

Lundgren, A.S. and Ljuslinder, K. (2011) '"The baby-boom is over and the ageing shock awaits": populist media imagery in news-press representations of population ageing', *International Journal of Ageing and Later Life*, 6(2): 39–71.

MacKinlay, E. (2014) 'Baby boomers ageing well? Challenges in the search for meaning in later life', *Journal of Religion, Spirituality & Aging*, 26(2–3): 109–21.

Mander, T. (2014) 'Longevity and healthy ageing – will healthcare be drowned by the grey tsunami or sunk by the demographic iceberg?', *Post Reproductive Health*, 20(1): 8–10.

Marshall, B.L. and Rahman, M. (2015) 'Celebrity, ageing and the construction of "third age" identities', *International Journal of Cultural Studies*, 18(6): 577–93.

Martin, R., Williams, C. and O'Neill, D. (2009) 'Retrospective analysis of attitudes to ageing in the *Economist*: apocalyptic demography for opinion formers', *British Medical Journal*, 339: b4914.

Marwick, A. (2001) *The Sixties: Cultural Revolution in Britain, France, Italy, and the United States, c. 1958–c. 1974*, London: A&C Black.

McInnes, G. (2016) '"Disgusting, selfish, immature": 10 reasons baby boomers are the worst generation', *The Rebel Online*, available from: http://www.therebel.media/10_reasons_baby_boomers_are_the_worst_generat ion [accessed 11 April 2016].

Meisner, B.A. (2020) 'Are you OK, boomer? Intensification of ageism and intergenerational tensions on social media amid COVID-19', *Leisure Sciences*, 43(1–2): 56–61.

Mendes, F.R. (2013) 'Active ageing: a right or a duty?', *Health Sociology Review*, 22(2): 174–85.

Minder, R. and Peltier, E. (2020) 'A deluged system leaves some elderly to die, rocking Spain's self-image', *New York Times*, 25 March.

Myles, J. (2002) 'A new social contract for the elderly', in G. Esping-Andersen (ed) *Why We Need a New Welfare State*, Oxford: Oxford University Press, pp 130–72.

O'Rourke P.J. (2013) *The Baby Boom: How It Got That Way (And It Wasn't My Fault) (And I'll Never Do It Again)*, New York, NY: Grove Press.

Orange R. (2020) 'Anger in Sweden as elderly pay price for coronavirus strategy', *The Observer*, 19 April.

Paxman, J. (2011) 'I am part of the most selfish generation in history and we should be ashamed of our legacy', *Mail Online*, available from: *http://www.dailymail.co.uk/news/article-2055497/JEREMY-PAXMAN-Baby-Boom ers-selfish-generation-history.html* [accessed 30 December 2020].

Robertson, A. (1997) 'Beyond apocalyptic demography: towards a moral economy of interdependence', *Ageing and Society*, 17(4): 425–46.

Russell, L.B. (1982) *The Baby Boom Generation and the Economy*, Washington, DC: Brookings Institute.

Sandberg, L. (2013) 'Affirmative old age – the ageing body and feminist theories on difference', *International Journal of Ageing and Later Life*, 8(1): 11–40.

Saharia, R.P. (2014) 'Agequake and its implications on economic growth', *Research Journal of Humanities and Social Sciences*, 5(1): 135–3.

Sepulveda, E.R., Stall, N.M. and Sinha, S.K. (2020) 'A comparison of COVID-19 mortality rates among long-term care residents in 12 OECD countries', *Journal of the American Medical Directors Association*, 21(11): 1572–4.

St Sauver, J.L., Boyd, C.M., Grossardt, B.R., Bobo, W.V., Rutten, L.J.F., Roger, V.L. and Rocca, W.A. (2015) 'Risk of developing multimorbidity across all ages in an historical cohort study: differences by sex and ethnicity', *BMJ Open*, 5(2): e006413.

Suokannas M. (2005) 'Cultural age and seniorism in an advertising context', *Kuluttajatutkimus. Nyt*, 1: 79–89.

Therborn, G. (1995) *European Modernity and Beyond: Trajectory of European Societies, 1945–2000*, London: Sage.

Thompson, D.C., Barbu, M.G., Beiu, C., Popa, L.G., Mihai, M.M., Berteanu, M. and Popescu, M.N. (2020) 'The impact of COVID-19 pandemic on long-term care facilities worldwide: an overview on international issues', *BioMed Research International*, article ID 8870249.

Timonen, V. (2016) *Beyond Successful and Active Ageing: A Theory of Model Ageing*, Bristol: Policy Press.

Verbruggen, C., Howell, B.M. and Simmons, K. (2020) 'How we talk about aging during a global pandemic matters: on ageist othering and aging "others" talking back', *Anthropology & Aging*, 41(2): 230–45.

Vervaecke, D. and Meisner, B.A. (2020) 'Caremongering and assumptions of need: the spread of compassionate ageism during COVID-19', *The Gerontologist*, 61(2): 159–65.

Vincent, J.A. (2009) 'Ageing, anti-ageing, and anti-anti-ageing: who are the progressives in the debate on the future of human biological ageing?', *Medicine Studies*, 1(3): 197–208.

Willetts, D. (2010) *The Pinch: How the Baby Boomers Took Their Children's Future – And Why They Should Give It Back*, London: Atlantic Books.

Williams, A., Wadleigh, P.M. and Ylänne, V. (2010) 'Images of older people in UK magazine advertising: toward a typology', *International Journal of Aging and Human Development*, 71(2): 83–114.

Woodspring, N. (2016) *Baby Boomers: Time and the Ageing Body*, Bristol: Policy Press.

Zeilig, H. (2014) 'Dementia as a cultural metaphor', *The Gerontologist*, 54(2): 258–67.

Zhang, J. and Liu, X. (2021) 'Media representation of older people's vulnerability during the COVID-19 pandemic in China,' *European Journal of Ageing*, 1–10.

3

Older adults and the pandemic in UK news media

Virpi Ylänne

Introduction

Language use in newspaper discourse reflects attitudes towards certain groups within society, but also reproduces and further promotes such attitudes. The media's tendency to misrepresent older adults as a homogeneous group has been widely reported (see, for example, Loos and Ivan, 2018 for a review). This chapter will investigate whether, and if so how, this was the case in UK news reporting in the first four months of the COVID-19 pandemic (spring 2020), and what inferences we can draw from the coverage about both the role of older adults in the newspaper discourse at the time and the role of the news media.

The context of the early stages of the pandemic in the UK will be known to readers, although there were regional differences. Following the World Health Organization's (WHO) declaration of a global pandemic on 6 March 2020, in the UK, lockdown was announced on 23 March 2020. But the first COVID-19 death had already occurred on 6 March (Scambler, 2020 p 142). The UK government has received widespread criticism for delaying the lockdown against scientific advice to 'test, trace, and isolate' much earlier (Ward, 2020, cited in Scambler, 2020 p 143), resulting in 'swathes of the vulnerable in the community and in care homes … amongst the highest casualties' (Scambler, 2020, p 143). Age scholars have highlighted how ageism has played a part in the response to the pandemic crisis (for example, Ayalon et al, 2021), accentuating societal inequalities. One example of such a critique is the response of the British Society of Gerontology (BSG) in its statement on 20 March 2020 (British Society of Gerontology, 2020). This followed the issuing of UK government advice on 16 March about social distancing and in particular the self-isolation of people over the age of 70 for a minimum of 12 weeks. The BSG raised an objection to 'any policy which differentiates the population by application of an arbitrary chronological age in restricting people's rights and freedoms … not all people over the age of 70 are vulnerable, nor all those under 70 resilient'. Although older adults have been more likely to develop severe illness from COVID-19 and comprise most cases of death from it across the globe, people of all ages have been seriously affected. It is older adults, though, who have often been at the centre of media coverage (Previtali et al, 2020). This chapter will investigate such coverage in UK news discourse.

Literature review

Previous research on newspaper portrayals of older adults has highlighted their focus on dependence and 'otherness'. Fealey et al (2012), for example, found that in Irish newspapers, older people's identities were constructed as 'victims'; 'frail, infirm, and vulnerable'; 'radicalised citizens'; 'deserving old'; or 'undeserving old'. These, collectively, assume a certain homogeneity and resort to negative stereotypes of vulnerability in older age. In contrast, radical older activists were represented as counter-stereotypical 'grey warriors', relying on readers interpreting them as atypical, and therefore still negatively based.

Rozanova's (2006, 2010) studies on Canadian news media have highlighted their alarmist stance by intimating the 'apocalyptic demography' of increased longevity (see also Chivers, 2021; Chapter 2). The texts displayed a strong association between ageing and disease and underlined the societal costs of ageing. On the other hand, 'successful ageing' ideology was also in evidence in the national newspaper under Rozanova's analysis, foregrounding individual choice and responsibility.

Similar themes have been reported in other cultural contexts, too (see, for example, Lundgren and Ljuslinder, 2011; Ishikawa, 2020; Xu, 2021). However, Koskinen et al (2014) report an absence of the 'burden' discourse in Finnish newspapers' coverage of older people and health. The authors suggest that this resonates with a Nordic model of healthcare, which promotes equal access to health and social services. Local healthcare policies, therefore, might influence the framing of news coverage.

Advocacy groups and bodies dealing with older people also regularly survey media portrayals of older adults. In the UK, the Centre for Ageing Better (2020) in England (see also Swift and Steeden, 2020) and the Older People's Commissioner for Wales (2021), for example, have recently commissioned reports, the findings of which reiterate previous academic research. The English report focuses on stereotypes of old age surrounding media coverage and the often negative language used in newspapers. The Welsh report similarly highlights ageism and a more common use of negative than positive language in the news, focusing on older people's ill health and care needs. It also looks at news coverage during the early stages of the pandemic and its potential for a critical stance towards public health information and government policy.

More recently, then, studies on how older adults are represented in the news media during the COVID-19 pandemic have started to appear, such as Morgan et al's (2021a, 2021b) studies of the New Zealand press. Their analysis revealed three main themes of representation: older people at risk; older people as passive; and older people as active. The risks comprised biological and epidemiological risks, and psychological and social risks. The former linked older age with increased risk of complications and death after contracting the virus. The latter were associated with the social isolation and loneliness resulting from the stay-at-home recommendation for people over the age of 70. As passive, older adults were depicted as spoken for and waiting to be protected, as opposed to taking part in discussions about their support and care. Relatedly, older adults were framed as a problem to be managed, and urged to take lockdown measures seriously. A more nuanced representation of older adults was as active beings, navigating the threat of the virus. Their voices were heard, and they were presented as volunteering and being online, for example. Yet, the articles nevertheless homogenised older cohorts: '[O]lder people were primarily portrayed as at risk or passive in the coverage of COVID-19 by the New Zealand news media' (Morgan et al, 2021b, p S140). We will compare this finding with UK data from the study on which this chapter is based.

Morgan et al (2021a) narrowed their examination to those articles early in the pandemic that covered the deaths of the 21 individuals comprising the New Zealand death toll at the time. Whereas articles with the theme 'unexpected community deaths' depicted the deaths as shocking, and provided biographical details of the deceased, the articles with the theme 'inevitable aged residential care deaths' described the deceased as frail, their deaths as caused by their vulnerability, and the individuals as anonymous (p 5). One finding from the study is that 'COVID-19 … made the death of older NZers newsworthy' (p 9) in a news context that typically tends to privilege cases of younger and traumatic deaths. Morgan et al (2021a) argue that journalists played an important advocacy role in supporting New Zealand's lockdown response to 'go hard and go early' (p 9), thus exemplifying the role of the news media in shaping public attitudes.

Another study about the first stage of the pandemic is that by Jen et al (2021), who examined explicit and implicit ageism in four US-based newspapers. A limited portrayal of older adults emerged where their vulnerability was highlighted by a preponderance of stories about infection, death rates and institutionalised care. In terms of language, the term 'elderly' was frequently used in these contexts. In contrast, the 'survivor' narrative offered a more positive image of resilient older adults, although potentially putting blame on those not thriving in old age. Encouragingly, in addition to the often ageist depictions, occasional opinion pieces offered a critique of ageist practices and discourses, too.

Vulnerability was also a predominant theme in Lagacé et al's (2021) study, which looked at the French Canadian press, in particular opinion and editorial (op-ed) and comment pieces, between the beginning of March and the end of May 2020 – a time period similar to the current study. The ageing process was discussed in almost half of the articles, mostly framing it as a process of decline, frailty and death. Overall, the authors suggest that the coverage contributed to 'collective manifestations of ageism' (p 6) at the time, and beyond. Vocabulary with negative connotations, such as 'vulnerable', 'alone', 'isolated' and 'death', was most frequent in reference to older adults, followed by 'more neutral' vocabulary, such as 'at risk' (p 5). More positive words, such as 'resilience' or 'grandparent (role)', were in the minority. Older adults were positioned as people who society needs to fight for and who must be protected. Older people's role as taking part in the fight against the virus was found in those few pieces (8 per cent) authored by older adults themselves.

Carney et al (2020) investigated older people's letters to the editors in the UK press about COVID-19 early in the pandemic, thus giving voice to older adults themselves, as opposed to how others represent them in newspaper discourse. The letters did not express the writers' fear of contracting the virus. Instead, their fear addressed the inevitable social isolation that accompanied the lockdown rules that obliged the over-70s to stay at home. Most talked about the problems this posed in relation to their role in the family as grandparents and as providers of childcare. Many made pleas for liberty. Of the 46 letters that formed the data, only two were about care homes and the deaths resulting from discharging older patients there from hospital without being tested for the virus (a topic frequently covered in news items at the time). This is in stark contrast to stories written by journalists, as discussed earlier. Carney et al conclude that '[t]here is a need for older people to participate in shaping responses to, and recovery from, the pandemic in a way that recognises their human rights and dignity' (p 3). The study demonstrates the benefits of investigating a range of different types of articles in newspapers. It also shows how older adults find it difficult to have their voices heard in the media unless they address the editors directly. We will now turn to the current study.

Data and methods of analysis

The data were collected from the online Nexis UK database, using the search terms old* (all variants of the word old, such as older) OR elderly AND (co-occurring with) corona OR covid OR pandemic. The period covered was between 23 March and 30 July 2020. A total of 67 news articles met the selection criteria (such as comprising UK news articles with a focus on older adults and excluding duplicates). In addition, ten articles about Captain Tom Moore were sourced (these will be discussed later; the articles referred to the protagonist's age and the word 'old', but not necessarily 'pandemic', 'covid' or 'corona'), so 77 articles form the final data sample. This comprises about 64,000 words. The articles varied in length from 103 to 2,843 words (with an average length of 841 words) and appeared in both local and national tabloid and broadsheet press and their online versions.

To address the main research question – 'How were older adults discursively represented in UK news discourse during the first four months of the COVID-19 pandemic?' – the articles were initially analysed thematically (Braun and Clarke, 2013), aided by NVivo 12 software to facilitate coding. The thematic analysis was conducted in a 'bottom-up', data-driven fashion based on how the news articles focused on older adults. Following an iterative process, four main themes were found to cover the main foci of the articles, and these will be discussed in this chapter.

Critical discourse analysis (CDA), more recently known as critical discourse studies (CDS) (see, for example, Phelan, 2020, p 285), emphasises the dialectical relationship between discursive practices and other social practices, and the constitutive role of discourse and language (see also Chapters 5 and 6). There are different approaches within CDS, such as the dialectical-relational approach (for example, Fairclough, 1995); the discourse-historical approach (for example, Wodak, 1996); the sociocognitive approach (for example, Van Dijk, 2008); and the social-semiotic approach (for example, van Leeuwen 1996). All these have been used in the analysis of media texts and the approaches have also been combined (for example, Richardson, 2007). CDS is primarily a language-based critical approach, which explores the relationship between language or a particular discursive event and the situation, institution and social structure that frames it. Along with ideology, power is a central concept in CDA/CDS and is examined both 'text- and discourse-internally … but also outside of discourse … in the ways in which particular texts and genres appear in social reality according to various motivations or particular groups holding and sustaining power and dominance' (Kryżanowski and Machin, 2020, p 63). Media analyses using CDS examine different levels of language, such as lexis (words), grammar, representation of social actors or argumentation.

In this study, we look at how the language of the articles reflects societal power structures and ideologies and consider the local context (newspaper) as well as the social context (such as the pandemic, the UK and intergenerational relations). Linguistic strategies used in the news discourse are seen as influencing how the articles are read and having a constitutive role in how older adults are positioned in the texts, shaping our understanding of older adults and older age. We will look at lexis referring to older adults, grammar in the headlines and the representation of the social actors in the news articles, drawing on the interpretive insights that can be gleaned via CDS.

Findings and discussion

Themes in the articles

'Risk' (31 articles or 40 per cent) was the most dominant theme in the articles, followed by 'death/death toll' (16 articles or 21 per cent). 'Support for older people' was the third most prominent (15 articles or 19 per cent) and, last, 'exceptional older individuals' featured as the main theme in 13 articles (or 17 per cent). Two articles that considered the impact of the pandemic to society more generally remained in an 'other' category.

As in Morgan et al's (2021b) study, the risks discussed varied from older adults being at a higher risk of contracting COVID-19, including in care homes, to their social isolation and loneliness, as targets of fraud or as victims of reduced access to medical interventions. The death/death toll themed articles were largely numerical updates on the pandemic fatalities, also relating to the risk theme. Support for older people involved coverage of organisations and communities looking after or advocating for older people and their needs during the pandemic, but also helping them to connect to others via technology. Exceptional older adults were mainly involved in fundraising activities and volunteering. We will now explore how these themes contribute to the 'othering' of older adults in these texts.

Othering via referential strategies

A CDA focus helps to uncover how older adults in these texts are 'othered'. 'Othering' has been defined as 'the practice of representing an individual or a social group … [as] distant, alien or deviant' (Coupland and Coupland, 2001, p 471), and Van Dijk (2014) talks about its contribution to an us–them positioning and hierarchical divisions between groups of people. Othering, therefore, is normally an intergroup perception and has the effect of homogenising and simplifying representations of individuals and groups.

In looking at how social groups are represented in texts, a focus on referential strategies and referring expressions is useful. Journalists must provide names and expressions to refer to the people in the events they are reporting, but there is always a choice involved. Referring expressions are nouns, noun phrases, pronouns and proper names used to identify an entity. In addition to referential meaning, the way people are named produces indexical meaning, which guides the reader's interpretation of the social meaning of the word(s) used. In this sense, referring expressions do more than 'just' refer – they have a symbolic meaning, which might challenge or confirm social stereotypes. Here, we will consider how older adults are referred to in the news texts.

Table 3.1: Categories of referring expressions

Expression	N
Older people – expressions that include the word 'older'	110 (31%)
(The) elderly – expressions that include the word 'elderly'	105 (30%)
Age in numbers or decades (for example, 'over-60s', '72-year-old')	45 (13%)
Residents – expressions that include the word 'resident' or a synonym	41 (12%)
Old – expressions that include 'old' as part of a noun phrase (for example, 'the very old')	12 (3%)
Patients – expressions that include the word 'patient' and/or for example dementia	10 (3%)
Pensioner(s) or OAP (old-age pensioner)	7 (5%)
Family role (for example, grandmother)	6 (2%)
Other (for example, Second World War veteran, NHS hero, name [excluding Tom Moore])	16 (5%)
Total	352

In the sample of 77 articles, 352 referring expressions to older adults via nouns or noun phrases were identified. We will return to proper names and titles later. Table 3.1 presents the main categories of expressions.

'Older people' was the most frequently occurring referring expression and featured in 35 articles. This is a generic term and arguably a neutral one. In addition to appearing as 'older people', 'older' also co-occurred with 'workers' (12 times), 'adults' (5), 'population' (5) and 'generation' (5), and with some more specific categories such as 'consumers' (1) and 'patients' (1). There were three instances of a possessive 'our older people'.

It is also important to consider the surrounding text for further information about the topic and the stance of the articles. With the aid of Sketch Engine corpus software, the concordance lines of the expression 'older people' were examined. These list every occurrence of the expression in the articles with its surrounding words. For example:

- phone calls with *older people* in self-isolation;
- one way of protecting *older people* against some of the worst symptoms;
- we provide critical services for *older people* and vulnerable adults;
- work by charities and organisations supporting *older people* is increasing all of the time.

This provided further evidence for the finding that older people in need of help and support was a prominent theme, together with risks, especially medical risks, even in cases where this more neutral term was used. In addition, Sketch Engine was used to find the most frequent collocates of the expression 'older people', that is, words that go together with the expression in the data. The preposition 'for' was in the top five collocates, also suggesting the positioning of 'older people' in the articles as recipients of help, support and so on.

'Elderly' was the second most frequent category and featured in 51 articles (so in many more articles than 'older people'). Here it is included both as a noun on its own as well as in 'the elderly', and as a modifier (for example, 'elderly people'). Mautner's (2007) corpus linguistic study investigated the term 'elderly' within a large online corpus of UK and US newspapers, magazines, books and other texts, also including spoken data, such as radio programmes. 'Elderly' and 'the elderly' had collocates pointing in a specific direction: '*elderly* being strongly associated with lexical items related to disability, care, victimhood and vulnerable social groups. The association is particularly noticeable with the nominalized adjective *the elderly*' (p 59). This provides illuminating evidence that it is particular groups of older adults who are assigned the label '(the) elderly'; that the expression is not the equivalent of 'old people'; and that 'elderly' does not equate to 'old'. Mautner argues that the term needs to be avoided in any general reference to older people, and indeed its general use has been discouraged in social and cultural gerontological literature.

In our data, the top collocates of 'elderly' were 'people', followed by 'vulnerable', 'relatives', 'patients', 'residents' and 'frail', echoing Mautner's findings. The use of 'elderly' achieves othering by homogenising older adults especially when co-occurring with 'vulnerable'. As discussed, the label already has this indexical meaning by itself but 'vulnerable' co-occurred with 'elderly' in 15 instances, and in a further six other expressions, for example 'vulnerable pensioners'. On the other hand, the use of 'elderly' is arguably more fitting in contexts where the focus is on older adults in vulnerable situations, such as in care homes during the first phase of the pandemic. For example, an article in the *MailOnline* reported that:

> Up to two thirds of *elderly patients* discharged from hospitals into a care home at the height of the pandemic were not tested for COVID-19, it was claimed today. NHS England data shows at least 25,000 patients were moved from hospitals to care homes between March 17 and April 15. But 16,000 weren't tested to ensure they were coronavirus-free before being moved in with other *elderly and vulnerable people*, The Times reports. (Chalmers, 16 July 2020, emphasis added)

Yet, talking about the same issue, the Older People's Commissioner for Wales, Heléna Herklots, is not reported to use the term 'elderly', and it is not used anywhere in this article: 'The situation we have seen in our care homes during the COVID-19 pandemic has been a tragedy, and I have concerns that *older people's* rights may not have been sufficiently protected in these settings and across health and social care more widely' (Gammie, 2020, emphasis added). Linking the situation with human rights and health and social care policies more generally may have affected the choice of the naming strategy in the article, in addition to the commissioner's own understandably more neutral vocabulary.

Older age indicated via reference to chronological age in years or decades was the third frequently used strategy. In Morgan et al's (2021b) New Zealand study, 32 per cent of the articles referred to a specific age and in our UK data, 39 per cent of the articles did so (52 per cent when articles about Tom Moore were included). This typically took the form of cohort reference via decades in relation to identifying groups at a higher risk of contracting COVID-19, or in death toll reports, or occasionally the age in years of individuals in focus. For example:

> *Over-65s* are six times more likely to be hospitalised with COVID-19 than those between 18 and 49. *Men over 80* are four times more likely to die as *those aged 60–79*, and for women the disparity is more than six times. (*i-Independent*, 25 June 2020, emphasis added)
>
> Oaklands Nursing Home has 15 of 20 residents with coronavirus-symptoms. One, Giuseppe Casciello, *95*, died on Monday. (*Mirror*, 4 April 2020, emphasis added)

Chronological references regarding age cohorts (such as the 'over-65s') construct a stance of a homogeneous group, typical of medical and epidemiological literatures. The use of the unmitigated 'are more likely' emphasises the status of the figures as facts and draws the reader's attention to an increased risk with age.

'Residents', 'care home residents' or near synonyms helped construct older adults as spatially distanced groups. 'Patients' and expressions such as 'untested patients' or 'dementia patients' referred to older adults primarily in hospital contexts, distinct from, albeit at times related to, the previous category. We can see that proper names were infrequent. This reflects the fact that older adults rarely featured as individual commentators. The few exceptions were adults of very advanced years, who had survived the virus – as in Jen et al's (2021) study – for example: 'BRUMMIE great gran Connie Titchen is all of 106 years old – and she has beaten coronavirus' (*Birmingham Evening Mail*, 16 April 2020). Alternatively, a few older celebrities afforded coverage as they highlighted social injustices, for example the British actor, 'Sir Tony Robinson has complained that older people have been "incarcerated" and "forgotten" during the coronavirus pandemic' (*Nottingham Post*, 30 April 2020). They were thus advocating for generic 'older people'. References to older adults via familial roles, such as grandparents, were also rare, and these were human interest stories, for example about families facing pandemic-related challenges.

The representation of older adults via referential strategies, then, arguably suppresses the heterogeneity of older adults via selective representation (Coupland, 2010 p 252), especially through the use of 'elderly' and its connotations and associated social stereotypes. On the other hand, this reflects the media attention on particular groups of older people.

Headlines

Newspaper headlines function to attract readers as well as alert them to the content of the text (Richardson, 2007, p 197). Headlines typically indicate a point of view (ideology) of the writer (and the newspaper at large) towards the topic. This is done via the grammar of transitivity. Transitivity refers to 'how actions are represented; what kind of actions appear in a text, who does them and to whom they are done – in short, the "*who* (or what) does *what* to *whom* (or what)"' (Richardson, 2007, p 54). The writer makes linguistic choices about how to represent an event's *participants* (typically by nouns or noun phrases), the event or the *process* itself (by the verb phrase) and the *circumstances* associated with the process (typically by adverbial and prepositional phrases).

In terms of participants, 56 of the 77 articles (73 per cent) referred to older adults in some way in the headline. Examples of these include:

- Age UK to make 'wellbeing calls' to *elderly* during coronavirus pandemic. (*St Helen's Star*, 24 March 2020, emphasis added)
- Homecare help for *elderly* axed during pandemic. (*Gazette*, 15 April 2020, emphasis added)
- COVID-19: *Elderly* abandoned to worst the virus can do, charities and providers warn. (*The Times*, 12 April 2020, emphasis added)
- 'ZoomWags' launched to help *over-65s* stay connected. (*East Anglian Daily Times*, 22 June 2020, emphasis added)
- More *over-50s* are claiming Universal Credit than under-25s, as *older* workers struggle in pandemic-hit job market. (*MailOnline*, 22 June 2020, emphasis added)
- Hard-up *over-75s* face losing TV access in midst of pandemic: BBC and ministers urged to 'sit down' and work out how to save free licences. (*MailOnline*, 3 June 2020, emphasis added)
- Concerns over *older people's* rights as pandemic hit Wales. (*The Western Mail*, 22 July 2020, emphasis added)

Looking at transitivity helps us uncover the role of older adults in the headlines. In terms of the process, in almost all these examples, it is people (or agents) other than the older adults who are doing things, or the passive voice is used, which here implies that the agents of the action are other than older adults (such as the government or care home management in examples one and two). The headlines in which older people are doing something almost exclusively refer to their dying.

Older people are mainly the recipients or targets of others' actions as in example one, where Age UK, a leading UK charity for older people, is presented as doing something and being behind the decision to act. In the second headline, the instigator of the 'axing' is not explicit, and in the third, it is charities and providers who are 'warning' and the virus is 'doing', whereas 'the elderly' are linked as the target of the passivised verb 'abandoned'. Passive voice is again used in 'launched' in the fourth case. In examples five and six, 'over-50s', 'older workers' and the 'hard-up over-75s' are doing things, but these actions are linked with something negative, such as 'struggl[ing]' or 'face losing'. In the last example, the only entity doing something is the pandemic.

Looking at the circumstances gives us further access to the ideological stance of the headlines. Age UK is doing something 'to' the elderly, which highlights the charity's role but also older adults as recipients of charitable actions. Homecare help exists 'for' the elderly, implying again their dependent status. The elderly are abandoned 'to', indicating their vulnerability in the context of the virus. The purpose of 'ZoomWags' is 'to help over-65s stay connected', which achieves the connotation that older adults face potential isolation and that they require assistance. In example five, the focus on the quantity in 'More over-50s' is used to highlight their financial difficulties, and the headline also alludes to intergenerational competition and tension in the job market with the comparison with 'under-25s'. The sixth example foregrounds a potential financial threat (amid the wider pandemic challenge) to those who are already 'hard-up'. The final example refers to 'older people's rights' being associated with 'concerns' (and thus potentially being violated) at the beginning of the pandemic, but the entity harbouring the concerns is unidentified as we only have the plural noun as the first word. This creates an implicature of two distinct groups: those who are concerned and those whose rights are under threat.

In sum, the headlines in these data typically communicate older adults' roles as recipients or targets of actions (or processes) and position them as lacking in agency, skill, financial resources or rights.

Exceptional individuals

It is 'important to recognise that casting a person or a group as "other" is not inherently and necessarily to marginalise or disparage them' (Coupland, 2010, p 241), although this typically tends to be the focus of research. In the period under investigation, there were many news items on exceptional older individuals, too. Many focused on 99-year-old Captain Tom Moore (TM), who raised millions of pounds for the UK National Health Service (NHS) and inspired other older adults to also fundraise.

In this coverage, TM was predominantly referred to (or nominated) formally by his military title, Captain, followed by his name, and categorised as a Second World War veteran, collectively indicating a respected social status and standing, in addition to his advanced age. With time, he was also referred to less formally by a more familiar 'Captain Tom', and later, after receiving a knighthood, 'Sir Tom'. A typical example from the data is as follows:

> A 99-year-old Second World War veteran has raised more than £12m for the NHS by walking 100 laps of his garden using a zimmer frame.
>   Captain Tom Moore, who turns 100 on April 30, wanted to complete the challenge at his home in Bedfordshire before his birthday to support medics on the frontline … who he says are 'national heroes'. …
>   His outstanding achievement was recognised by Matt Hancock, the health secretary, during the Wednesday evening press conference at Downing Street. (*The Telegraph*, 14 April 2020)

This article, and the others, provide details about TM's background, his military career, his recent medical problems, the care he received from the NHS and his daily routine, and he is interviewed and quoted, thus given voice. These discursive strategies achieve individualisation (van Leeuwen, 1996), in stark contrast to articles about collectivised 'older people' and the 'elderly'. Across the ten articles about TM, he is described as an 'inspiration', 'a role model', an 'NHS hero', 'an unexpected hero', 'a national treasure', 'very stoic and controlled' (in a quote from his daughter), 'remarkable', to have 'captured the public imagination with his astonishing feat', to have 'show[n] optimism and energy', and his efforts 'heroic'. He is represented as active, 'walking laps of his garden', although 'clutching his walking frame', implying the extra effort involved and indexing his agedness. Othering here works by TM being presented as atypical and positively exceptional.

The news value of surprise and 'superlativeness' (Bednarek and Caple, 2014) framed the media coverage of TM. In addition, as Henry Mance wrote in the *Financial Times* (25 April 2020): 'Britons have a largely uncomplicated reverence for two things: the memory of the second world war and the NHS. Captain Tom bridges them.' The wide coverage of TM across various media afforded a 'feel good' factor among other, more sombre, news about the pandemic and positively portrayed an old individual playing a useful role in society. Yet, the spotlighting of TM and the results of other similar fundraising efforts obscured the need to fundraise for what is a nationalised health service.

Conclusion

CDA involves the explication and contextualisation of the data at different levels. We have seen that the referential strategies in the texts under study in this chapter and the transitivity in the headlines achieved 'othering' via collective expressions that often connoted vulnerability and positioned older adults as the recipients of others' actions. These related to the themes of risk and support for older people. Even though the texts displayed some critique of government action and, for example, highlighted inadequacies and shortages in health providers' supplies, the construction of vulnerable populations was arguably simplistic in its main focus on 'the elderly' (see also Chapter 2). We also need to acknowledge the priorities of news texts and their associated news values in determining what gets reported. At a more macro level, the strategies used, and the stories covered, helped construct older adults as needing protection and stricter self-isolation than younger populations in the early phase of the pandemic. The death toll coverage also played its part in constructing the virus as a particular concern for older cohorts. This suggests intergenerational differences and responsibilities (and potentially tensions) in the first few months. Individualisation was almost exclusively evident in the stories about exceptional people. And exceptional older adults were those performing active and useful social roles.

UK news coverage in the first four months of the COVID-19 pandemic continued the trend of representing older adults as largely a homogeneous group, foregrounding their vulnerability, dependency on others and passivity or, at times, their exceptional status. We can link this representation with the ageism reported in many previous studies. Older people were mainly presented in roles whereby things were done to or for them, with the exception of Captain Tom Moore and a few other similar fundraisers, who were depicted as exceptional heroes. There was a tendency for a problem orientation in relation to older age in the context of the pandemic, but also more generally. The pandemic was presented as multiplying the challenges faced by older adults, both in terms of health risks and access to healthcare, but also in terms of social exclusion and vulnerability. Yet, older adults' voices were rarely present. In the later articles in the sample, there were some critical voices about the treatment of care home residents, for example, but these came from institutional representatives, celebrities or family members as advocates for the residents.

In the context of a health crisis, older people as at risk arguably needed highlighting, such as the risks and fatalities experienced in care homes. However, a predominant news media positioning of older adults as vulnerable, risks expressions of 'compassionate ageism' (Vervaeke and Meisner, 2021), or 'benevolent ageism', via a potentially paternalistic stance and the perpetuation of a dependency-support script of old age. This arguably also fuels disassociation from the category 'old' those older adults who identify as ageing 'well', constructing othering between and within older cohorts. Later in the pandemic, other age groups at risk, such as university students, appeared in the news as vulnerable. While those reports also exhibited ageist sentiments, the protagonists were afforded much more visibility and agency than the nameless older adults in the data analysed in this chapter, demonstrating that ageist portrayals themselves are multidetermined.

Note

I wish to thank Charlotte Griffin, Charlotte Joyce, and Cecily Edwards for their help with the data coding.

References

Ayalon, L., Chasteen, A., Diehl, M., Levy, B.R., Neupert, S.D., Rothermund, K., Tesch-Römer, C. and Wahl, H.-W. (2021) 'Aging in times of the COVID-19 pandemic: avoiding ageism and fostering intergenerational solidarity', *Journals of Gerontology: Psychological Sciences*, 76(2): e49–e52.

Bednarek, M. and Caple, H. (2014) 'Why do news values matter? Towards a new methodological framework for analysing news discourse in critical discourse analysis and beyond', *Discourse & Society*, 25(2): 135–58.

Braun, V. and Clarke, V. (2013) *Successful Qualitative Research*, London: Sage.

British Society of Gerontology (2020) 'BSG statements on COVID', available from: https://www.britishgerontology.org/publications/bsg-statements-on-covid-19 [accessed 27 March 2020].

Carney, G.M., Maguire, S., Byrne, B. and Gray, A.M. (2020) 'Caged and forgotten: older people's letters to the editor about COVID-19', *Research Update*, 134, September, available from https://ark.ac.uk [accessed 15 July 2021].

Centre for Ageing Better (2020) *Doddery but Dear? Examining Age-related Stereotypes*, London: Centre for Ageing Better, available from: https://www.ageing-better.org.uk/publications/ [accessed 1 December 2020].

Chalmers, V. (2020) 'Up to two thirds of elderly patients "were discharged from hospitals to care homes without a COVID-19 test at the height of the pandemic"', *MailOnline*, 16 July [accessed via Nexis UK, 26 January 2021].

Chivers, S. (2021) '"With friends like these": unpacking panicked metaphors for population ageing', *Societies*, 11(3): 69.

Coupland, N. (2010) '"Other" representation', in J. Jaspers, J.-O. Östman and J. Verschueren (eds) *Society and Language Use*, Amsterdam: John Benjamins, pp 241–60.

Coupland, N. and Coupland, J. (2001) 'Language, ageing and ageism', in P.W. Robinson and H. Giles (eds) *The New Handbook of Language and Social Psychology*, Chichester: John Wiley & Sons, pp 467–86.

Fairclough, N. (1995) *Critical Discourse Analysis*, London: Longman.

Fealey, G., McNamara, M., Pearl Treacy, M. and Lyons, I. (2012) 'Constructing ageing and age identity: a case study of newspaper discourses', *Ageing and Society*, 32(1): 85–102.

Gammie, J. (2020) 'Call for probe into Covid-19 care home testing: "Older people's human rights infringed as testing delayed"', *The Western Mail*, May 22, p. 2.

Ishikawa, M. (2020) 'Media portrayals of ageing baby boomers in Japan and Finland', doctoral dissertation, Faculty of Social Sciences, University of Helsinki.

Jen, S., Jeong, M., Kang, H. And Riquino, M. (2021) 'Ageism and COVID-related newspaper coverage: the first month of the pandemic', *Journals of Gerontology: Social Sciences*, 76(9): 1904–12.

Koskinen, S., Salminen, L. and Leino-Kilpi, H. (2014) 'Media portrayal of older people as illustrated in Finnish newspapers', *International Journal of Qualitative Studies on Health and Well-being*, 9: 25304.

Kryżanowski, M. and Machin, D. (2020) 'Media analysis in/and critical discourse studies', in C. Cotter and D. Perrin (eds) *The Routledge Handbook of Language and Media*, Abingdon: Routledge, pp 62–76.

Lagacé, M., Doucet, A., Dangoisse, P. and Bergeron, C. (2021) 'The "vulnerability" discourse in times of COVID-19: between abandonment and protection of Canadian Francophone older adults', *Frontiers in Public Health*, 9: 662231.

Loos, E. and Ivan, L. (2018) 'Visual ageism in the media', in L. Ayalon and C. Tesch-Römer (eds) *Contemporary Perspectives on Ageism: International Perspectives on Ageing*, Cham: Springer Open, pp 163–76.

Lundgren, A.S. and Ljuslinder, K. (2011) '"The baby-boom is over and the ageing shock awaits": populist media imagery in news press representations of population ageing', *International Journal of Ageing and Later Life*, 6(2): 39–71.

Mance, H. (2020) 'The age of heroes. Henry Mance talks to 99-year-old Captain Tom Moore, Britain's unlikely hero of the coronavirus crisis – and asks what the war veteran's sudden fame tells us about our response to the pandemic', *Financial Times*, 25 April [accessed via Nexis UK, 1 February 2021].

Mautner, G. (2007) 'Mining large corpora for social information: the case of *elderly*', *Language in Society*, 36(1): 51–72.

Morgan, T., Carey, M., Gott, M., Williams, L., Egli, V. and Anderson, N. (2021a) 'More than mortality data: a news media analysis of COVID-19 deaths in Aotearoa, New Zealand', *Kōtuitui: New Zealand Journal of Social Sciences Online*, 16(2): 419–31.

Morgan, T., Wiles, J., Williams, L. and Gott, M. (2021b) 'COVID-19 and the portrayal of older people in New Zealand news media', *Journal of the Royal Society of New Zealand*, 51(suppl 1): S127–S142.

Nexis UK, NexisLexis Butterworths, available from: https://advance.lexis.com/bisnexishome/?pdmfid=1519360&crid=9d45f6ea-6201-4166-88fb-3c85464d62d3 [accessed 1 February 2021].

Older People's Commissioner for Wales (2021) *Portrayal of Older People in News Media*, Cardiff: Older People's Commissioner for Wales.

Phelan, S. (2020) 'Critical discourse analysis and media studies', in J. Flowerdew and J.E. Richardson (eds) *The Routledge Handbook of Critical Discourse Studies*, Abingdon: Routledge, pp 285–97.

Previtali, F., Allen, L.D. and Varlamova, M. (2020) 'Not only virus spread: the diffusion of ageism during the outbreak of COVID-19', *Journal of Aging & Social Policy*, 32(4–5): 506–14.

Richardson, J.E. (2007) *Analysing Newspapers: An Approach from Critical Discourse Analysis*, Basingstoke: Palgrave Macmillan.

Rozanova, J. (2006) 'Newspaper portrayals of health and illness among Canadian seniors: who ages healthily and at what cost?', *International Journal of Ageing and Later Life*, 1(2): 111–39.

Rozanova, J. (2010) 'Discourse of successful ageing in The Globe and Mail: insights from critical gerontology', *Journal of Aging Studies*, 24(4): 213–22.

Scambler, G. (2020) 'COVID-19 as a "breaching experiment": exposing the fractured society', *Health Sociology Review*, 29(2): 140–8.

Sketch Engine, available from: https://www.sketchengine.eu/ [accessed 1 August 2021].

Swift, H. and Steeden, B. (2020) *Exploring Representations of Old Age and Ageing: Literature Review*. London: Centre for Ageing Better, available from: Exploring-representations-of-old-age-review.pdf (ageing-better.org.uk) [accessed 1 December 2020].

Van Dijk, T.A. (2008) *Discourse and Context:. A Sociocognitive Approach*, Cambridge: Cambridge University Press.

Van Dijk, T.A. (2014/1992) 'Discourse and the denial of racism', in A. Jaworski and N. Coupland (eds) *The Discourse Reader* (3rd edn), London and New York, NY: Routledge, pp 425–39.

Van Leeuwen, T. (1996) 'The representation of social actors', in C.R. Caldas-Coulthard and M. Coulthard (eds) *Texts and Practices: Readings in Critical Discourse Analysis*, London: Routledge, pp 32–70.

Vervaeke, D. and Meisner, B.A. (2021) 'Caremongering and assumptions of need: the spread of compassionate ageism during COVID-19', *The Gerontologist*, 61(2): 159–65.

Wodak, R. (1996) *Disorders of Discourse*, London: Longman.

Xu, W. (2021) *Ageism in the Media: Online Representations of Older People*, Linköping, Sweden: Linköping University.

4

Present-time witches: media and the intersecting discourses of age, gender and mental health in Ghana

Monika Wilińska and Doris Boateng

Introduction

A tall and slender silhouette in black, always with a large pointy hat shading the face, and often surrounded by birds and cats. The witch is always mysterious but also mischievous; she always engages in dark magic. When she fails, she howls, but when she succeeds, her wicked and terrifying laughter penetrates the surroundings with an incredible force. Witches are commonly portrayed as middle-aged and older women who live alone, far away from anyone else and when they interact with others, they do that among themselves. They use broomsticks to fly to faraway places, but also to hover above ordinary lives, spreading fear and terror.

That is a typical popular culture's image of a witch in the Western imaginary. The image has been recreated in countless stories, artworks and pictures. From the Biblical mentions of witches in the ancient world, through *Maleus Mallificarium*[1] in the Middle Ages (Broedel, 2003), to the contemporary Disney production of *Maleficent* (2014), the images of witches as dangerous and possessed by malicious spirits have prevailed. But these have not been just images; they are also part of larger societal discourses including all 'meaningful practices that form the identities of subjects and objects' (Howarth and Stavrakakis, 2000, pp 3–4). In this, the distance between green-faced images of the Wicked Witch of the West from the 20th century (*The Wizard of Oz*, 1939) and the Salem witch trials from the 17th century, is not so great. Concrete media representations and social and material practices are all intertwined and reliant on each other. They constitute vital aspects of an overarching societal discourse that delineates the contours of witches and witchcraft.

As much as the figure of a witch seems to penetrate diverse temporal and spatial contexts, its shape and character may differ substantially. In this chapter, we turn our attention to the ways in which witches are constructed in Ghana, a country of the Global South. Contrary to Western images of witches as far away from ordinary life, the witches from the Global South seem to be deeply embedded in everyday life. Typically, witches are mothers, grandmothers, mothers-in-law and sisters-in-law. These are women who live in their local communities, they are known to everybody and they look just like everyone else – until the moment when they are accused of possessing supernatural powers and using them to inflict harm or death onto another family or local community member (Riedel, 2018). As such, a witch from a Global South is 'one of us' who has unexpectedly gone awry.

Regardless of the context, a witch is considered a powerful figure, and it is her power that has for centuries made her a target of public crusades and cruel trials. After all, a witch is typically a woman in late middle-age. Badoe (2005) emphasises that a study of witches is intrinsically related to the study of gender and sexuality. For example, using cases from her home country of Ghana, she demonstrates how, at times, the accusations of witchcraft can be directed at successful and independent women who are, as a result, reminded in a very crude way about the rules of a patriarchal system and men's control. The feminist discourses around witches are not, however, unanimous. Some appropriate a figure of a witch as a symbol of power, freedom and resistance; a figure not to be afraid of, but a figure to aspire to. Rountree (1997) explicates that by bringing together the ideals of goddesses and witches who all emanate inner power and independence, and who, because of that, are feared by men but appreciated by women. Others, however, are more cautious about the universal usage of 'the witch' as a symbol unifying and appealing to women across times and spaces (for example, Sempruh, 2004). There is still a great deal of mystery concerning witches, and this relates not only to their character, but also to their appropriation in the mainstream social space.

In this chapter, we therefore attempt to unmask some of the mysteries surrounding the figure of a witch by focusing on modern-day witches and the ways in which they are constructed in the media in one of the countries of the Global South – Ghana. Ghana is one of the countries known for the persistence of not only witch-hunt practices, but also witch refugee camps, established to host women accused of witchcraft (Federici, 2010).

The chapter proceeds as follows. The next section places our study within the field of research exploring the intersection of age, gender and the media. Thereafter, we introduce the particularities of everyday life for ageing women in Ghana and discuss the problem of mental ill health in that context. The core of the chapter focuses on the discussion of modern-time witches through the perspective of interlinked media, cultural and political practices. In the final section of the chapter, we discuss the changing position of the media and its role in the construction of social phenomena in countries of the Global South.

The construction of women and ageing in and via the media

The relationship between women, ageing and the media has never been straightforward. For the most part, the media have been heavily criticised for under-representing older women (see, for example, Lauzen and Dozier, 2005; Beugnet, 2006; Anderson and Han, 2008; Lewis et al, 2011). This process of the symbolic annihilation of older women, as explained by Bauman and de Laat (2012), pushes older women away from the mainstream culture on the basis of their presumably lost beauty, young age and vitality. Further, when older women appear in the media, their images are very often stereotypical and presented via the prism of judgements made on the basis of physical appearance (see, for example, Lemish and Muhlbauer, 2012; LaWare and Moutsatos, 2013). In addition, there seems to be a limited scope of potential roles that older women may take up in the media (Oró-Piqueras, 2012). Because of that, studies point to the individualistic discourses permeating the media when discussing older women and their lives. For example, studies focusing on the media coverage of older mothers in Canadian newspapers and television (Campbell, 2011) and UK newspapers (Shaw and Giles, 2009; Budds et al, 2013) reveal the underlying logic of individual responsibility and choice that guides the media in approaching that topic. For instance, older women who are pregnant are commonly 'blamed' for the potential risks associated with pregnancies at an older age (Ylänne, 2016).

On the other hand, it has been recognised that the media can have an important role in destabilising rigid roles and can be purposefully used to alter dominant stereotypes. For example, Lövgren (2013) gives an example of the Swedish media and the word '*tant*' (which can mean both 'auntie' and 'granny', or 'little old lady'), commonly used to refer to older women. Drawing on several types of media, she demonstrates the apparent ambivalence in the use of this word, which ranges from negative to positive depictions of female ageing. In a similar vein, Coupland (2013), reflecting on various appropriations of grannyhood in the media, recognises the variety of uses, but at the same time cautions about the underlying logic of removing diverse voices of older women from the media. In general, the diversity of older women is a non-existent topic in the media. Reflections on the career of female comedians by Mock (2012) and on the actress Judi Dench by Krainitzki (2014) provide the grounds to discuss the potential of acting for age and gender stereotypes, stepping outside them, and challenging them. This is in line with Harpin's (2012) reading of several contemporary British theatre plays featuring older women as main heroines – the presence of older women and their voices on stage can be seen as signs of change.

In this chapter, we recognise that the media have an important role in shaping societal discourses, but that process is far from being one directional.

Thus, we refer here to the phenomenon of co-constructing discourses and practices (Couldry, 2009). Such an approach maintains that media content is as much affected by the media industry and its logics as it is by an expression of audiences' practices, hopes and fears (Altheide, 2013; van Dijck and Poell, 2013). Thus, in order to reach a deeper and more nuanced understanding of the media's role in contemporary societies, we focus on the interactive processes that are involved in the creation and reception of various media contents (Iversen and Wilińska, 2020). More specifically, in this chapter we demonstrate the interaction between media, political and societal discourses and their outcomes for shaping the contemporary images of witches and witchcraft in Ghana.

Gender, ageing and mental health in Ghana

In almost every society, differentiations are made on the basis of age and gender. People's age and gender often determine their access to resources in their community, as well as the options and choices available to them. These differentiations in social lives are also reflected in people's internal states such as their emotions, meaning making and predisposition to certain health conditions. Due to the gendered nature of social life, mental health also tends to be gendered (WHO, 2002). There have been different schools of thought on the gendered nature of mental health. For some time, there have been heated debates over the differences between the mental health of men and women in Ghana. Some argue that women have more psychopathology than men, while others claim that men have more; others think that both genders suffer equally, but from different maladies (Rosenfeld and Smith, 2010).

In addition, although both sex and age are fundamentally biological, they exponentially get defined in social terms – as gender and ageing – as a person goes through the life cycle. Consciously and unconsciously, in tacit and explicit ways, gender and age come to play in socialisation, the formation and maintenance of social ties, productive activities at home and elsewhere, and encounters with health risks and their physical and mental outcomes. A person's gender and age determine their social standing, and the demands society will make on them, which eventually holds outcomes for their mental health. Mental health problems are among the most important contributors to global burdens of disease and disability. Examples of mental health problems are depressive and anxiety disorders, eating disorders and schizophrenia. These conditions have been gendered in the way they are seen to be either masculine or feminine. For example, depression and anxiety are considered to be more feminine because of their emotional overtones (Fusco, 2017), or been known to be more associated with one gender than the other (Rosenfeld and Smith, 2010).

It has been argued that gender differences in mental health disorders transcend differences related to the rates of prevalence among men and women and include several factors that can affect risk or susceptibility, diagnosis, treatment and adjustment. Gender differences in the prevalence of mental disorders vary across age groups as well; for example, conduct disorder, the commonest psychiatric disorder, often occurs in childhood, with three times as many boys as girls being affected (Ogundele, 2018). During adolescence, girls tend to have a higher prevalence of depression and eating disorders and engage more in suicidal ideation and suicide attempts than boys, who are more prone to engaging in high-risk behaviours and committing suicide (Lemstra et al, 2008). Age and gender also influence intentions to seek professional psychological help, as women tend to exhibit more favourable intentions to seek help from mental health professionals than men (Mackenzie et al, 2008).

In Ghanaian society, both gender and age are key determinants of a person's access to healthcare generally but are even more critical for mental healthcare. Further, one's geographical location and socioeconomic status add to one's gender and age, leading to differential access to quality mental healthcare (Ofori-Atta et al, 2010). Again, differential gender roles between men and women mediate the relationship between age and mental health. Women bear the majority of the care burden and are therefore expected to be strong to take care of their children, grandchildren and the family in general. In many instances, they are expected to modify their physical and psychological wellbeing for the sake of their dependants (Khlat et al, 2000).

Ageing in Ghana has become problematic for many women due to several sociocultural and socioeconomic challenges they face. The more a woman advances in age, the more her status in the Ghanaian society weakens. Her social networks begin to diminish and if she cannot afford certain services, then she is at the mercy of the larger society, which may scorn or ridicule her or even accuse her of being 'a witch'. Because mental health problems are often related to low income, widowhood and social isolation, older women living in poverty tend to bear the brunt of witchcraft accusations. There is therefore a need for a gender approach to mental health to provide guidance for the identification of appropriate responses from the mental healthcare system from all stakeholders, as well as from public policy (Afifi, 2007).

Present-time witches: intersecting media, cultural and political practices

The issues of witchcraft and witches remain prevalent and highly relevant in today's Ghana. One of the material artefacts illuminating this are so-called 'witch camps', or sanctuaries that offer refuge to women accused of dark magic. There are nine sanctuaries located in more remote, northern parts of the country, which host up to 1,000 women (Riedel, 2018). Such sanctuaries and the women who live there demonstrate that gender is only one of many perspectives implicated in the social construction of witches. Age and ageing appear to be equally pronounced although not equally recognised (Crampton, 2013). Similarly, everyday practices provide further evidence suggesting that issues of mental health and ill health tend to feature profoundly in the societal discourses concerning witches in Ghana.

Witch camps or sanctuaries have, for a long time, attracted the attention of the media, policies and human rights organisations. However, that attention has not led to concrete actions and measures that would aid the situation of the women residing in them. One of the key concerns brought to the public eye has been the inhuman conditions and violence that women have had to endure while living in the camps. Tragically, thus, the places of refuge can turn into places of further abuse (Sossou and Yogtiba, 2015). On the other hand, witch camps are also recognised as potentially important for the process of healing and reconciling. In this, they are seen as only consequences of a bigger problem than the accusations of witchcraft.

Witches as victims of poverty and superstition

Ghanaian media abound with stories of witchcraft. From locally produced movies, to documentaries and news coverage, one frequently comes across an article on witchcraft. Perhaps the first and internationally produced media that highlighted the plight of 'witches' in Ghana was the documentary by Yaba Badoe dubbed *The Witches of Gambaga* (2010). This has been widely acclaimed in both national and international contexts. It won the Best Documentary Award at the 2010 Black International Film Festival and second prize in the documentary competition at Africa's largest film festival – FESPACO – in Burkina Faso (Ekine, 2012). A synopsis of the documentary is given as follows:

> The Witches of Gambaga is a haunting 55-minute documentary film about a community of women condemned to live as witches in Northern Ghana. Made over the course of 5 years, this disturbing expose is the product of a collaboration between members of the 100 strong community of 'witches', local women's movement activists and feminist researchers, united by their interest in ending abusive practices and improving women's lives in Africa. Painful experience and insight combine to generate a uniquely intimate record of the lives of women ostracized from their communities. Told largely by the women themselves, their incredible stories and struggles are rendered comprehensible to a wide range of audiences by the director's narration. Completed in July 2010, Fadoa Films Ghana and UK, Directed by Yaba Badoe, Co-produced by Yaba Badoe and Amina Mama. (African Women's Development Fund, 2011)

In watching the documentary, certain key issues immediately come to the fore. The stark poverty in the communities where such witchcraft accusations occur compels one to wonder whether witchcraft accusations have a direct correlation with poverty. It appears that the poorer a person or community is, the more likely they are to believe that somebody else, in this case the 'witch', is responsible for their woes. Such associations are further strengthened by the images that accompany media reporting on witches and witchcraft. For example, articles in print media often portray impoverished neighbourhoods and, if women are presented, they are often photographed against walls that are bare, unpainted and falling apart.

The second key issue is the feminisation of witchcraft in Ghana. In the documentary, one male narrator is heard saying that although both men and women are witches, female witches tend to use their witchcraft to cause harm, while male witches use theirs to protect their families. Due to such beliefs, there is a widespread stigma associated with witchcraft, causing people to persecute and sometimes kill those who are accused.

In addition to this, widespread superstition and the alarming increase in the number of self-styled spiritualists, who claim to possess the ability to cast out demons, have resulted in some serious abuses of 'witches' in the country. In the past, such accusations and subsequent abuses were either few or did not get to the notice of the mainstream population. However, due to technological advancement and the increasing use of social media, such events now get publicised for many people to see. The media coverage of topics related to witchcraft and witches emerges, therefore, as an important reminder of practices that many people in the country would like to disassociate themselves from.

The local movie industry also abounds with stories of witchcraft and black magic. In most such movies, the 'witch' is portrayed as a middle-aged or older woman who is jealous, greedy and generally evil, and uses her witchcraft to kill and/or destroy other people's good fortunes. Such films end up stoking negative emotions in viewers about witchcraft. This, unfortunately, then ends up causing people to lynch those they accuse of witchcraft, sometimes to death.

From cultural practice to the media and politics

In November 2010, the Ghanaian public were horrified to see front-page pictures of an older woman in Tema (one of the districts in the capital city, Accra), who had been burnt to death for being a witch. The 72-year-old woman had been tortured into confessing to being a witch by a pastor, who, with the assistance of four others, poured kerosene on the woman and set her ablaze. She later succumbed to her injuries after she was rescued and taken to the hospital. This story was reported by the *Daily Graphic*, a state-owned newspaper, and was later picked up by the international news portal, *The Guardian* (29 November 2010). The report sparked outrage across the country, with many influential groups and individuals issuing statements to categorically condemn the act and calling for the arrest and prosecution of the individuals involved. The victim's son, a 48-year-old businessman, indicated that the mother had never suffered from any known mental health condition, except for forgetfulness and other symptoms of old age. The so-called symptoms of old age and forgetfulness are very often lost in societal debates regarding witchcraft. In practice, these may be signs of mental health problems that make women who experience them easy targets for accusations. This, in particular, refers to very old women living in remote locations where social awareness concerning mental health issues is much lower. Thus, any changes in behaviour, such as forgetting, being confused or absent-minded, can be read as evidence of contact with evil powers.

On 12 January 2018, a two-year-old Ghanaian girl with blue eyes was reported to be a witch. This story broke on Facebook and other social media platforms, with pictures circulating of the little girl. Due to the interactive nature of social media, people who were familiar with the condition could post comments to educate sharers of the picture that the little girl's bluish eyes stemmed from a rare condition called Waardenburg Syndrome (WS). Usually, the belief that people use their witchcraft to kill, destroy and wreak havoc on others is the reason why people accused of witchcraft are lynched in many parts of the country. In the instance of this little girl, many factors might have accounted for her life being spared. First, there were beliefs that went with the picture that she could be a god, or that her family had been cursed. Second, the girl's age could have been a factor, meaning that she could not be destructive at this age. And third, the education that followed the sharing of her picture prevented her from getting killed. This example highlights the great role of social media in contemporary societal discourses and practices. The swift mobilisation of social media, aiming at saving the accused girl and preventing another potentially tragic event, demonstrates the use of media for activism purposes. Yet, the example illuminates one of the key issues surrounding the witchcraft accusation, namely that any difference in physical appearance or behaviour can be used as a sign of contact and alignment with evil forces. While physical features can be quickly recognised and diagnosed as a sign of illness, changes in mental state are less often discussed in terms of underlying problems with mental health or mental illness.

In the years since the November 2010 incident, many other similar incidents have been reported in various news outlets, each of which receiving attention from various circles in society, although that attention appears to die down quickly. While the media attend to cruel incidents and report the wrongdoing, efforts to follow up on the issues at hand are minimal. By drawing attention only to the most severe cases that many people condemn and are appalled by, the witchcraft reporting does not seem to engage with the underlying structures and aspects of everyday life that make such acts possible. The same applies to the public debates arising at the outset of such reporting, which tend to single out the events and criminalise the acts but fail to discuss wider structures and common elements of culture that uphold witchcraft accusations.

In July 2020, another unfortunate news story, of a 90-year-old woman who was lynched to death in her village after a fetish priest in the area had suggested that she was a witch, hit the Ghanaian media. The whole event was filmed on a mobile phone by one of the bystanders and uploaded thereafter on social media. The video and its content initiated a renewed public debate and actions regarding witches and witchcraft in Ghana, sparking outrage across the country.

The manner in which the nonagenarian had been subjected to severe beatings, leading to her untimely death, was cruel. Many groups and influential individuals issued statements against this event, insisting that the time had come for the country to have an open and honest discussion about witchcraft accusations and the ways in which they have been gendered over the years. In the context of that event, the role of the media had also been elevated. For example, in one of the articles in *Daily Graphic*, reflecting on the so-called 'Ghana's day of shame', the following statement was made: 'God bless the video (wo)man and the video technology. You can imagine how many such lynches have gone unreported because nobody filmed them' (31 July 2020).

Social media and digital technology were assigned here the role of an important witness that can testify to the committed abuse and cruelty. The event was portrayed as belonging to a series of events that typically remain unknown. The media debates that followed emphasised the backwardness of people engaging in witchcraft accusations, and the need for criminalising such acts. Both the President of Ghana and the Minister of Gender, Children and Social Protection gave speeches and posted online comments in which they condemned the act from the point of view of human rights abuse and proposed changes to the legislative system. All this resulted in the arrest and prosecution of several members of the crowd who took an active part in the lynching and contributed to the death of the older woman.

The reporting and subsequent public discussion regarding the crime, but also the woman who was killed, were focused on the individual. The full name of the victim and her funeral pictures (staged photographs portraying older people in festive outfits) were used in the media reporting, instead of, as mentioned earlier, anonymous images of impoverished areas and neighbourhoods. Words such as '*madame*' and '*grandma*' appeared in public, signalling the respect paid to the victim. This could be read as a way of bringing the victim closer to the audience and a way of magnifying the cruelty and inhumanity of the killing. At the same time, the discussion and subsequent actions at the political level kept on drawing a boundary between the law-abiding majority and the criminal minority. For example, a notion that the events of July 2020 were 'Ghana's day of shame', as the chief executive of the mental health authority expressed, were not widely recognised. The notion of shared responsibility for such cruel practices has not fully entered the mainstream discourse and debates.

From public and political debates to media practices

The Ghanaian society is notoriously religious (with Christianity, Islam and traditional beliefs constituting the main religions) and tends to attribute many events and incidents to the supernatural. When misfortune hits a community, the tendency to suspect and accuse someone or something as the cause is common. Those who are accused often do not get the chance to speak up to defend themselves. They are at the mercy of the community who decide what kind of punishment best fits the 'crime'. It would take other family members and the social ties of the accused to defend and protect them. Because women are socialised and expected to be submissive and docile, outspoken and/or eccentric older women are those most typically accused of witchcraft. In some ways, such accusations are used to send 'warning signals' to other women to fit with the status quo and not to push the boundaries of their society, but the punishments meted out to accused 'witches' are becoming increasingly extreme.

Since the July 2020 incident, there have been many stories of accused 'witches' who have come out to share their ordeal and how they escaped from witch camps, or other hidden witch camps and the treatment of inmates. Ghanaian media appear to not only report the events but also create a space for the accused women to share their stories and experiences. In this way, the media open up the dominant societal discourse regarding witchcraft by representing the perspective of mistreated and abused women who seek refuge and understanding. Modern Ghana, an online news portal, reported that as many as 17 other women had been lined up for lynching in the village where the 90-year-old woman was murdered. One of the escapees, 69-year-old Hawa Yakubu, recounted thus: 'I was about to have a bath, but they refused to allow me to shower and dragged me out of the house' (modernghana.com, 30 July 2020). Earlier, 3 News, another online news portal, had reported Hawa Yakubu of indicating that 'I had to admit to their demands that I'm a witch to save my life. I would have been dead by now' (3News.com, 29 July 2020).

Hardly a month after these incidents, a local radio station reported on a 60-year-old Meri Ibrahim, who together with other older women were alleged to have bewitched a gentleman and were thus brutalised until they confessed to being witches. In her words, Ibrahim narrated her ordeal as: '[S]ee, see how they have cut my hand, see the wounds they have inflicted on me. If we had not accepted that we were witches, they would have killed us' (Nkilgi FM, 29 August 2020).

Unfortunately, there does not appear to be a clear, concerted effort by the government or civil society to better protect and safeguard the lives of these modern-times witches, who may meet their untimely death simply because someone or a group of people decides they are not worthy of living, either because their lives did not fit the prescribed ways of being, or because they began exhibiting some 'out-of-ordinary' features.

Discussion

This chapter offers a critical reflection on the knowledge and production of images of older women as witches through societal and cultural practices involving traditional and new media. In this, we have discussed the media as integral to societal lives that are neither constant nor obsolete but rapidly changing. By the same token, we have problematised the ageing, gender and media connections in the context of the Global South and the insights such discussions provide worldwide.

This chapter aimed to shed some light on the contemporary figure of a witch in Ghana. The discussion advanced here portrays a highly problematic picture. On the one hand, the societal discourse including media and political practices focuses on witchcraft accusations and the resultant abuse and violence. In this, the debate about witchcraft and witches is only partial. On the other hand, the so-called witches are hardly ever invited to partake in that discourse. Instead, they are largely portrayed as silent victims who undergo trial by ordeal at the mercy of a mob who are only too happy to 'rid' society of 'those who use dark magic'.

The intricate relationship between the media, ageing, gender and mental health in Ghana has also been presented. The media landscape provides an avenue for making visible an age-old problem, which hitherto has remained hidden and/or unknown. Clearly, many old women have been murdered in the past, but currently, the media are being widely used to shed light on the problem and have caught the needed government and civil society attention for addressing the situation. The media play critical roles in setting the agenda and ensuring that dispassionate discussions are held, and critical paths followed, to ensure the success and development of economies. As evidenced in this chapter, that critical role may be enacted in many different ways, for example, revising the vocabulary used to refer to older women accused of witchcraft, or creating spaces for women to tell their own stories using their own voices. The emergence of social media and their meaning in the countries of the Global South also seem to provide another impetus for informing society about the cruelty and severity of witch-hunting practices. Above all else, the rapidly spreading images of witch-hunting in social media raise awareness of the problem and make it visible to a large majority of the Ghanaian population. This not only brings the problem closer to the average citizen but may also encourage and mobilise a collective action aimed at preventing further wrongdoing.

However, the media also present problems in their reportage of mental ill health among older people. In many instances, media houses have been accused of choosing sensationalism in place of professionalism in their reports. Such sensational headlines, relating to older women who are accused of witchcraft or who, due to some mental health challenges, 'confess' to being witches, are far too common in Ghana. Coupled with televised drama on witches and the harm they can cause with their witchcraft, the media inadvertently create fear among the population who may not know how to counter those 'dark powers' other than killing those who possess them.

In conclusion, we iterate the important role of the media in highlighting the ills of society and taking the lead in seeking redress for the vulnerable in society. However, the media have also been used as a tool for portraying ageing, gender and mental health in a negative light in the Global South. In this, we demonstrate that media are important, but not the only social practice that contributes to the production of images of witches. Above all else, this chapter provides a critical insight into a very contemporary and pertinent societal problem that mainly affects older women, and especially those who, due to poor mental health, become easy targets for witchcraft accusations and the ensuing abuse.

Note

[1] A 16th-century text written by two clergymen – H. Kramer and J. Sprenger – criminalising witchcraft. The text has been commonly referred to as a handbook for witch-hunting.

References

Afifi, M. (2007) 'Gender differences in mental health', *Singapore Medical Journal*, 48(5): 385–91.

African Women's Development Fund (2011) '"The Witches of Gambaga": a documentary by Yaba Badoe', available from: http://awdf.org/the-witches-of-gambaga-a-documentary-by-yaba-badoe/ [accessed 22 October 2020].

Altheide, D. (2013) 'Media logic, social control, and fear', *Communication Theory*, 23(3): 223–38.

Anderson, K.A. and Han, J. (2008) 'An exploration of ageism and sexism in obituary photographs: 1967–1997', *Omega: Journal of Death & Dying*, 58(4): 335–45.

Badoe, Y. (2005) 'What makes a woman a witch?', *Feminist Africa*, 5: 37–51.

Baumann, S. and de Laat, K. (2012) 'Socially defunct: a comparative analysis of the underrepresentation of older women in advertising', *Poetics*, 40(6): 514–41.

Beugnet, M. (2006) 'Screening the old: femininity as old age in contemporary French cinema', *Studies in the Literary Imagination*, 39(2): 2–20.

Broedel, H.P. (2003) *The Malleus Maleficarum and the Construction of Witchcraft: Theology and Popular Belief*, Manchester: Manchester University Press.

Budds, K., Locke, A. and Burr, V. (2013) '"Risky business": constructing the "choice" to "delay" motherhood in the British press', *Feminist Media Studies*, 13(1): 132–47.

Campbell, P. (2011) 'Boundaries and risk: media framing of assisted reproductive technologies and older mothers', *Social Science & Medicine*, 72(2): 265–72.

Couldry, N. (2009) 'Theorising media as practice', *Social Semiotics*, 142: 115–32.

Coupland, J. (2013) 'The granny: public representations and creative performance', *Pragmatics and Society*, 4(1): 82–104.

Crampton, A. (2013) 'No peace in the house: witchcraft accusations as an "old woman's problem" in Ghana', *Anthropology & Aging Quarterly*, 34(2): 199–212.

Ekine, S. and Manji, F. (eds) (2012) *African Awakening: The Emerging Revolutions*, Capetown, Dakar, Nairobi and Oxford: Fahamu/Pambazuka Press.

Federici, S. (2010) 'Women, witch-hunting and enclosures in Africa today', *Sozial. Geschichte Online*, 3: 10–27.

Fusco, J. (2017) 'How gender differences affect mental health outcomes', *Perspectives*, 9(1), article 6, available from: https://scholars.unh.edu/perspectives/vol9/iss1/6 [accessed 13 April 2022].

Harpin, A. (2012) 'The lives of our mad mothers: aging and contemporary performance', *Women & Performance: A Journal of Feminist Theory*, 22(1): 67–87.

Howarth, D. and Stavrakakis, Y. (2000) 'Introducing discourse theory and political analysis', in D. Howarth, A.J. Norval and Y. Stavrakakis (eds) *Discourse Theory and Political Analysis*, Manchester: Manchester University Press, pp 1–23.

Iversen, S.M. and Wilińska, M. (2020) 'Ageing, old age and media: critical appraisal of knowledge practices in academic research', *International Journal of Ageing and Later Life*, 14(1): 121–49.

Khlat, M., Sermet, C. and LePape, A. (2000) 'Women's health in relation with their family and work roles: France in the early 1990's', *Social Science and Medicine*, 50(12): 1807–25.

Krainitzki, E. (2014) 'Judi Dench's age-inappropriateness and the role of M: challenging normative temporality', *Journal of Aging Studies*, 29: 32–40.

Lauzen, M. and Dozier, D. (2005) 'Maintaining the double standard: portrayals of age and gender in popular films', *Sex Roles*, 527(8): 437–46.

LaWare, M.R. and Moutsatsos, C. (2013) '"For skin that's us, authentically us": celebrity, empowerment, and the allure of anti-aging advertisements', *Women's Studies in Communication*, 36(2): 189–208.

Lemish, D. and Muhlbauer, V. (2012) '"Can't have it all": representations of older women in popular culture', *Women & Therapy*, 35(3–4): 165–80.

Lemstra, M., Neudorf, C., D'Arcy, C., Kunst, A., Warren, L. and Bennett, N. (2008) 'A systematic review of depressed mood and anxiety by SES in youth aged 10–15 years', *Canadian Journal of Public Health / Revue Canadienne De Sante'e Publique*, 99(2): 125–29, available from: *http://www.jstor.org/stable/41995056* [accessed 30 January 2021].

Lewis, D.C., Medvedev, K. and Seponski, D.M. (2011) 'Awakening to the desires of older women: deconstructing ageism within fashion magazines' *Journal of Aging Studies*, 252: 101–9.

Lövgren, K. (2013) 'The Swedish tant: a marker of female aging', *Journal of Women and Aging*, 25(2): 119–37.

Mackenzie, C.S., Scott, T., Mather, A. and Sareen, J. (2008) 'Older adults' help-seeking attitudes and treatment beliefs concerning mental health problems', *The American Journal of Geriatric Psychiatry*, 16(12): 1010–19.

Mock, R. (2012) 'Stand-up comedy and the legacy of the mature vagina', *Women & Performance: A Journal of Feminist Theory*, 22(1): 9–28.

Ofori-Atta, A., Read, U.M., Lund, C. and MHaPP Research Programme Consortium (2010) 'A situation analysis of mental health services and legislation in Ghana: challenges for transformation', *African Journal of Psychiatry*, 13(2): 99–108.

Ogundele, M.O. (2018) 'Behavioural and emotional disorders in childhood: a brief overview for paediatricians', *World Journal of Clinical Pediatrics*, 7(1): 9–26.

Oró-Piqueras, M. (2012) 'Narrating ageing: deconstructing negative conceptions of old age in four contemporary English novels', *Journal of Aging Studies*, 27(1): 47–51.

Riedel, F. (2018) 'The sanctuaries for witch-hunt victims in Northern Ghana', *Modern Africa: Politics, History and Society*, 6(1): 29–60.

Rosenfield, S. and Smith, D. (2010) 'Gender and mental health: do men and women have different amounts or types of problems?', in T.L. Scheid and T.N. Brown (eds) *A Handbook for the Study of Mental Health: Social Contexts, Theories, and Systems*, Cambridge: Cambridge University Press, pp 256–67.

Rountree, K. (1997) 'The new witch of the west: feminists reclaim the crone', *Journal of Popular Culture*, 30(4): 211–29.

Sempruch, J. (2004) 'Feminist constructions of the "witch" as a fantasmatic other', *Body & Society*, 10(4): 113–33.

Shaw, R.L. and Giles, D.C. (2009) 'Motherhood on ice? A media framing analysis of older mothers in the UK news', *Psychology & Health*, 24(2): 221–36.

Sossou, M.-A., Joseph A. and Yogtiba, J.A. (2015) 'Abuse, neglect, and violence against elderly women in Ghana: implications for social justice and human rights', *Journal of Elder Abuse & Neglect*, 27(4–5): 422–7.

Van Dijck, J. and Poell, T. (2013) 'Understanding social media logic', *Media and Communication*, 1(1): 2–14.

WHO (World Health Organisation) (2002) 'Gender disparities in mental health', available from: www.who.int/mental_health/media/en/242.pdf [accessed 26 October 2020].

Ylänne, V. (2016) 'Too old to parent? Discursive representations of late parenting in the British press', *Discourse & Communication*, 10(2): 176–97.

References to online news items:

https://www.facebook.com/446173902168681/posts/1667635173355 875/?d=n

https://www.graphic.com.gh/features/opinion/ghana-s-day-of-shame-lynching-old-witch.html

https://www.kyfilla.com/08/video-woman-escapes-lynching-over-witchcraft-allegations/

https://www.modernghana.com/news/1019777/other-17-old-women-lined-up-for-lynching-in-kafaba.html

https://3news.com/one-of-17-old-women-accused-of-witchcraft-by-kafaba-spiritualist-shares-ordeal/

5

Portrayals of older people with dementia in Taiwanese newspapers

Chin-Hui Chen and Yan-Hua Huang

Introduction

This chapter aims to extend studies on media representations of older adults by focusing on those with dementia. According to the World Health Organization (WHO, 2021), dementia is mainly characterised by cognitive deterioration, usually, but not inevitably, as a consequence of biological ageing. It is a progressive syndrome divided into three stages (namely, early, middle and late stage) and involving a number of symptoms, such as forgetfulness, losing track of time, becoming lost and confused, having communication difficulties or being increasingly aggressive. Dementia is one of the leading causes of older people's disability and dependency and a common cause of death. Because there is no cure, it has been regarded as society's worse terror (Zeilig, 2015).

There are more than 55 million people living with dementia worldwide and there are 10 million new cases of dementia every year (WHO, 2021). The prevalence of dementia can have a big economic and social impact on family, carers and society. It is suspected that older people living with dementia may therefore experience greater social ageism compared with other older adults (O'Connor and McFadden, 2012; Yun and Maxfield, 2020). The combating of social ageism against older adults with dementia will be difficult if the general public are not encouraged to understand dementia or older people with this condition and many misperceptions and negative social attitudes prevail (de Carvalho Pelegrini et al, 2020).

Previous scholarly investigations of attitudes towards dementia have already suggested that people with non–medical backgrounds and lower educational attainment tend to have less positive and more stereotypical attitudes towards it, mainly due to their lesser knowledge (Blay and Peluso, 2010; Rawlins et al, 2015; Kimzey et al, 2016). Popular stigmatisation of dementia can be problematic given that it may prevent individuals from acknowledging their dementia symptoms, and this will increase the time it takes for them to receive appropriate medical assistance (Koch and Iliffe, 2010). Perhaps more importantly, managing social stigma is crucial because of its impact on affected people's expectations regarding the quality of life they might experience (Burgener et al, 2015).

Cooperation between the media, government and educational institutions in any given society can contribute in important ways to reducing this stigma, along with any associated social discrimination against those with dementia. But to achieve that goal, one must attain a clearer picture of the media landscape around dementia, for instance by studying how older people with dementia are portrayed in the press.

Arguably, the media are a major influence on how people perceive dementia before they really come to understand it. The power of the media derives from our constant exposure to their messages, which – irrespective of whether they are misleading – cultivate a sense of what the world is like (Gerbner et al, 1986) and, eventually, define reality itself for the audience (Howitt, 2013). Moreover, as pointed out by Fowler (2013), news is socially and ideologically produced rather than neutrally constructed to reflect facts. This chapter aims to present the role the media play in shaping our understanding of dementia, and potentially perpetuating ageism. Also, it intends to diversify cultural insights by focusing on Taiwanese data, because, as revealed in the following literature review, the scholarly discussion on this topic so far has mainly derived from Western cultural contexts.

Literature review

The review that follows addresses media (mainly news) representations of dementia and of those living with it. The representational strategies employed as the main themes of news articles mostly suggest that dementia is an object to fight against, having a catastrophic nature.

For instance, in Kirkman's (2006) study, based on New Zealand news data, dementia was depicted as an active agent, stealing one's time, and – via a military metaphor – as an enemy. Similarly, van Gorp and Vercruysse (2012) noticed that in Belgian news, dementia was likened to an 'invader': a devil, a thief or a monster taking possession of people living with it. Its catastrophic nature is realised in the depiction of dementia as fearsome, relentless, cruel and powerful, especially via the voices of medical experts and long-suffering caregivers (Clarke, 2006). In the British press, the invocation of fear has generally proceeded via the use of militaristic metaphors that position the disease as a major cause of death, as a competitor against other diseases (Brookes et al, 2018), or as a tsunami, striking people who have no chance to prepare for it (Peel, 2014).

However, different from these studies, positive representations of dementia have started to emerge, although they are rather rare. For example, Doyle et al (2012) found that Australian newspapers' reporting of dementia was less sensationalised, both in headlines and in content. Additional linguistic evidence for this emerging pattern is the use of less outdated, negative and inappropriate language.

Media representations of older people living with dementia

When it comes to the discursive construction in newspapers of older people living with dementia, a number of representational strategies can be observed, such as portraying them in terms of lacking a voice, losing personal identity and personhood, and being receivers of others' help.

As argued by Kirkman (2006) and Bailey et al (2021), first-person accounts of dementia experiences and other narratives giving voice to those with the condition are rare. Usually, the accounts of men are presented via the voices of their wives, daughters or daughters-in-law. Such portrayals tend to imply that the individual's desires and needs are scant. According to van Gorp and Vercruysse (2012), individuals with dementia are portrayed essentially as having bodies but no minds. Brookes et al (2018), meanwhile, report that British media representations of people with dementia tend to anonymise them. Both these sets of findings suggest the existence of a representational strategy in which people with dementia lack personal identity and personhood.

Furthermore, people living with dementia have often been positioned as on the receiving end of others' help, assistance and care in the news. Such portrayals have been discussed in two studies (Kirkman, 2006; van Gorp and Vercruysse, 2012). Individuals going missing is a popular theme, sometimes reported in a humorous vein, and this storyline positions them as receivers of help from the police and charities (Kirkman, 2006).

Two studies have examined visual rather than discursive representations of older people with dementia and argue that the visual images in the news appear to be models of a certain age or gender cohort, and the images are either negative or idealised. For example, as claimed by Kessler and Schwender (2012), German weekly news magazines prefer to represent female and 'old-old' individuals living with dementia as a means of attracting readers' attention and arousing fewer negative feelings. They also notice that visual images of those with dementia can sometimes be exaggeratedly positive. These two visual representational strategies might function to avoid evoking readers' fear of dementia or to make the images appear rather idealised (Kessler and Schwender, 2012). Brookes et al (2018) further found that the most common imagery of individuals with dementia in the news was limited to their disembodied hands, often bruised and wrinkled. Vulnerability, fragility and deterioration are hence suggested by such images.

As the foregoing review implies, non-Western studies on the news' representations of older people with dementia remain extremely scarce. The analysis in this chapter, hence, aims to examine whether there are culturally specific ways to report news about this social cohort in Taiwanese news and what ideological implications can be inferred about how older people with dementia are perceived in Taiwan.

Methodology

The data in this study consisted of news items on older people with dementia as reported in the *United Daily News*, *Liberty Times*, *China Times* and *Apple Daily* – the four most-read quality Chinese-language newspapers in Taiwan (Rainmaker International Corporation, 2018). Four months, one from each season of 2019, were randomly selected to sample the relevant articles from the four news sources (for details, see Table 5.1). Keywords including the Chinese words/phrases meaning 'dementia', 'memory loss' and 'Alzheimer's disease' were used to locate news articles about older people with all types of dementia. If the articles were only about the disease, they were not included in our analysis. This sampling approach yielded 5,190 references spread across 181 articles.

We selected van Leeuwen's (2008) approach to critical discourse analysis (CDA), from among various others (such as van Dijk, 1993; Fairclough, 2001; Weiss and Wodak, 2007), to study discursive representations of older people living with dementia in Taiwanese news. Unlike other linguistically oriented forms of CDA, which address grammatical issues such as nominalisation, passive agent deletion and transitivity (see also Chapter 3), van Leeuwen's framework of CDA seeks to draw up the socio-semantic inventory or the sociological relevance of the coding categories that he introduced to decode in which contexts social actors are represented in media discourses.

Therefore, the chosen approach, which can be applied to analysing news representations of any social group, involved coding several dimensions, as follows. We analysed the *actions* that older people living with dementia were actively and passively associated with (activation and passivation); the *social relationships* they were depicted as having (relational identification); how they were *socially categorised* (social classification); how they were *labelled* in terms of what they were supposedly capable of doing (functionalisation); and whether they were *identified* by their full names, first or last names only, or titles (nomination).

Table 5.1: Sampling months

Newspaper	Sampling months (in 2019)
Liberty Times	March, June, September, December
China Times	February, April, August, October
Apple Daily	January, May, August, December
United Daily News	February, June, September, November

To further discern the relative salience of the representational strategies already discussed, simple frequency reports are provided alongside our qualitative analysis. All extracts presented in the findings have been translated from Chinese into English.

Findings

Activation

In terms of activation, the sampled Taiwanese newspaper items overwhelmingly depicted people living with dementia as active agents (doers or performers) of verbal processes (actions as realised in verbs or gerunds) that suggested their loss of abilities due to dementia.

For instance, older people with dementia were often reported to leave home alone, but because of their health condition, their subsequently reported actions included wandering around the streets and eventually losing contact with their family or losing their way home:

> Extract 1: An older man, Fang, with dementia ... left home for a walk at night on the 6th of May but *forgot his way home*, which was only hundred metres away. (*Apple Daily*, 8 May 2019, emphasis added)

Actions related to communication, expression or responses by older people with dementia could also be observed in the Taiwanese newspapers. However, when they were mentioned, the emphasis tended to be on failure. In Extract 2, for example, the older woman was the active agent of the actions of 'expressing' and 'answering', but the nature of the communication was framed as unsuccessful by the phrase 'unable to' and the word 'fail'. In this case, even though the older character played an active role in two actions, the emphasis was on her losing her abilities to communicate:

> Extract 2: The police ... asked the older woman about her personal information and home address, but she, because of dementia, was *unable to express herself clearly and failed to answer* these questions. (*United Daily News*, 5 September 2019, emphasis added)

Also, when the individuals with dementia or suspected dementia in the sampled news accounts were portrayed as standing, walking or lying down, they were said to limp, falter, behave in an absent-minded manner or simply be 'spaced out':

> Extract 3: An elderly grandpa, aged 90s, living alone in the Taiping area, left home, walked for five kilometres, and got lost. He *sat on the*

ground in a limp and weak manner in the pouring rain. (*China Times*, 16 August 2019, emphasis added)

The sampled Taiwanese newspapers seldom reported on how older people with dementia might contribute to society, instead focusing on their causing problems or harming themselves. Such actions included swallowing sharp objects (Extract 4) and entering highly dangerous places, often to look for someone who was not actually there (Extract 5).

> Extract 4: 80-year-old Taichung grandmother Lai has suffered from dementia for many years. She *always puts objects into her mouth* so her family members, for her safety, put away everything small enough to be swallowed. Even so, one day, she *swallowed a safety pin, causing stomach bleeding*. (*China Times*, 7 August 2019, emphasis added)
>
> Extract 5: An older woman with dementia *looks for her son on highway ramp* (*China Times*, 9 February 2019, in the headline, emphasis added)

Older people with dementia were also reported to 'die' (another action they performed as active agents) in Taiwanese newspapers. However, the status of being deceased per se was typically characterised as the consequence of tragic acts such as accidentally falling (Extract 6), starving (Extract 7) or committing suicide. Because they had dementia, their falling and helplessly starving to death seemed to be normalised in the news articles.

> Extract 6: An old man with dementia … left home at night and was suspected to have *fallen into the fifty-metre-deep valley*. (*Liberty Times*, 11 June 2019, emphasis added)
>
> Extract 7: A mother with dementia, living in Tao-Yuan City, had been abandoned by her son, Zhang, for years … and was left helpless and *starved to death*. … She was found six days after she died. (*Apple Daily*, 6 May 2019, emphasis added)

Older people with dementia, of both genders, were occasionally reported to be engaged in sexual harassment. In Extract 8, a story about an older American woman harassing a staff member dressed as Donald Duck while vising a Disney theme park, was reported in *Apple Daily* in Taiwan, and her action was attributed to her being 'crazy'. Such an action, in another news article about an older Taiwanese man harassing his caregiver (Extract 9), was ironically marked as a surprise by means of a contrasting word, 'but'. This seems to imply that a man at the age of 80 who has dementia should be asexual, so the action of showing his own 'lust' was unexpected, and hence newsworthy.

Extract 8: A 60-year-old woman *crazily harassed* Donald Duck and even reached in and rubbed his body. ... Disney did not file a complaint because they suspected that the old woman could be living with dementia. (*Apple Daily*, 28 December 2019, emphasis added)

Extract 9: Diagnosed with dementia *but not "losing lust"*: 80-year-old man climbed onto his female caregiver's bed to molest her (*China Times*, 7 October 2019, in the headline, emphasis added)

It was also uncommon among the sampled Taiwanese news items to see portrayals of older people with dementia that focused on what they were still capable of doing. However, seven reports did do so. These highlighted such individuals' remaining functions, including working (Extract 10), self-care (Extract 11) and teaching or demonstrating traditional skills (Extract 12). Notably, however, the ability of dementia sufferers to engage in such activities was usually implied to be exceptional (using 'but' or 'still' to trigger this implication; see Extracts 10 and 11) and linked to their being younger than most others with dementia (with 65 usually regarded as a cut-off point; see Extract 10).

Extract 10: *But* even if they suffer from dementia, people *may still have the ability to work and participate in society, especially those younger than 65* who are still physically fit. (*United Daily News*, 23 September 2019, emphasis added)

Extract 11: As indicated by Dr Zheng-Nan Shen. ... People with mild dementia *still have the ability to take care of themselves*, so staying in the community or family to receive care is OK. (*China Times*, 5 August 2019, emphasis added)

Extract 12: Elderly people with dementia personally dictate, *demonstrate, and teach* the skills of making rice dumplings. Young children studied these techniques carefully. The intergenerational interactions were pleasant. (*Liberty Times*, 5 June 2019, emphasis added)

Passivation

The passivation of older people with dementia mainly consisted of depicting them on the receiving end of others' actions, such as assistance, support or care (see Extract 13). They were also frequently represented as targets to be found (see Extract 14), due to their being lost, which, as we have seen, was a major theme of the Taiwanese news reports.

Extract 13: Cao Wenlong (71 years old), [who] used to be the Director of the Dementia Centre at Dalin Tzu Chi Hospital in Chiayi County ... *is now taking care of* his 90-year-old *mother with dementia*, chatting and singing with her. (*Liberty Times*, 18 September 2019, emphasis added)

Extract 14: An elderly man living with dementia, aged 90s, left home three days ago and lost contact. ... The police and a rescue team ... *found* him ... in the mountains. (*Apple Daily*, 10 January 2019, emphasis added)

They were also positioned as patients (Extract 15) who were treated, diagnosed and/or trained by medical experts. Alongside medical discourses about dementia, older people with this condition had certain features ascribed to them (which is one form of passivation), detailing the symptoms of dementia that they might have, for instance, being sick, weak, disabled, senile, forgetful, mentally disoriented, confused, difficult to reason with (Extract 16), spaced out and troubled by incontinence.

Extract 15: A grandpa in Taoyuan got lost frequently. ... The family was concerned and took him to *a doctor who diagnosed him to have dementia* (*United Daily News*, 10 November 2019, emphasis added)

Extract 16: A grandma has lived with dementia for many years, and *her being difficult* sometimes makes her like a child. (*China Times*, 20 April 2019, emphasis added)

Other attributions commonly seen in our data were loneliness and solitude (Extract 17), both of which emphasised helplessness and vulnerability as defining characteristics of older people with dementia. Such characteristics were further reinforced by their vulnerable roles as victims of deception, accidents and threats (Extract 18), or being exposed to bad weather conditions, such as rain and cold weather (Extract 19).

Extract 17: Police officers arrived at the scene and found an old man surnamed Zhang *sitting alone* by the ditch beside the road. (*Apple Daily*, 6 January 2019)

Extract 18: There have been more cases of *exploitation of the property* owned by *victims living with dementia*. (*Liberty Times*, 8 September 2019, emphasis added)

Extract 19: There was drizzle outside and the temperature was *cold*. The old man, surnamed Jian, was not holding an umbrella and was *not warm*, just like that, standing *in the rain*. (*Apple Daily*, 4 January 2019, emphasis added)

Older people with dementia were also passivated as carriers of other attributions indicating their emotional disturbance/instability, usually triggered by accidents, or becoming lost (Extract 20). They were also naturally positioned as targets of attempts to provide them with comfort or calm them down.

> Extract 20: An old man *got lost* on Zhengxin Road and needed police assistance. A police officer, Zhu, immediately went to help and provided care. He found that *the old man was in a trance, anxious*, and frequently said that he was looking for the chief of his neighbourhood. (*Liberty Times*, 3 September 2019, emphasis added)

Relational identification

In the sampled Taiwanese newspaper articles, older individuals with dementia were socially associated with certain other groups. The articles often associated them with family members, mostly offspring who were worried about what had happened to them – typically, accidents and loss of contact. In the data, police officers, medical/caregiving experts including doctors, nurses and professional caregivers, rescuers, volunteers and young children were other social groups that interacted with those with dementia.

Social classification

The newspapers also tended to socially classify individuals with dementia in terms of their health condition, by means of the label 'dementia patients', but also refer to them as 'seniors' or 'old people'. Comments on their advanced age, or specific references to their chronological ages, were also found. The data suggested that any age above 70 was regarded as noteworthy in the context of dementia, or the consequences deemed relevant to that condition, with the number of mentions of 70- to 79-year-olds (n=19) nearly quadruple the number of mentions of 60- to 69-year-olds (n=5). There were an additional 35 mentions of the ages of older people with dementia who were aged 80 years and above.

Modes of address suggestive of generational differences were also used by Taiwanese journalists. Interestingly, in 42 of the 181 sampled news articles, they positioned older people with dementia as 'grandma', 'grandpa' or 'uncle' despite there being no mention of a corresponding grandchild, nephew or niece (Extract 21). The choice of such address forms arguably offered newspaper readers a perspective from which they could relate to the central figures in the news items, that is, in terms of an intergenerational or even pseudo-familial relationship. More examples of age-specific or gender-specific classifications of older people living with dementia will be presented later in this chapter, along with a discussion of the use of only their surnames.

Extract 21: *Grandma Sun* (78 years old), with dementia, took the elevator downstairs alone at 7.30 and disappeared without a trace. ... The police found *Grandma Sun* on the road about 2 kilometres away from the building. (*Apple Daily*, 12 August 2019, emphasis added)

Functionalisation

In contrast to the frequency with which they classified people with dementia into various social groups, the sampled Taiwanese newspapers seldom functionalised them. One example functionalised an older man with dementia as an actor. However, this term, emphasising his professional identity, was immediately followed by his tragic end as a nursing-home resident, dying due to dementia with no family around him (Extract 22). His achievement as a veteran actor was not detailed, and this example of functionalisation did not enhance his individuality. Among the 181 articles, only 13 (7%) functionalised older people with dementia. The functions included actors (n=6), unpaid trainees (n=3), presidents (n=2), a cultural tour guide (n=1) and a teacher (n=1).

> Extract 22: *Hou Jie*, a 73-year-old *veteran actor, passed away* yesterday. ... He suffered dementia and stroke in his later years and broke up with his family. He ended up living alone and entered the nursing home. (*Liberty Times*, 6 December 2019, emphasis added)

Nomination

Clear identification of older people with dementia by their full name or title was exceptional in our Taiwanese data sample. Those who received such full nomination were usually celebrities or well-known politicians, such as the actor just discussed or Taiwan's ex-president, Chen Shui-bian (Extract 23).

> Extract 23: Former Taiwanese *President Chen Shui-bian* ... suffered from dementia and incontinence. (*Apple Daily*, 1 May 2019, emphasis added)

In most cases, older people with dementia were nominated only with their last name – for example, '陳姓老翁' and '湯姓老婦', which literally translate as 'Chen older man' and 'Tang older woman' – along with other referential terms suggestive of their older-age identity, generally by means of the word '老', meaning 'old'. When they were presented as old, gender-specific indicators were also used, such as '翁', meaning an elderly man, or '婦', meaning a married woman who is not young. It is reasonable to argue that mere references to people's surnames do not help establish their

Table 5.2: Nature of actions by role-allocation types and number of occurrences

Nature of actions	Activation	Passivation
Actions with positive connotations	10	0
Actions with negative connotations	75	118

Table 5.3: Relational identification

Relational identification type	Number of articles
Family members	101
Medical staff	49
Police officers	43
Caregivers	18
Volunteers	8
Rescuers	3
Friends	3
Lovers	3
Young children (as pupils)	2
Colleagues	2

individuality – the key function of nomination – and only constitute a piece of almost random information, supplementing their social classification as aged or gendered.

The relative salience of the abovementioned representational strategies should be clear from the following tables. For instance, as shown in Table 5.2, when older people living with dementia were activated or passivated in relation to actions, many actions had more negative connotations (n=75 for activation, n=118 for passivation) than positive ones (n=10 for activation).

Among the various types of relational identification (see Table 5.3), older people with dementia were most likely to be depicted with their family members (in 101 articles), followed by people who provided help, care and support, that is, medical staff, police officers, caregivers, volunteers and rescuers (a total of 121 mentions). Other kinds of social connections, suggestive of romance (lover), friendship (friends) or professional identities (teaching young children and working with colleagues) were found in relatively few news articles (with numbers ranging from two to three per season). This representational pattern seems to suggest that the lives of older people with dementia in Taiwan are mainly family centred. In fact, older people in Taiwan do prefer to be taken care of at home when they

Table 5.4: Social classification types

Type	Articles (n)
Health condition	110
Age-specific	80
Gender-specific	75
Professional identity	13

Table 5.5: Nomination types

Types of nomination	Articles (n)
Last names	33
Full names	11
Titles	8

become dependent (Ministry of Health and Welfare, 2017) and, in general, this preference is honoured (Ministry of Health and Welfare, 2019). This could explain why older people with dementia were likely to be reported as socially connected with their family members in Taiwanese newspapers, or conversely, as being in danger because they had left the family home.

As shown in Table 5.4, the sampled Taiwanese news articles socially classified older people with dementia into a number of social groups. In 110 articles, they were referred to as 'patients', highlighting their health condition, while 80 classified them in terms of their age identity, and their gender was mentioned in 75 articles. Professional identities, on the other hand, were mentioned in only a small minority of articles (n=13). The top category, other than having dementia, was age.

While observing whether and how older people were nominated in Taiwanese newspapers, the occurrences of titles and full names were both low (see Table 5.5). In less than one fifth of the sampled articles that mentioned names at all, only family names were mentioned.

Discussion and conclusions

This chapter has examined how a large sample of mainstream Taiwanese newspaper reports represented older people living with dementia in 2019, with the aim of ascertaining how they are ideologically and culturally constructed in Taiwan. The results revealed an overwhelmingly derogatory representation of this social group. This section summarises the identified representational patterns and provides additional contextualisation of the findings.

The words and phrases used in the examined news items consistently highlighted the frailty of the individuals and other problems – for themselves and others – that their condition caused. More specifically, they were represented as active agents of actions that caused others trouble, which also naturalised their need for others' assistance. The social networks with which the older people with dementia were associated further reflected those who helped, cared for and worried about them.

Decisions regarding the newsworthiness of individuals living with dementia appear to have been rooted in stereotypical expectations about the consequences of the condition (Wei and Tsai, 2002; Chang and Hsu, 2020), rather than extremely bad or surprising news. That is, the sampled Taiwanese newspapers exhibited a clear preference for detailing the negative experiences that older people with dementia had, such as becoming victims, being abandoned, losing control of their lives, lacking self-discipline or feeling helpless and vulnerable.

The referential strategies used to denote individuals with dementia in Taiwanese newspapers involved extensive social categorisation, and reflected a corresponding lack of individualisation. Their health-related and age identities were particularly highlighted. The observed juxtapositions of having dementia and being older only served to reinforce the stigmatisation of ageing and discrimination against those above a certain age (usually 70). Constantly describing individuals with dementia in relation to their advanced chronological age could have the ideological effect of reinforcing negative stereotypes of older age (Johnson et al, 2005). Moreover, the public might come to perceive that the main risk factor for the diagnosis of dementia is 'only' the increase of age, or even that it is just a normal part of the ageing process (Cahill et al, 2015), despite the existence of various other reported risk factors, including diabetes, smoking, mid-life hypertension and mid-life depression (WHO, 2021).

When the sampled Taiwanese newspapers referred to older people with dementia via modes of address indicating intergenerational relationships, they seemed to be inviting their readers to interpret the stories in question from the perspective of grandchildren, that is, as if the reported incidents might happen to their own grandparents. This referential strategy could encourage more empathy towards the subjects of such stories (and, by extension, other older people with this condition), especially when coupled with tragic content.

Importantly, however, this representational strategy has never been found in Western studies. To explain this discrepancy, the influence of Confucianism should be taken into consideration. In Chinese-speaking communities, Confucianism is considered a unique cultural root that guides people to live in deep association with their families. For instance, as indicated in *Mencius* (a representative book of Confucian doctrines), people are urged to practise the saying '老吾老以及人之老', meaning 'treating the elders in your family with respect, and then extending that respect to elders in other families' (An, 2008). This helps to explain why Taiwanese journalists and their readers may not think it odd to refer to older people with dementia as grandparents or uncles, even when no corresponding family members are present or mentioned. Indeed, it is plausible that Taiwanese journalists would consider this referential strategy an effective means of triggering empathy from readers, since in Taiwanese cultural contexts, loving other older people as if they are your own family elders is a pre-existing ideological and mental resource that can be drawn on when reading news articles about older people living with dementia.

Other naming strategies that were used to write about older people with dementia, coupled with a lack of functionalisation, could lead readers to perceive them as incapable and as making few contributions to society. Individuals living with dementia inevitably undergo a process of decline, but its progression can be quite slow; certainly, those with mild dementia do not lose all their abilities instantly. In Taiwanese news representations, however, the focus is solely on what they have lost, or the most severe stage of the condition, while their personhood, individual voice and the remaining functions that define their uniqueness are generally disregarded.

Those older people with dementia who, exceptionally, were described by their full names, denoting an identifiable individual identity, were all well-known celebrities or politicians. Their being chosen as subjects of reportage arguably illustrates a contrast between being a successful person and taking on the status of someone with dementia. This could create an ideological effect of advancing fear of dementia by implying to readers that even high-achieving people cannot escape its problematic consequences. From that viewpoint, the use of full names functions chiefly to remind us of what we know about such well-known figures, adding further drama to the unexpected downturn in their lives caused by the power or cruelty of dementia.

The representational patterns that reflect more negativity in Taiwanese newspapers are more likely found in Western studies. However, this could be due in part to the latter's earlier sampling periods (for example, Kirkman, 2006; Doyle et al, 2012; Kessler and Schwender, 2012). Cross-cultural research, meanwhile, has established that Taiwanese news is more likely than its Western counterparts to depict older people as vulnerable (Chen, 2015). Moreover, according to Harwood et al (2001), older people in Eastern countries may be more likely to be perceived as living with decreased validity than those in Western countries. As such, journalists with such a mindset in Taiwan might paint older people with dementia in a more negative light – for example, as feeble, deceived and vulnerable – than those working in Western news industries.

To conclude, the problem-oriented framing of individuals with dementia and the predominant negativity is concerning (Kirkman, 2006; van Gorp and Vercruysse, 2012). The following recommendations could improve such representational patterns in Taiwanese press contexts. First, it is reasonable to call for more diversity (Clarke, 2006; Spiteri and Pennington, 2018) in the portrayals of older people living with dementia, by reporting more of their own voices to highlight that they also have their own thoughts and feelings (Moore and Hollett, 2003; Swaffer, 2014). More accounts of their experiences of coping with their health conditions through medical means would also be welcome (Tariot, 2003; Herrmann et al, 2007), as this could bring hope to others with dementia. News stories about how they continue to make a contribution to society (Langdon et al, 2007; Beard et al, 2009; Genoe, 2010), or how caregivers enjoy interacting with them in care–communication processes, should also be encouraged. This would help to combat the stereotype that once a person is diagnosed with dementia, they can be regarded as having lost all abilities and they become merely a source of trouble to others – a view that tends to evoke more fear than sympathy.

References

An, Y. (2008) 'Family love in Confucius and Mencius', *Dao*, 7(1): 51–5.

Bailey, A., Dening, T. and Harvey, K. (2021) 'Battles and breakthroughs: representations of dementia in the British press', *Ageing & Society*, 41(2): 362–76.

Beard, R.L., Knauss, J. and Moyer, D. (2009) 'Managing disability and enjoying life: how we reframe dementia through personal narratives', *Journal of Aging Studies*, 23(4): 227–35.

Blay, S.L. and Peluso, E.T.P. (2010) 'Public stigma: the community's tolerance of Alzheimer disease', *The American Journal of Geriatric Psychiatry*, 18(2): 163–71.

Brookes, G., Harvey, K., Chadborn, N. and Dening, T. (2018) '"Our biggest killer": multimodal discourse representations of dementia in the British press', *Social Semiotics*, 28(3): 371–95.

Burgener, S.C., Buckwalter, K., Perkhounkova, Y. and Liu, M.F. (2015) 'The effects of perceived stigma on quality of life outcomes in persons with early-stage dementia: longitudinal findings: part 2', *Dementia*, 14(5): 609–32.

Cahill, S., Pierce, M., Werner, P., Darley, A. and Bobersky, A. (2015) 'A systematic review of the public's knowledge and understanding of Alzheimer's disease and dementia', *Alzheimer Disease & Associated Disorders*, 29(3): 255–75.

Chang, C.Y. and Hsu, H.C. (2020) 'Relationship between knowledge and types of attitudes towards people living with dementia', *International Journal of Environmental Research and Public Health*, 17(11): 1–13.

Chen, C.H. (2015) 'Advertising representations of older people in the United Kingdom and Taiwan: a comparative analysis', *The International Journal of Aging and Human Development*, 80(2): 140–83.

Clarke, J.N. (2006) 'The case of the missing person: Alzheimer's disease in mass print magazines 1991–2001', *Health Communication*, 19(3): 269–76.

De Carvalho Pelegrini, L.N., Hall, A., Hooper, E., Oliveira, D., Guerra, F., Casemiro, F.G. and Mioshi, E. (2020) 'Challenges in public perception: highlights from the United Kingdom-Brazil Dementia Workshop', *Dementia & Neuropsychologia*, 14(3): 209–15.

Doyle, C.J., Dunt, D.R., Pirkis, J., Dare, A., Day, S. and Wijesundara, B.S. (2012) 'Media reports on dementia: quality and type of messages in Australian media', *Australasian Journal on Ageing*, 31(2): 96–101.

Fairclough, N. (2001) 'Critical discourse analysis as a method in social scientific research', *Methods of Critical Discourse Analysis*, 5(11): 121–38.

Fowler, R. (2013) *Language in the News: Discourse and Ideology in the Press*, London: Routledge.

Genoe, M.R. (2010) 'Leisure as resistance within the context of dementia', *Leisure Studies*, 29(3): 303–20.

Gerbner, G., Gross, L., Morgan, M. and Signorielli, N. (1986) 'Living with television: the dynamics of the cultivation process', in B. Jennings and Z. Dolf (eds) *Perspectives on Media Effects*, Mahwah, NJ: Lawrence Erlbaum Associates, pp 17–40.

Harwood, J., Giles, H., McCann, R.M., Cai, D., Somera, L.P., Ng, S.H., Gallois, C. and Noels, K. (2001) 'Older adults' trait ratings of three age-groups around the Pacific rim', *Journal of Cross-cultural Gerontology*, 16(2): 157–71.

Herrmann, N., Gauthier, S. and Lysy, P.G. (2007) 'Clinical practice guidelines for severe Alzheimer's disease', *Alzheimer's & Dementia*, 3(4): 385–97.

Howitt, D. (2013) *The Mass Media and Social Problems*, Oxford: Pergamon.

Johnson, M.L., Bengtson, V.L., Coleman, P.G. and Kirkwood, T.B. (eds) (2005) *The Cambridge Handbook of Age and Ageing*, Cambridge: Cambridge University Press.

Kessler, E.M. and Schwender, C. (2012) 'Giving dementia a face? The portrayal of older people with dementia in German weekly news magazines between the years 2000 and 2009', *Journals of Gerontology Series B: Psychological Sciences and Social Sciences*, 67(2): 261–70.

Kimzey, M., Mastel-Smith, B. and Alfred, D. (2016) 'The impact of educational experiences on nursing students' knowledge and attitudes toward people with Alzheimer's disease: a mixed method study', *Nurse Education Today*, 46: 57–63.

Kirkman, A.M. (2006) 'Dementia in the news: the media coverage of Alzheimer's disease', *Australasian Journal on Ageing*, 25(2): 74–9.

Koch, T. and Iliffe, S. (2010) 'Rapid appraisal of barriers to the diagnosis and management of patients with dementia in primary care: a systematic review', *BMC Family Practice*, 11(1): 1–8.

Langdon, S.A., Eagle, A. and Warner, J. (2007) 'Making sense of dementia in the social world: a qualitative study', *Social Science & Medicine*, 64(4): 989–1000.

Ministry of Health and Welfare (2017) *Survey Report on the Status of the Elderly in the Year of 2017*, Taipei: Ministry of Health and Welfare, available from: https://dep.mohw.gov.tw/dos/cp-1767-38429-113.html [accessed 5 March 2019] (in Chinese).

Ministry of Health and Welfare (2019) *Reference Manual for Dementia Common Care Centres and Community Service Bases*, Taipei: Ministry of Health and Welfare, available from: https://1966.gov.tw/LTC/cp-4474-48200-201. html [accessed 27 June 2019] (in Chinese).

Moore, T.F. and Hollett, J. (2003) 'Giving voice to persons living with dementia: the researcher's opportunities and challenges', *Nursing Science Quarterly*, 16(2): 163–7.

O'Connor, M.L. and McFadden, S.H. (2012) 'A terror management perspective on young adults' ageism and attitudes toward dementia', *Educational Gerontology*, 38(9): 627–43.

Peel, E. (2014) '"The living death of Alzheimer's" versus "take a walk to keep dementia at bay": representations of dementia in print media and carer discourse', *Sociology of Health & Illness*, 36(6): 885–901.

Rainmaker International Corporation (2018) *The Fourth Quarter of Media Survey Report in 2018*, Taipei: Rainmaker International Corporation, available from: http://www.xkm.com.tw/HTML/report/rngresearch/ 2018Q4RNMM.pdf [accessed 25 June 2021] (in Chinese).

Rawlins, J., Mcgrowder, D.A., Kampradi, L., Ali, A., Austin, T., Beckles, A. and Dialsingh, I. (2015) 'Attitude towards Alzheimer's disease among undergraduate students of University of the West Indies, Trinidad and Tobago', *Journal of Clinical and Diagnostic Research*, 9(9): 19–25.

Spiteri, L. and Pennington, D. (2018) *Social Tagging for Linked Data across Environments: A New Approach to Discovering Information Online*, London: Facet Publishing.

Swaffer, K. (2014) 'Dementia: stigma, language, and dementia-friendly', *Dementia*, 13(6): 709–16.

Tariot, P.N. (2003) 'Medical management of advanced dementia', *Journal of the American Geriatrics Society*, 51(2): 305–13.

Van Dijk, T.A. (1993) 'Principles of critical discourse analysis', *Discourse & Society*, 4(2): 249–83.

Van Gorp, B. and Vercruysse, T. (2012) 'Frames and counter-frames giving meaning to dementia: a framing analysis of media content', *Social Science & Medicine*, 74(8): 1274–81.

Van Leeuwen, T. (2008) *Discourse and Practice: New Tools for Critical Discourse Analysis*, New York, NY: Oxford University Press.

Wei, S.L. and Tasi, Y.F. (2002) 'Senile dementia: related knowledge and attitudes of the general population in the Hualien area', *Tzu Chi Medical Journal*, 14(2): 97–104 (in Chinese).

Weiss, G. and Wodak, R. (eds) (2007) *Critical Discourse Analysis*, London: Palgrave Macmillan.

WHO (World Health Organization) (2021) Dementia, available from: https://www.who.int/news-room/fact-sheets/detail/dementia [accessed 31 December 2021].

Yun, S. and Maxfield, M. (2020) 'Correlates of dementia-related anxiety: self-perceived dementia risk and ageism', *Educational Gerontology*, 46(9): 563–74.

Zeilig, H. (2015) 'What do we mean when we talk about dementia? Exploring cultural representations of "dementia"', *Working with Older People*, 19(2): 12–20.

6

Older LGBTQ+ persons
in Canadian newspapers

Laura Hurd and Raveena Mahal

Introduction

In recent years, a number of scholars have argued that media representations are powerful drivers of cultural norms and social behaviours. On the one hand, media depictions may improve the status of marginalised groups by illuminating their diverse human experiences and challenging existing social barriers to inclusion (Ayoub and Garretson, 2017). On the other hand, media portrayals may also reinforce stereotypes and social inequities (Couldry, 2012) and negatively impact how individuals view themselves and their places within society (Gomillion and Giuliano, 2011). In particular, they may symbolically annihilate disadvantaged groups by rendering them invisible and reproducing dominant and exclusionary cultural and political norms and structures (Gross, 2001).

Considerable research has examined media representations of ageing, focusing on later life more generally as well as the marginalisation of particular groups of older adults, including lesbian, gay, bisexual, transgender, queer and other gender-minority and sexually diverse (LGBTQ+) persons. The former literature has suggested that older adults have typically been depicted in three dominant ways in advertising, television, film, literary works and news media. Collectively, these various media have largely under-represented older adults, reinforcing their invisibility in Western societies (Lumme-Sandt, 2011; Edström, 2018). Where older adults have been present in the media, their depictions have typically adhered to a binary of negative versus positive ageing (Gilleard and Higgs, 2000; Katz, 2005). Negative or fourth-age narratives have reflected undesirable, ageist stereotypes as they synonymise experiences of growing older with deteriorating health, dependence and obsolescence (Rozanova et al, 2016; Tortajada et al, 2018) (see also Chapter 2). For example, print news media often depict older adults as familial and social burdens who threaten the sustainability of health care systems (Lundgren and Ljuslinder, 2011). In contrast, a growing number of studies have found that older adults are increasingly depicted with positive or third-age aspirational narratives that emphasise youthfulness, health, consumption and ageing as both a choice and a personal responsibility (Hurd Clarke et al, 2014; Markov and Yoon, 2020). Sandberg and Marshall (2017, p 3) have argued that third-age narratives have excluded LGBTQ+ individuals as they have positioned successful ageing in terms of heterosexuality or 'hetero-happiness' (see also Chapter 9).

Despite increases in both the relative frequency and positive nature of LGBTQ+ depictions over time, both younger and older cohorts remain under-represented in Western media (Gross, 2001; Westwood, 2019). Where they are present, gay men, followed by lesbian women, have made up the majority of popular depictions, with bisexual and transgender individuals, especially transgender men, largely absent (Tsai, 2010; Capuzza, 2014). A similar pattern has emerged with respect to ageing LGBTQ+ persons, whereby these relative inclusion disparities and media absences have been even more pronounced (Westwood, 2019). Altogether, media portrayals have generally excluded those who are not cisgender, White, middle-class, non-disabled and young to middle-aged (Nölke, 2018; Petermon and Spencer, 2019).

Contemporary depictions of both younger and older LGBTQ+ individuals have tended to reinforce several recurring narratives and stereotypes. These portrayals have often been constructed through a heteronormative lens of respectability (Krainitzki, 2015; Waggoner, 2018). For example, beginning in the 1990s, as media representations became more positive, depictions of LGBTQ+ individuals and their families focused on normalisation, emphasising the ways in which they were similar to cisgender heterosexuals, and de-emphasising difference (Landau, 2009; Åkerlund, 2019). Similarly, advertising has tended to underscore that 'love is love' and that 'all types of families are wholesome' (Nölke, 2018, p 242). Other narratives have positioned LGBTQ+ individuals as victims. Exemplified by the 'bury your gays' (Waggoner, 2018, p 1877) trope that is found in film and television storylines, LGBTQ+ characters frequently and disproportionately meet a premature demise (Rodriguez, 2018). Lesbians have typically been framed as 'burly, tomboys, and dykes' in mainstream and entertainment print and television news (Rodriguez, 2018, p 2), and as nonsexual, tragic and evil or dangerous figures in fictional television portrayals (Waggoner, 2018; Parker et al, 2020). Representations of transgender individuals have often pathologised their bodies and identities (Billard, 2016), trivialised their experiences as a form of deceptive 'dress-up' (Åkerlund, 2019, p 1319) and treated them as a danger to children in certain spaces (Koch-Rein et al, 2020). Finally, Capuzza (2014) found that news stories tended to limit the contexts in which transgender voices were directly cited, allowing them to speak about their own personal narratives, but employing the use of advocates and experts when addressing transgender issues more broadly.

To date, no studies have examined how older LGBTQ+ persons have been portrayed in contemporary Western news media. The limited existing research has selectively focused on how older gay and lesbian individuals have been depicted in North American films, television shows and 20th-century novels (Krainitzki, 2015; Hess, 2019). Thus, the purpose of our study was to address this gap, build on previous considerations of the representations of younger and middle-aged LGBTQ+ persons, and explore the ways in which older gender-minority and sexually diverse people have been constructed and portrayed in the Canadian news media. In this chapter, we build from our previous content and thematic analysis of newspaper and magazine stories, which found that older LGBTQ+ persons were largely invisible and represented either as victims of discrimination or as extraordinary individuals (Hurd et al, 2020). Drawing on four representative stories from the original study, we use critical discourse analysis (CDA) (Fairclough, 2003) to examine how older LGBTQ+ persons' identities, experiences and social statuses were discursively constructed as invisible, victims and extraordinary.

Theoretical framework

The study draws on queer theory, which problematises heterosexist and binary understandings of both gender identity and sexual orientation (Lewis, 2016). Queer theory challenges heteronormativity, or the systematic privileging of heterosexuality, and the resultant and pervasive homophobia and transphobia (Sullivan, 2003; Marcus, 2005). Highlighting the ways in which identities are performed, fluid and emergent, queer theory acknowledges and celebrates diverse gender and sexual identities 'as cultural forms independent from rather than imitative of heterosexuality' (de Lauretis, 1991, p 3; Siverskog, 2015; King, 2016). Queer theory has historically ignored the experiences of ageing and older sexual-minority and gender-diverse persons (Brown, 2009). However, a growing number of scholars have identified that queer theory powerfully illuminates the ways that ageing intersects with heterosexism (Sandberg, 2008; Siverskog, 2015; King, 2016). In particular, queer theory draws attention to and explicates the systemic exclusion of old, LGBTQ+ individuals (King, 2016; Sandberg and Marshall, 2017) and their simultaneous invisibility and hypervisibility in the media (Gross, 2001; Kia, 2016).

Study design and methods

Our previous study (Hurd et al, 2020) analysed Canadian newspaper and magazine stories that were published in English between 1 July 2016 and 30 June 2017 and either focused on or peripherally included LGBTQ+ individuals aged over 50. The target sources for the original study included three national newspapers (*National Post*, *The Globe and Mail* and *Metro Canada*), 13 provincial newspapers, one national online news website (www.cbcnews.ca) and five popular magazines (*Chatelaine*, *Canadian Living*,

Maclean's, *Reader's Digest* and *Zoomer*). Our systematic search[1] yielded a sample of 190 stories, which had been published online (53 stories) as well as in various newspapers (133 stories) and magazines (4 stories). As well as being diverse in terms of where they had been published, the sample was comprised of different types of stories, including 99 news articles, 83 features, seven editorials and one book review. In our original content analysis, we focused on whether older LGBTQ+ adults were centrally or peripherally positioned within the narrative, which sexual and gender identities were most commonly depicted and whose voices were included through the use of supporting quotations. Identifying the ways in which older LGBTQ+ persons were depicted, our content and thematic analysis resulted in the identification of three overarching themes, namely that older LGBTQ+ persons were socially invisible, and depicted as either victims of discrimination and exclusion or as extraordinary individuals.

In the present CDA, these categories are positioned as the three dominant LGBTQ+ ageing discourses found in the stories. CDA investigates the interplay between text, discursive practices and broader social inequities, as language is seen to construct, reinforce and challenge hegemonic power systems (Fairclough, 2003) (see also Chapters 3 and 5). Thus, we coded the article texts and associated photographs in an iterative, collaborative process, focusing on how the news media used language and discursive strategies to construct older LGBTQ+ persons as invisible, victims and extraordinary. Whereas a single story was chosen to reflect how older LGBTQ+ persons were depicted as invisible or as victims, two stories were used to examine the third and final theme, namely older LGBTQ+ adults as extraordinary. This was done in order to fully capture the nuance of each of the categories as well as to represent the four sexual-minority and gender-diverse identities that appeared most often in the sample, namely the ageing LGBTQ+ community as a whole, as well as older gay, lesbian and transgender individuals. We considered how prominently the older LGBTQ+ adults were positioned, how their voices were included and how their sexual, gender and other identities were constructed, situated and contextualised within each of the four representative stories. We coded not only for the explicit language and imagery used to construct these three discourses, but also for the underlying assumptions propagated by the journalist. This served the larger goal of considering how the stories shaped, buttressed and changed the disadvantage, exclusion and heteronormativity faced by older LGBTQ+ persons.

Findings

Media silence: the invisibility of older LGBTQ+ persons

Largely under-represented in Canadian print and online news media (Hurd et al, 2020), older LGBTQ+ adults were often discursively silenced or narrowly depicted in the stories in which they did appear. This was evident not only through the small number of stories found, but also through the journalists' choice of directly quoted experts, the positioning of older LGBTQ+ adults in relation to their own experiences and the ways in which those experiences were often characterised. Of the 20,000 news and magazine stories that the initial search yielded, only 190 articles explicitly referenced LGBTQ+ ageing and/or older adults. The bulk of these stories came from only four sources, including *CBC News*, *The Globe and Mail*, *Toronto Star* and *Montreal Gazette*. Rather than depicting a diversity of experience, these stories primarily focused on older gay, cisgendered, White men. The stories tended to centre on events in major Canadian cities rather than rural communities and were typically published in conjunction with Pride festivities in June. While the majority (88 per cent) of the stories included supporting statements from a variety of sources, fewer than half of these (43 per cent) exclusively relied on quotations from older LGBTQ+ persons. Instead, the stories typically included interviews with experts who were younger or ambiguously aged in combination with, or in lieu of, older LGBTQ+ individuals.

A representative example of the discursive silencing of older LGBTQ+ persons can be found in a *Montreal Gazette* story published in August 2016 and entitled 'LGBT seniors' next frontier in rights battle; discrimination' (McIntosh, 2016). The story discussed the long-term care needs of older, Canadian LGBTQ+ adults in Calgary, Alberta. While the article highlighted an important and seldom-discussed issue facing LGBTQ+ older people, these older adults were not given the opportunity to independently voice their specific needs and experiences as they were never directly quoted. Instead, author Emma McIntosh included supporting quotations from three authoritative sources, including Kelly Ernst (the executive director of a local LGBTQ+ service agency), Michael Phair (a gay, former city councillor and coordinator of the Edmonton Pride Seniors Group) and Julie Kerr (a government employee of Alberta Health Services). Phair, in particular, was positioned as having insider knowledge of the specific experiences of LGBTQ+ older people in care homes and the types of solutions they were seeking, as he disclosed: 'There have been instances that we've heard about where people have been bullied.' In this way, Phair was used as a proxy for LGBTQ+ persons, from whom the audience did not directly hear.

The journalist used three generalised assumptions that further silenced and misrepresented the experiences of the LGBTQ+ ageing community. First, the story made the assumptive claim that homophobic discrimination was not a lifelong and daily reality, but rather something that characterised older LGBTQ+ adults' younger years and threatened their ageing futures. This was evident in both the title of the article, which stated that '[d]iscrimination' was the 'next frontier in [their] rights battle', and the introductory sentence that claimed that older LGBTQ+ persons 'may find themselves fighting discrimination all over again' as they 'get older and enter nursing homes'. Second, the narrative was predicated on the assumption that LGBTQ+ older people were 'people who have been out of the closet for decades', ignoring the reality that this is not always the case and that coming out is typically a continual process that can begin at any point in the lifecourse. Finally, the repeated use of the word 'bullying', or an associated derivative, softened and mischaracterised what was systemic, homophobic discrimination.

Additionally, a narrative disruption occurred half way through the story, which called into question whether or not long-term care facilities in Calgary were actually inclusive, welcoming and safe spaces for older LGBTQ+ adults. On the one hand, Ernst contended that 'there is a gap here … there's really no LGBT seniors' homes in Calgary at all'. Consequently, LGBTQ+ older people were described as being at risk from 'bullying' and 'traumatic experience[s]' and in need of 'measures to protect' them. The use of the word 'bullying' on three occasions and 'protect' twice underscored the vulnerability and neglect experienced by LGBTQ+ older people as a result of systemic problems in Alberta's provincial social support system. On the other hand, and standing in stark contrast to the narrative that older LGBTQ+ people were at risk, Julie Kerr, acting as a spokesperson for the government, argued: 'It's not an issue that has arisen to us in a way that indicates to us that there's an unmet need in the long-term care facilities or senior housing areas in Calgary.' Kerr's 'us' versus 'them' language, in combination with her disavowal of the problem, undermined Phair and Ernst's characterisation of these issues as an established and pressing concern. Rather, Kerr de-emphasised any potential failings of the government by highlighting two alternative narratives. First, she noted that her government was 'working to create a more welcoming environment in general', homogenising the needs of all LGBTQ+ individuals, regardless of age. Second, she indicated that necessary changes were being made through the implementation of general LGBTQ+ sensitivity training initiatives, framing discrimination as purely the product of a lack of concern and awareness on the part of health care professionals. Although Kerr indicated that she 'wants to hear if they are experiencing discrimination', she put the onus on LGBTQ+ older people, already framed as a marginalised and vulnerable group, to come forward and challenge her assumptions.

Finally, older LGBTQ+ adults were further discursively silenced and symbolically annihilated in both the story conclusion and choice of accompanying image, which both served to decentre them from the narrative. The photograph, devoid of any older LGBTQ+ adults, instead featured the mayor of Calgary, Naheed Nenshi, aged 44, marshalling the city's annual Pride parade, surrounded by young people, wearing a t-shirt emblazoned with the phrase 'Straight not narrow', thereby proclaiming his own 'straight' (or heterosexual) allyship. The discrepancy between the story's focus on LGBTQ+ ageing and the associated image served to reinforce the centring of younger individuals. This dissonance was further perpetuated in the story's final remarks where Ernst stated: 'Now is the time to do the education and the prep work for future generations.' In this way, the demands for societal change appeared to only be for younger individuals as the story concluded by noting that the long-term care needs of older LGBTQ+ persons constituted a future and growing concern, rather than a pressing current reality for today's older people that demanded immediate attention.

Older LGBTQ+ persons as victims of discrimination and exclusion

As well as being invisible, in more than half of the stories included in the original study, older LGBTQ+ persons were depicted as victims of ongoing and historical discrimination and exclusion who had struggled to come out or transition in a social context characterised by ubiquitous homophobia and transphobia. These stories highlighted the emotional suffering, interpersonal difficulties, systemic barriers and marginalisation that older LGBTQ+ persons had experienced over the course of their lives. While homosexuality was decriminalised in many Western countries in the 1960s, the road to gaining widespread legal protections and civil rights has been a long and difficult process. An illustrative example can be found in an October 2016 story that was published in the *Toronto Star* and entitled: 'He was convicted for being gay' (Jacobs, 2016). The story was a first-person account of the life of 93-year-old gay Englishman, George Montague, and his ongoing fight for an apology from the British government due to his wrongful conviction of gross indecency in 1974.

The construction of Montague as a victim occurred via three complementary discursive strategies that collectively subverted the historical framing of LGBTQ+ persons as deviant, engendered empathy in the audience and created a narrative of injustice. To begin, the author highlighted three social roles in such a way that they positioned Montague as a sympathetic, respectable man who closely approximated heteronormative, masculine ideals. First, Montague was described as a military man, who had bravely joined the Second World War effort because, as he put it, '[t]he war was on, everywhere was getting bombed, and I wanted join up'. His obvious pride in this role was evident in one of the included photographs that depicted a young, uniformed Montague grinning at the camera. Next, the author noted that Montague had provided 40 years of dedicated service to the Boy Scouts' Association, 'working with severely disabled boys', where he was taught to 'always be totally honest'. Finally, the author stated that Montague had been a faithful partner, first to his wife, and later to Somchai, his same-sex lover of 21 years. Underscoring the importance of both his volunteer work and his marital history, a classic black-and-white wedding photo was included that featured a contented, 35-year-old Montague and his beaming bride, surrounded by 12 Boy Scouts and four Boy Scout leaders all dressed in matching uniforms. Another more recent photo depicted an elderly Montague with his arm draped lovingly over a middle-aged Somchai's shoulders. In the related text, Montague described his relationship as follows: 'Somchai and I have been together for 21 years in complete harmony, and we shall be together until the day we die.' Positioning Montague as a military man, a civic-minded volunteer and a faithful partner, the story challenged the historical equating of homosexuality with emasculation, immorality and promiscuity.

Next, the author used two discursive tools, namely juxtaposition and first-person narrative, to undermine the credibility of Montague's public indecency conviction. Set against the backdrop of his established respectability, the author introduced the incongruous label of 'criminal'. The implausibility of this latter status was highlighted through a strategic use of an em-dash in the opening sentence of the feature article, as the journalist contended that 'George Montague has been many things during his long and colorful life: World War II veteran, entrepreneur, father, grandfather, Scout leader — and criminal'. Whereas the title of the article signalled the absurdity and injustice of his criminality ('He was convicted for being gay'), the journalist's four ensuing sentences established how systemic discrimination was at the root of his conviction. In particular, the journalist explained how Montague had been charged as a result of a 'British law that targeted gay men'. The story then relied on an uninterrupted, first-person account of the events that had transpired to illuminate the injustice Montague had endured and to further engender empathy in the reader. Indeed, the entire remainder of the story was told in Montague's own words as he described, in 49 sentences, how his treatment had been 'very unjust' and questioned 'How can I be guilty for being born the way I was?' The construction of Montague as a victim was also achieved through the sanitisation of his sexuality as well as that of public toilets in gay culture. Buttressing the narrative that he was a respectable and moral man, Montague downplayed the sexual activity typically associated with those spaces. Rather, he emphasised how they were sites of personal expression and sociality for gay men, as he asserted: 'The only way to meet other men was to go to the public gents' toilet. People would write poems or their phone numbers on the wall. They wouldn't do anything naughty; just use their eyes, and talk and meet people.' By employing 'anything naughty' as a sanitised euphemism for sex and highlighting the non-sexual activities that took place, Montague challenged the historical associations between public toilets, gay men and sexual deviance. This framing underscored Montague's description of his own arrest as he stressed his innocence when he was found 'alone and doing nothing wrong' in a public toilet stall in a 'targeted' police raid. Positioned as an innocent victim who happened to be in the wrong place at the wrong time, Montague and his experience were thereby emblematic of the historical injustice endured by gay men as a result of homophobic discrimination in the British police and legal systems.

Extraordinary older LGBTQ+ persons

Finally, three quarters of the stories in the sample included narratives that described older LGBTQ+ adults who had risen above their experiences of discrimination to become extraordinary role models, activists and pioneers. Found primarily in feature stories, this recurring theme of resilience entailed accounts of how older LGBTQ+ persons had overcome societal oppression and exclusion. The narrative of resilient transformation was commonly employed, constructed through the use of a 'before and after' story arch, which juxtaposed an individual's dark past with their happy present and future. A representative story included a feature article that was published in the *Toronto Star* in July 2016, entitled: 'At 50, Breagh Williams is walking in her first Trans March' (Battersby, 2016). This story contrasted two distinct time periods in Williams' life. Her past was characterised by, as the journalist put it, a 'lifetime of isolation' that included being raised in foster care and becoming permanently separated from her sister as a result, as well as later being rejected by her few friends who 'stopped returning calls when she came out'. This period of time was also framed as one of suffering and vulnerability as 'for most of [Williams'] life showing her true identity put a target on her'. The journalist included ten different examples of previous hardships and experiences of discrimination that Williams had endured, ranging from 'lost jobs' and being 'sexually and physically abused' to homelessness. The use of the transition adverb 'then' in the following sentence demarcated between Williams' lonely and difficult past and hopeful present/future as a result of gaining access to key resources ten months prior: 'Then in October she found help through Fred Victor, a local charity, which offered housing, medical and social supports.' Previously forced to take on life's challenges alone, Williams had 'since found community', stating 'I felt like I was home' upon first entering the health centre. As a result, Williams had found inner strength and self-acceptance such that experiences of discrimination were now 'like water off the duck's back' as she was determined to 'live loud and proud'. This transformation was validated by supporting quotations from King, the leader of a mutual aid group for older transgender women that Williams attended: 'It's a wonderful thing, and it's so great to hear her saying positive things about herself.' King described Williams' transformational journey towards resilience, stating that '[s]he's like a butterfly', thereby further reinforcing the 'before and after' narrative contrast through metaphor.

The other key way that the stories in our sample framed older LGBTQ+ persons as extraordinary was by positioning them as accomplished pioneers who had paved the way for future generations. A representative example included an article that was published on the *CBC News* website in December 2016 and entitled: 'Great-grandmothers celebrate 50th anniversary as a couple' (Beaudette, 2016). Using three discourses of success, the story celebrated the '50-year romance' of lesbian couple Jean Baker (aged 76) and Sharon Colter (age not included). The first of these three discourses consisted of the underlying and repeated narrative that Baker and Colter had successfully performed heteronormative roles and ideals through motherhood and their long-term, monogamous partnership. Similar to accounts of older heterosexual couples, the feature article was framed as a classic love story in which Baker and Colter had embarked on a 'whirlwind romance' in 1966 followed by a committed, lifelong journey filled with adventure, challenges and family. Central to this narrative was the use of repetition as the journalist referred to the women as doting mothers, grandmothers and/ or great-grandmothers on 14 different occasions. Indeed, beginning with the article headline, noted above, the women were referred to as 'great-grandmothers' rather than a lesbian or gay couple who were celebrating their 50th anniversary. The word lesbian was never used in the story while gay was used four times, but only once when describing them as a couple. Baker and Colter's family roles were constructed as their primary identities in the story, which worked to increase their palatability and close the presumed gap between the women and the heterosexual audience.

The second discourse positioned the women as brave pioneers who had successfully redefined the nature and performance of heteronormative roles, including that of spouse, mother and woman. Amid the backdrop of institutionalised and systemic homophobia, the women had built a family and maintained a long-term relationship. The story described how the couple had moved in together the day after Baker picked up Colter outside a local bar, with the following line: 'Wanna go for a ride and raise a little hell?' From there, the couple were framed as lifelong renegades who had decided not to formalise their relationship once same-sex marriage had been legalised in Canada because, as they put it, after 40 years of being together, it was 'just a piece of paper'. Another example of their subversion of heteronormative roles was found in the recounting of their escapades as avid, competitive and same-sex disco and ballroom dancers, beginning in the 1970s. Additionally, Colter, in particular, was depicted as having transgressed female appearance norms as Baker noted that, when she first met her, she looked similar to 'John Wayne'. In three of the accompanying photographs, which showed the pair affectionately posed together throughout their middle-aged years, Colter was seen sporting a masculine, ruffled tuxedo, standing in contrast to Baker's more traditional feminine aesthetic.

The final success discourse underpinning the story was the narrative of transcendence over homophobia, which was primarily conveyed by the couple's daughter, Allison Nelson. Nelson noted that rural Canada in the 1970s was characterised by '[d]on't ask, don't tell', which meant 'not talking about [their being gay] with anyone' for fear that their 'kids would be bullied' even as others 'talked about [them] behind their backs'. Nelson stated that while the homophobia was palpable, '[n]obody wanted to say anything about it, but they let us be. There weren't any pitchforks or anything like that.' Nelson attributed her mothers' ability to overcome the prejudicial attitudes and behaviours of others at the time to their extraordinarily genuine and generous natures: 'My parents were so great and so giving, and they helped out anyone and everybody, and they were so warm, you know, how can you turn your back on that because of somebody's sexuality?'

Discussion and conclusions

Deepening our previous thematic and content analysis (Hurd et al, 2020), this chapter has reported on the findings of a CDA of four representative Canadian news stories, highlighting the ways that the three original themes were discursively constructed. First, a story about the long-term care needs of ageing LGBTQ+ adults demonstrated how they were often invisibilised in the stories, as their voices were never directly quoted. Instead, the journalist misrepresented their experiences of discrimination and coming out and their future care needs were framed as a debate by experts, who ultimately decentred older LGBTQ+ adults from their own narrative and instead privileged the needs of younger generations. These findings echo those of previous studies, which have found that the media typically under-represent and thereby discursively silence older LGBTQ+ individuals (Lumme-Sandt, 2011; Capuzza, 2014; Krainitzki, 2015; Edström, 2018). As such, media depictions, and the lack thereof, highlight the ways in which ageism intersects and augments homophobia and transphobia, resulting in issues pertaining to older LGBTQ+ adults being assigned low news value or newsworthiness (Caple and Bednarek, 2016). Moreover, the lack of media representation amplifies the marginalisation and exclusion experienced by ageing LGBTQ+ individuals in society more broadly.

Second, older LGBTQ+ persons were often framed as victims of discrimination and exclusion, as was depicted in a story about George Montague, a gay man who was wrongfully convicted of gross indecency. Constructing a narrative of injustice, the article sought to foster a sense of empathy from the audience by disrupting historical associations between gay men and deviance. Therefore, his palatability was discursively established through the use of juxtaposition, a first-person narrative structure, the highlighting of his respectable social roles and the sanitisation of both his sexuality and public toilet culture. Paralleling the findings of previous research (Landau, 2009; Capuzza, 2014), these portrayals highlight the ways in which older LGBTQ+ persons experience an accumulation of systemic inequity over the lifecourse, leading to poor social outcomes (Fredriksen-Goldsen, 2018). These fourth-age representations also serve to reproduce and bolster ageist and heterosexist associations between ageing, gender-diverse and sexual minorities, physical decline and social devaluation (Gilleard and Higgs, 2000; Sandberg and Marshall, 2017). Such portrayals also point to the need for continued social change through policy development and the challenging of existing cultural norms that privilege youthfulness and heterosexuality within Canada.

Third, the stories frequently positioned ageing LGBTQ+ adults as extraordinary individuals due to their resilience and/or pioneering accomplishments. The narrative of resilience was often discursively constructed via a 'before and after' story arch, as was evidenced in an article about transgender woman, Breagh Williams. In contrast, stories that embodied a pioneer narrative were typically accounts of exceptional accomplishments such as that of an older lesbian couple celebrating their 50th anniversary, who had been successful conformists and extraordinary disruptors of heteronormative standards. The portrayal of older LGBTQ+ individuals as exceptional figures firmly positioned them in third-age narratives that emphasised the importance of inner fortitude for ageing well. In other words, the stories often suggested that successful ageing was possible for older LGBTQ+ persons even in the face of personal biographies characterised by discrimination, social exclusion and personal suffering. That said, these portrayals also worked to limit older LGBTQ+ persons' pathways to being deemed newsworthy and thus culturally visible as the only available options for representation included that of fourth-age victims or third-age models of successful resilience (see also Chapter 2).

The current analysis points to the need for greater media attention to be paid to representations of the diversity of experience among older LGBTQ+ adults. Mainstream newspapers are important sources of information about events and issues experienced by community members of all social locations. As such, the news media not only orient and educate their readers, but also socially construct reality through their identification of what constitutes news and how groups of people are framed (Gross, 2001; Couldry, 2012; Caple and Bednarek, 2016). Even as they may reinforce societal homophobia, transphobia and heterosexism, the media also have the power to challenge existing norms and ideologies, by offering up alternative, inclusive, normalising and more progressive depictions of marginalised or othered individuals (Weibull, 1992). This was evidenced in all the stories highlighted in this chapter, which, in some ways, offered subversive and humanising portrayals of older LGBTQ+ persons, while also emphasising their respectability in limited, heteronormative terms. In an increasingly globalised world in which localised news has become internationally accessible, the Canadian media have a contributing role to play in both the perpetuation and disruption of dominant narratives associated with ageing LGBTQ+ persons both nationally and abroad.

In conclusion, this study adds to the existing research, which has, to date, primarily examined media representations of younger LGBTQ+ persons or older cisgender, heterosexual adults. The present analysis adds to queer theorising by illuminating the cultural invisibility and narrow depictions of older LGBTQ+ persons in Canadian news media. Such portrayals reflect the social exclusion of ageing LGBTQ+ individuals in the media and society more broadly (Siverskog, 2015; King, 2016; Sandberg and Marshall, 2017). Our study underscores the importance of media representation in the fostering of social inclusion as well as the repudiation of discriminatory cultural tropes and everyday social practices, particularly for marginalised communities (Gomillion and Giuliano, 2011).

Acknowledgement

This study was supported by a Social Sciences and Humanities Research Council of Canada Insight Grant (#435-2017-0165).

Note

[1] We searched each publication using the following terms: LGBT*, gay*, lesbian*, bisexual*, transgender*, queer*, asexual*, pansexual*, gender fluid, transexual*, transsexual*, transman, trans man, transmen, trans men, transwoman, trans woman, transwomen, trans women, two-spirit, two-spirited, homosexual*, same-sex, gender variant, non-binary and intersex*.

References

Åkerlund, M. (2019) 'Representations of trans people in Swedish newspapers', *Journalism Studies*, 20(9): 1319–38.

Ayoub, P.M. and Garretson, J. (2017) 'Getting the message out: media context and global changes in attitudes toward homosexuality', *Comparative Political Studies*, 50(8): 1055–85.

Battersby, S. (2016) 'At 50, Breagh Williams is walking in her first Trans March', *Toronto Star*, 1 July.

Beaudette, T. (2016) 'Great-grandmothers celebrate 50th anniversary as a couple', *CBC News*, 13 December, available from: www.cbc.ca [accessed 26 July 2017].

Billard, T.J. (2016) 'Writing in the margins: mainstream news media representations of transgenderism', *International Journal of Communication*, 10: 4193–218.

Brown, M.T. (2009) 'LGBT aging and rhetorical silence', *Sexuality Research & Social Policy*, 64(4): 65–78.

Caple, H. and Bednarek, M. (2016) 'Rethinking news values: what a discursive approach can tell us about the construction of news discourse and news photography', *Journalism*, 17(4): 435–55.

Capuzza, J.C. (2014) 'Who defines gender diversity? Sourcing routines and representation in mainstream U.S. news stories about transgenderism', *International Journal of Transgenderism*, 15(3–4): 115–28.

Couldry, N. (2012) *Media, Society, World: Social Theory and Digital Media Practice*, Cambridge: Polity.

de Lauretis, T. (1991) 'Queer theory: lesbian and gay studies: an introduction', *Differences: A Journal of Feminist Cultural Studies*, 3(2): 3–28.

Edström, M. (2018) 'Visibility patterns of gendered ageism in the media buzz: a study of the representation of gender and age over three decades', *Feminist Media Studies*, 18(1): 77–93.

Fairclough, N. (2003) *Analysing Discourse: Textual Analysis for Social Research*, New York, NY: Routledge.

Fredriksen-Goldsen, K. (2018) 'Shifting social context in the lives of LGBTQ older adults', *Public Policy & Aging Report*, 28(1): 24–8.

Gilleard, C. and Higgs, P. (2000) *Cultures of Ageing: Self, Citizen and the Body*, New York, NY: Routledge.

Gomillion, S.C. and Giuliano, T.A. (2011) 'The influence of media role models on gay, lesbian, and bisexual identity', *Journal of Homosexuality*, 58(3): 330–54.

Gross, L. (2001) *Up from Invisibility: Lesbians, Gay Men, and the Media in America*, New York, NY: Columbia University Press.

Hess, L.M. (2019) *Queer Aging in North American Fiction*, Cham: Springer.

Hurd, L., Mahal, R., Ng, S. and Kanagasingam, D. (2020) 'From invisible to extraordinary: representations of older LGBTQ persons in Canadian print and online news media', *Journal of Aging Studies*, 55: 100877.

Hurd Clarke, L., Bennett, E.V. and Liu, C. (2014) 'Aging and masculinity: portrayals in men's magazines', *Journal of Aging Studies*, 31: 26–33.

Jacobs, A. (2016) 'He was convicted for being gay', *Toronto Star*, 30 October.

Katz, S. (2005) *Cultural Aging: Life Course, Lifestyle, and Senior Worlds*, Peterborough, ON: Broadview Press.

Kia, H. (2016) 'Hypervisibility: toward a conceptualization of LGBTQ aging', *Sexual Research and Social Policy*, 13(1): 46–57.

King, A. (2016) 'Queer categories: queer(y)ing the identification "older lesbian, gay and/or bisexual (LGB) adults" and its implications for organizational research, policy and practice', *Gender, Work and Organization*, 23(1): 7–18.

Koch-Rein, A., Haschemi Yekani, E. and Verlinden, J.J. (2020) 'Representing trans: visibility and its discontents', *European Journal of English Studies*, 24(1): 1–12.

Krainitzki, E. (2015) 'Ghosted images: old lesbians on screen', *Journal of Lesbian Studies*, 19(1): 13–26.

Landau, J. (2009) 'Straightening out (the politics of) same-sex parenting: representing gay families in US print news stories and photographs', *Critical Studies in Media Communication*, 26(1): 80–100.

Lewis, H. (2016) *The Politics of Everybody: Feminism, Queer Theory, and Marxism and the Intersection*, London: Zed Books.

Lumme-Sandt, K. (2011) 'Images of ageing in a 50+ magazine', *Journal of Aging Studies*, 25(1): 45–51.

Lundgren, A.S. and Ljuslinder, K. (2011) '"The baby-boom is over and the ageing shock awaits": populist media imagery in news-press representations of population ageing', *International Journal of Ageing and Later Life*, 6(2): 39–71.

Marcus, S. (2005) 'Queer theory for everyone: a review essay', *Signs: Journal of Women in Culture and Society*, 31(1): 191–218.

Markov, C. and Yoon, Y. (2020) 'Diversity and age stereotypes in portrayals of older adults in popular American primetime television series', *Ageing & Society*, 41(12): 2747–67.

McIntosh, E. (2016) 'LGBT seniors' next frontier in rights battle; discrimination', *Montreal Gazette*, 13 August.

Nölke, A. (2018) 'Making diversity conform? An intersectional, longitudinal analysis of LGBT-specific mainstream media advertisements', *Journal of Homosexuality*, 65(2): 224–55.

Parker, K.M., Sadika, B., Sameen, D., Morrison, T.G. and Morrison, M.A. (2020) 'Humanizing lesbian characters on television: exploring their characterization and interpersonal relationships', *Journal of Lesbian Studies*, 24(4): 395–413.

Petermon, J.D. and Spencer, L.G. (2019) 'Black queer womanhood matters: searching for the queer history of Black Lives Matter in television dramas', *Critical Studies in Media Communication*, 36(4): 339–56.

Rodriguez, J.A. (2018) 'Lesbian, gay, bisexual, transgender, and queer media: key narratives, future directions', *Sociology Compass*, 13(4): 1–10.

Rozanova, J., Miller, E.A. and Wetle, T. (2016) 'Depictions of nursing home residents in US newspapers: successful ageing versus frailty', *Ageing & Society*, 36(1): 17–41.

Sandberg, L. (2008) 'The old, the ugly and the queer: thinking old age in relation to queer theory', *Graduate Journal of Social Science*, 5(2): 117–39.

Sandberg, L.J. and Marshall, B.L. (2017) 'Queering aging futures', *Societies*, 7(3): 21.

Siverskog, A. (2015) 'Ageing bodies that matter: age, gender and embodiment in older transgender people's life stories', *NORA – Nordic Journal of Feminist and Gender Research*, 23(1): 4–19.

Sullivan, N. (2003) *A Critical Introduction to Queer Theory*, New York, NY: New York University Press.

Tortajada, I., Dhaenens, F. and Willem, C. (2018) 'Gendered ageing bodies in popular media culture', *Feminist Media Studies*, 18(1): 1–6.

Tsai, W.S. (2010) 'Assimilating the queers: representations of lesbians, gay men, bisexual, and transgender people in mainstream advertising', *Advertising & Society Review*, 11(1): 1–36.

Waggoner, E.B. (2018) 'Bury your gays and social media fan response: television, LGBTQ representation, and communitarian ethics', *Journal of Homosexuality*, 65(13): 1877–91.

Weibull, L. (1992) 'The status of the daily newspaper: what readership research tells us about the role of newspapers in the mass media system', *Poetics*, 21(4): 259–82.

Westwood, S. (ed) (2019) *Ageing, Diversity and Equality: Social Justice Perspectives*, New York, NY: Routledge.

PART II

Imagined ageing in promotional and fictional contexts

7

Ageism and the promotion of agelessness in Brazilian advertising

Gisela G. S. Castro

Introduction

Although ageing is a global phenomenon, the growth rates of older populations have been particularly rapid in developing countries (Ha and Hodgson, 2020). The increasing number of older people in the Brazilian population stands out. Fewer babies are being born and longevity is more widespread in Brazil than before. But while an increasing number of people are now living longer, with more opportunities for active, gratifying lives, we cannot disregard the persistent and vexatious social, cultural and economic forms of inequality that compromise the quality of life of a growing number of disadvantaged older men and women.

The current Brazilian population stands at more than 213 million people (IGBE, 2021a). The long-held predominance of children and young adults in demographics, and population pyramids, is no longer a reality. With more than 34.4 million people aged 60 or over, Brazil is slowly coming to terms with its ageing population. Just over 34 per cent of Brazilian households have at least one adult aged 60 or over (Núcleo 60+, 2021).

The fast-growing, radical modification of the age distribution of the Brazilian population means that the current youth-centric approach in media portrayals of older adults needs urgent research attention. Brazilian advertising, in general, has too often ignored or misrepresented older consumers (Debert, 2003, 2018; Castro, 2018), who have accumulated substantial spending power but, nonetheless, mostly remain unseen or are poorly portrayed in stereotyped roles. These modes of presentation are inappropriate for today's ageing Brazilian society.

In this chapter, we address advertising to critically reflect on what it means to age in an ageist consumer society in modern Brazil. In much the same way as in other countries, Brazilian media portrayals of older people affect the way older adults view themselves and are viewed in society. Brazilian media in general have operated according to the 'conspiracy of silence' denounced by Simone de Beauvoir (1977) decades ago. Beauvoir notably used this expression to refer to the 'unspoken consensus to not mention this' attitude that kept the dire living conditions of older French people hidden from public debate.

This chapter takes a critical stance on the persuasive language of Brazilian advertising and discusses how negative assumptions about ageing still inform Brazilian media. We first present the fundamental sociocultural basis of this discussion, and then provide empirical data as a basis for critical reflection on the topic.

We begin by examining advertising in Brazil and its role in forming a social stance on ageing, and present a brief description of the methodological procedures behind the empirical corpus of six multi-platform audiovisual commercials selected for this chapter. We then discuss the prevalence of ageism in Brazilian society and problematise the notion of 'successful ageing'.

The chapter then proceeds to examine the promotion of agelessness in Brazilian advertising. This leads to a discussion on ageism from the point of view of a beauty industry commercial, followed by a seemingly counterintuitive display of mastery of information and communication technology (ICT) skills in a banking sector advert. Towards the end of the chapter, we address Woodward's (2006) argument about the 'youthful structure of the look' and the strong appeal of emotional storytelling, to further discuss ageism and the promotion of agelessness in Brazilian advertising. The chapter closes with a reflection on the sociocultural construction of meanings of ageing in the Brazilian imaginary, the role of promotional cultures in the production of subjectivities and the social engagement of academic research, which actively takes part in the struggle to combat ageism in Brazil.

Advertising

In Brazil, as in the rest of the world, we can understand advertising as a complex type of persuasive cultural media text by the promotional industry, with powerful economic, social and cultural significance. It simultaneously addresses and establishes target audiences as it performs the role of promoting consumerism. The affective potential and mode of address in advertising rhetoric contribute to disseminating ways of being and lifestyles associated with the logic of consumer culture (Merlin, 2017; Castro, 2018).

Ageism is still flagrantly disregarded, albeit widespread in Brazil. In the Brazilian reality, as in other countries, advertising finds ways to produce different styles of rhetoric in the rich diversity of contemporary everyday life. The transformation of older age into a consumer market segment, together with the discursive construction of an ageless way of being, may result in various forms of social bullying and age-based discrimination. Despite the recent radical demographic change, today's youth-driven ethos relegates older people in Brazil – especially older women – to varying degrees of social ostracism and oppression. In a major study on ageing in Brazil, 81 per cent of respondents stated that ageism is a problem in Brazilian society (Sesc and Fundação Perseu Abramo, 2020). The same study shows that 8 per cent of respondents aged 50 or over had experienced age discrimination.

Brazilian anthropologist Guita Grin Debert (2018) argues that we must distinguish the older people depicted in commercials from older members of the public, so as not to incur what she labels 'a referential illusion'. Advertising campaigns help to create ideal role models for older adults, while consumer culture is mainly interested in affluent, healthy and active older people. Still, as Debert (2018, p 83, translated from Brazilian Portuguese) notes, 'not rarely, antagonistic representations of old age – dependency and power – may be presented during the same commercial break'. Finally, studying images of ageing in advertising means considering that these messages may have multiple interpretations.

This chapter critically reflects on ageism and the promotion of the ageless ethos in contemporary Brazilian advertising, according to which individuals are presumed to take responsibility for the way they are said to 'choose' to age. This author acknowledges the argument that older people should be regarded in broader terms than solely their chronological age – a premise that supports the ageless ideal – but strongly rejects the neoliberal claim that ageing is simply a matter of individual 'choice'.

We should be keenly critical of the anti-ageing conception of 'successful' ageing that is somewhat subsumed in the glorification of agelessness. This belief claims that people paradoxically never really grow old but remain 'ageless' as they diligently struggle to maintain a youthful appearance and vitality throughout their senior years. Based on her influential study of Brazilian advertising from the 1990s, Debert (2003, p 137) notes:

> [I]mages of ageing in Brazilian advertising are active in the production of what I call 'reprivatising ageing', which ensures its transformation in a problem for individuals who were incapable of getting involved in motivating activities and who neglected adopting patterns of consumption and lifestyle that would ultimately enable them to avoid old age and its problems.

Research (Debert, 2003, 2018; Castro, 2018) shows that we are experiencing changes in the way marketing and advertising address old age and longevity in Brazil. Several decades ago, we would more often see a stereotypical presence of older adults in secondary roles. Today we find memorable characters, and older people playing leading roles. Anti-hegemonic models challenge the common sense of frailty and social devaluation, traditionally ascribed to older people. However, negative stereotypes have not completely disappeared. The elusive boundaries that separate humour from scorn expose the insidious presence of ageism.

Methodology

Considering that Brazilian advertising is widely acknowledged and highly praised internationally,[1] this chapter builds on existing interdisciplinary literature on age, consumption and media studies to critically examine empirical data from advertising, marketing and demographic studies (for example, Cetic. Br., 2020). According to official figures (IBGE, 2021b),[2] television is present in 96.7 per cent of Brazilian households, while 75 per cent of Brazilians have an internet connection. Since the majority (52.9 per cent) of advertising investment in Brazil focuses on broadcast television, and 28.2 per cent on the web, our reflections are empirically grounded in six audiovisual commercials for leading brands from different market sectors, as part of wider marketing strategies for the products and brands they are designed to promote.

For this purpose, we consider interdisciplinary perspectives in sociocultural research on ageing (Calasanti and Slevin, 2006; Woodward, 2006; Calasanti, 2016; Debert, 2018; Gullette, 2019; Raisborough, 2019) and the media (Ylänne, 2012, 2018; Davis, 2013; Kuschick and Machado, 2016; Castro, 2018). We also take into consideration market and public sector studies (AARP, 2019; UN, 2020, 2021; WHO, 2021) to discuss issues such as ageism, negative stereotypes, the double standard of gendered ageing, as well as the promotion of the ageless ethos in Brazilian media and consumer cultures.

As we know, age is linked to various other social categories. Among the social policies in effect in Brazil, 60 is the age at which one is entitled to a series of social benefits. In marketing segmentation, individuals aged 50+ (sometimes 45+) are commonly classified as 'senior consumers', although 60+ is more widely adopted in Brazilian marketing research today (AARP, 2019; Kakulla, 2021).

Our selection of six television adverts that feature older adults was achieved by randomly searching the database of three well-known Brazilian advertising news websites.[3] We used a three-year timeframe (2018–20), and Portuguese search words for the 'elderly', 'ageing', 'old age', 'seniors', the 'silver market' and '60+'. A table was created with the search results, with information such as the brand name, market sector, year of production, a brief description and the link to each advert. For a final selection of the commercials that would be featured in this chapter, the main criterion was linked to the cultural aspect that their rhetoric helped us to highlight. This decision justifies the inclusion of one advert that was not produced in the timeframe originally selected. Since it allowed us to discuss a given cultural aspect in an exemplary way, a 2015 production was included. Whenever possible, the selected adverts are grouped by market sector.

Ageism and the changing meanings of ageing

The Brazilian communication and media researchers Kuschick and Machado (2016, p 145) studied the meanings of older age in *Veja*, a leading Brazilian weekly news magazine, from 1968 to 2014. Their main finding was a steady increase in presenting 'positive ageing as a reflex of one's own individual actions'. This has helped to consolidate a set of ideas that reduce ageing to 'a series of questions of individual, private order' among its broad, affluent reader base (Kuschick and Machado, 2016, p 147).

In cultural gerontology, 'active', 'positive' and 'successful' ageing are viewed as controversial concepts. This is true worldwide, including in Brazil. We cannot fight against ageism without contesting age-based relations. Calasanti (2016, p 1095) claims that 'like power relations based on gender, race, or ethnicity, the concept of age relations conveys the ways that age serves as a social organizing principle such that different age categories gain identities and power in relation to one another' (see also Chapter 1). Therefore, older adults suffer from an unequal distribution of authority, status and income, and are also culturally devalued. This does not result from personal attitudes of prejudice against older people but is a side-effect of the way social institutions, such as the media, and everyday life operate. 'To leave age relations unexplored reinforces the inequality old people face, one that shapes their relations of oppression, and one that we reproduce for ourselves if we live long enough' (Calasanti and Slevin, 2006, p 14).

As Raisborough (2020, p 2) argues:

> Endorsed by the World Health Organisation 'active ageing' aims to increase and extend older people's participation and inclusion in society, not least by their remaining productive and healthy. By promoting self-responsibility for our ageing, active ageing policies promise the personal and social benefits of autonomy and well-being while reducing the number of frail, dependent, economically unsecure older people and thus the personal and social costs of ageing.

Since the active ageing agenda is embedded with the neoliberal ethos of individual self-responsibility, this notion is promoted, just as health and social care provision is being downsized by austerity measures in Brazil, and many other parts of the world. As Raisborough (2020, p 3) eloquently argues, '"active ageing" policies form part of an "anti-welfare agenda" ... and promote neoliberal subjectivities'.

As this author has posed before (Castro, 2018), one of the main goals of modern neoliberal capitalism is to promote not only goods and services, but also certain models of subjectivity in line with the requirements of the system. In no way does this ethos address the pressing fact that access to resources and opportunities is unequally distributed, and even more so in developing countries such as Brazil.

The invisibility of older people and the problematic forms of their presentation in Brazilian media are largely supported by widespread, unchecked ageism. According to the World Health Organization (WHO) newsletter *Valuing Older People*, 'unlike other forms of discrimination, including sexism and racism, ageism is socially acceptable, strongly institutionalized, largely undetected and unchallenged' (Officer et al, 2016, p 3). In the more recent *Global Report on Ageism* (WHO, 2021), 'ageism refers to the stereotypes (how we think), prejudice (how we feel) and discrimination (how we act) directed towards people on the basis of their age. It can be institutional, interpersonal or self-directed' (see also Chapter 1). The report exposes this as an insidious scourge on society and goes on to make a strong call for urgent action against the various forms of ageism.

For Gullette (2017, p xiii), 'compared to sexism, racism and transphobia, ageism is the least censured, the most acceptable and unnoticed of the cruel prejudices'. In her words, 'by being sprung on us late, ageism differs from racism and sexism, the born-into-them biases' (Gullette, 2017, p xix). Ageism turns youth into a powerful social imperative – something to be maintained and displayed throughout one's entire life. This is clear within the Brazilian context of rampant plastic surgery, Botox, dermal fillers and other aesthetically motivated clinical anti-ageing procedures that form a type of culture that only finds beauty in youthful-looking adults, while shaming others whose appearance is regarded as evidence that they have 'let themselves go'.

To discuss the insidious presence of ageist messages in Brazilian advertising, the remaining sections of this chapter examine empirical data from audiovisual commercials that represent older men and women. Produced by local advertising agencies and aired in commercial breaks during regular programmes in Brazilian broadcast or cable television, as well as in social media platforms such as YouTube, these adverts are examined for their multimodal, underlying cultural messages. We regard the neoliberal take on ageing as a private, individual matter that can be dealt with by consumption rituals, practices and products.

Promoting agelessness

Let us now examine two cases from Brazilian advertising that openly promote the ageless ideal, each in their own, unique way. The first is a television commercial produced in 2019 (Nutren Senior, 2019). We see members of two generations from the same families being asked similar, but slightly different questions. While the younger members seem to be quite comfortable talking about what they want to be when they grow up, the adults find it hard to answer the 'question that has never been posed'. In this advert for a multinational brand of nutritional-supplement drinks and shakes, we are persuaded that there is little difference between growing up and growing old. The motivating, underlying message – 'it is never too late' – encourages everyone to make their dreams come true, regardless of their age. Ironically, this seemingly uplifting lesson is tinged with age denial.

One of the problems with the ageless ideal is precisely this: in resisting the possible frailty and constraints of advanced age, and the finitude of life, it denies ageing altogether. Furthermore, the 'never too late to dream' lesson is given on behalf of the marketing strategy for a nutritional product, based on controversial scientific evidence. The Harvard Medical School (2020) considered these costly supplements to be more of a hype than actual help in keeping healthy. In addition, this approach disregards the fact that a significant segment of the Brazilian population is unemployed and undernourished.

Produced in 2019 for a private health insurance company for older people in Brazil (Prevent Senior, 2019), the title of our next commercial reads like a manifesto, and a declaration of principles: 'We believe in empowering adults+.' The company is now involved in a major corruption scandal related to medical malpractice, and the omission of information about COVID-19-related deaths in its network of hospitals and clinics.

Classifying its target audience as 'adults+' suggests that anyone who is not a baby, child or adolescent can (and should) be 'empowered'. The trademark expression coined for this company in Brazilian Portuguese can be understood both as a euphemism and as an invented, ageless category, so that the empowered 'adult pluses' are supposed to refrain from growing old as they age. The piece was produced to be aired in major cinema chains in Rio de Janeiro and São Paulo, the two largest cities in Brazil. It reads like a short documentary film. From this persuasive advert, which shows several different people speaking directly at the camera, as a testimonial, one learns that while growing up is fine, growing old is negative, limiting and even hurtful. After all, if ageing is 'all in your head', as some of the speakers suggest, one can – and must – resist old age. It is not hard to understand why ageless ideology informs the clearly motivational tone of this commercial.

When we take a critical stance on the type of empowerment that is allegedly being promoted in this advert, we find the neoliberal defence of the 'entrepreneurial self' (Dardot and Laval, 2016). While society is entirely disregarded by neoliberalism, every aspect of one's personal life is turned into a matter for scrutiny and strict individual management. In this way, one is persuaded to individually take on responsibility for actively managing one's own health and wellbeing, under any circumstances. At first glance, there seems to be nothing wrong with this statement. But if we take a closer look, from the standpoint of a health insurance company in Brazil, it ultimately means that medical assistance is only needed if one is not disciplined in conscientious self-care. This call to arms to consumer empowerment implies that the company should not be required to provide a service to empowered 'adult plus' clients who should know better.

Ageing is now part of the global debate on public policies that are more clearly focused on social and human development. This debate includes the campaign against all forms of ageism and age discrimination. The World Health Organization (2021) and the United Nations (2002, 2020, 2021) have been working to tackle ageing and ageism, to foster changes in government and societies' attitudes towards older people. It is crucial to encourage social inclusion for all ages in this endeavour, in addition to a dignified presentation of older men and women in the media worldwide.

Ageism and the beauty industry

The next Brazilian television commercial we turn to brings to the screen a popular middle-aged actress with a thriving career on the stage and in films and television in Brazil. She stars in this advert for a leading manufacturer in the local perfume and cosmetics industry (O Boticário, 2020), in a bid to make skincare routines more widespread among the immense Brazilian middle-class strata. The advert is shot in a testimonial format, as if she is simply talking to the public. In the opening scene, she complains in a good-natured way about people taking to the web to find out how old she really is. While she glances at her laptop, the search words are shown in the foreground. She reproaches this with a smile: "Oh, come on, folks. Such an outdated thing to do!" (translated from original Portuguese). She then proceeds to disclose 'the secret' to her clear, smooth skin, by saying: "when the topic is such beautiful-looking skin, the real secret is to invest in the best products". She then introduces the range of cosmetics that this commercial is selling and shows viewers how to apply the serum. The whole script is made to sound and look honest, spontaneous and straightforward. Cosmetics are suggested as something any ordinary person can use as they go about their everyday chores – not too fancy, not too complicated and with promising results.

This commercial reinforces the neoliberal message about the moral duty of engaging in diligent, daily anti-ageing routines, dubbed as 'self-care' or 'beauty' maintenance, to Brazilian audiences. In this way, people are reminded that you are primarily judged by the way you look, especially if you are a woman. Visible signs of ageing must be avoided, since they keep you from looking 'your best'. It is important to stress that these internalised, intimidating, sexist and ageist (mis)conceptions power a youth-centric, anti-ageing consumer culture in Brazil.

As a creative strategy, this advert clearly resorts to the prestige of a well-liked national celebrity to endorse the brand and its new product line. The celebrity selected is not usually seen in adverts, and this works as a further reason for audiences to believe in the alleged authenticity of her words, since she apparently 'reveals the secret' of her grooming routine with the new line in question. No one really knows her exact age, but most people would agree that she looks friendly and attractive for someone who is middle-aged. For the fan base in the struggling Brazilian middle classes, the message is quite clear: no matter how old you are, to look good one needs to engage in 'skin care', by investing in often costly cosmetic products that promise excellent results thanks to the powerful ingredients in their formula. Science and self-help are intertwined in a message that downplays the importance of age, and attempts to equate self-care with self-worth.

Ageism and technology

Let us now consider the very successful advertising campaign for a major Brazilian bank (*Itaú App*, 2020) featuring two friendly old ladies in their 80s. They cheerfully show off how keen they are to use the latest technology to remotely access their bank accounts and make all their payments. In one of the bank's latest commercials, one of the women confesses that she misses going to the bank, while they both comment on how easy it is to use the online banking application, and to maintain the mandatory social distancing during the pandemic.

One way to critically read this advert rests on the broadly accepted assumption that the younger generations display a 'natural' resourcefulness and skill in digital technologies. This claim resonates with the so-called 'digital divide' in Brazil (Silveira, 2003; Pedrozo, 2013). The disconnection between chronological age and accompanying patterns of behaviour forms a widely used strategy to attract attention to a specific advert. Based on this idea, these adverts intend to innovate by presenting old ladies who have a total mastery of the latest technology.

Although at first glance this type of depiction may be interpreted as resisting ageist beliefs, we must consider that older characters are often used to develop a creative line of adverts that do not necessarily target older consumers. In the advertising campaign, the purpose is to reassure the bank's house-bound clientele that their internet banking application is so safe and easy to use that even so-called digital 'novices' can gain full control.

The 'tech-savvy' old ladies also pose as role models for what is now considered an 'appropriate' Brazilian bank customer. The message is that we must all embrace change, and keep up with all things modern, regardless of our motivation, capability or skills. These changes include the forceful and often vexing reconfiguration of banking services. In Brazil, banks increasingly cut costs by dismissing the employees responsible for individualised, face-to-face interactions, in favour of autonomous self-service in the automated, preconfigured flows of internet banking.

Ageism, agelessness and the youthful structure of the look

A commercial for the Brazilian branch of an international online marketplace (OLX, 2015) is another example of an advert aimed at younger audiences that cast older characters. The scene of this 2015 production shows an interaction between a grandson and a grandfather. The latter is played by a very friendly-looking grey-haired old man who displays surprising grace in an unexpected hip-hop performance. According to an ingrained stereotype, the viewer would expect this routine to be played by a young Black person, whereas this old White man cheerfully sings and dances to rap music. The lyrics resonate with the commercial message, advising that he wants to sell his bike in order to make money to take his wife for a holiday in the beautiful, sunny northeast coast of Brazil. This type of humour, which implies that the scene is so out of place it could only be considered a joke, could be classified as ageist.

Brazilian advertising often operates according to 'the youthful structure of the look' described by Woodward (2006). This refers to the fact that, by default, viewers are positioned in an uncritical 'younger than', superior position in relation to the older person or persons depicted in the scene. In the ideology of a youth-centric visual culture, 'age is largely deemed a matter for comedy or sentimental compassion' (Woodward, 2006, p 164).

It can be said that ageism plays a part in the habits of the Brazilian advertising industry. This cultural milieu values constant innovation, and it somehow seems to equate accumulated life experience with a lack of flexibility to follow the fast-paced flow of inevitable market changes and transformations. There has recently been some concern in fostering racial, gender and sexual diversity in the Brazilian advertising industry, although age is often neglected in diversity campaigns and efforts. The lack of age diversity in the workplace leads to Brazilian advertising professionals' difficulties in dealing with something as unfamiliar as ageing or ageism. When asked to gear their rhetoric towards older segments of the public, it is not uncommon for content producers to unconsciously translate their lack of empathy into a lack of solidarity. Fortunately, the situation is changing, and specialised consultancy firms in the longevity market are now a growing part of the Brazilian marketing scenario.

Another major point when considering the advertising industry in Brazil, and elsewhere, concerns the overwhelming valorisation of the glamour of creation, and the adrenaline of production, at the expense of the slow and laborious process of reflection on one's work. Critical capacity is eroded in the race to meet escalating demands within extremely tight deadlines. In other words, speed characterises the incessant flow of sound, text and images on the screens on which Brazilian advertising professionals spend the majority of their time. There is little opportunity to reflect on their own practices, and the demands of each new client often supersede the social dimensions of their work.

Where there is emotion, there is value?

Reflecting on the stereotypes and values linked to old age and ageing in the current Brazilian advertising rhetoric, the strong appeal of emotional storytelling stands out in 'Where there is love, there is beauty' (O Boticário, 2020), a commercial for a local perfume and cosmetics brand. It tells the touching story of an 80-year-old man who enrols on a professional make-up course, where he is the oldest, least-qualified student. Narrated in the first person, the advert details the man's difficulties as he toils and perseveres towards his goal. He could not be more motivated: he is doing it for love.

As we see him tenderly applying make-up to an elderly woman's face, we learn that his wife had been gradually losing her eyesight. He sprays her with perfume, and says that he promised she would never have to lose her beauty. The woman smiles. In the final scene, the couple sway in a tender dance. Photographs of real-life characters pop up on the screen, as we learn that this is a true story. The highly sentimental commercial takes advantage of the added value of an account-shaped narrative based on real people's lives.

Brand communication strives to evoke emotional engagement with consumers. The Brazilian brand that commissioned this sentimental commercial is well- known for its range of perfumes, and lesser known for cosmetics. The sentimental story of a tenacious old man who turned into a make-up artist for the love of his life, helps to consolidate this lesser-known aspect of the brand in a memorable way. Affect activates the memory. It is easier to remember things that have moved us, and made us emotional, and this is the reason behind the emotionally charged storytelling strategy employed in the advert. The narrative is so involving that it is easy to ignore the sexist, ageist undertone, and claim that a woman's key worth is in her looks. The message appears to suggest that if she loses her beauty, she loses everything, as far as the male perspective is concerned. This reinforces the biased notion that every woman must strive to always show what is said to be the best version of herself. This, in turn, requires actively engaging in daily, and often laborious, hair and make-up routines. This is viewed as a demonstration of love, for the husband to take over when his wife is no longer able to continue.

Conclusion

In this chapter, we have engaged in a critical analysis of Brazilian commercials, to demonstrate how ageism, and other forms of prejudice, taint advertising rhetoric. Our investigation into images of ageing in Brazilian advertising considers ageism as an insidious form of prejudice that permeates the most diverse social instances, and gives rise to disrespect, aggression and neglect.

By focusing on the types and contexts of portrayals of older people in Brazilian advertising, we reflect on the question of how Brazilian media help to challenge or further reinforce ageism. Based on the empirical data analysed, we problematise the paradoxical ageless ideal of growing up without growing old in Brazil as a negative by-product of the neoliberal ethos of the entrepreneurial self. In our view, the sociocultural dimension of ageing, including the production of subjectivities should be examined.

Our critical analysis of the ways advertising in Brazil presents older adults is based on the premise that images, sounds and the tenor of discourse affect the way that societies relate to this age group. Negative stereotypes, prejudice and demeaning moral values insidiously permeate practices and discourse on ageing. These can, in turn, be reinforced, or rejected. As mentioned earlier, media discourse participates in the construction of the social imaginary, by producing an affective charge that modulates our interactions in the world.

This reflection considers the affective dimension of media images of ageing elicited in Brazilian advertising rhetoric, albeit recognising the active role of the recipient in communication. We also consider the dialectical aspect of the social structure of discourse. Our discussion on the images of ageing elicited in Brazilian advertising rhetoric has sought to emphasise the work of affectivity, creating bonds of identification and belonging, in the rituals of exclusion, forms of sociability and production of subjectivities in modern Brazil.

Advertising plays a major role in financing media and shaping cultural production. Far broader than purchasing behaviour per se, consumption practices are linked to media visibility in highly complex, multifaceted sociocultural flows. This often generates a blurring of lines between creative and promotional content. In the realm of what has been named in media and cultural studies as promotional cultures (Davis, 2013), the production of subjectivities largely unfolds by means of communicative practices that are governed by the logics of consumption.

A number of the Brazilian commercials examined in this chapter promote certain types of subjectivity as if they are the only appropriate and dignified way to be. By considering the affective power of the media within contemporary Brazilian consumer culture, we claim that these narratives of consumption take part in the social pedagogy that feeds into inequality, dominance and oppression. Viewed as complex and multi-layered texts, some Brazilian advertising narratives mobilise well-established stereotypes, and often produce ageist portrayals, even when they apparently challenge the hierarchies existing between the old and the non-old.

As we draw attention to the effects of contemporary mediated images of ageing in the way Brazilian media informs the construction of subjectivities, we argue that the struggle against ageism and age discrimination in Brazil is part of the social engagement of academic research. This type of study should be viewed as an undertaking in favour of new, inclusive and respectful forms of social interaction among generations in Brazil, and worldwide. We need more nuanced media representations of ageing, together with diverse narratives of ageing experiences. From the standpoint of critically reflecting on some of the ways older adults are presented in creative contemporary Brazilian advertising, this research seeks to disseminate ideas, and foster a debate on ageing and the media. Our hope is that it adds to this discussion in a meaningful way.

Notes

[1] According to Cannes Lions' (2021) *State of Creativity* report, Brazil is the third leading country in advertising creativity, next to the United States and the UK, while New York, London and São Paulo are judged to be the world's most creative cities.

[2] The figures show investment in advertising in Brazil as monitored by the institution that gathers data from the main advertisers, media outlets and advertising agencies, *CENP Meios − Painel 2021* [CENP Media − 2021 Panel], available from: https://cenp.com.br/cenp- meios?id=20 [accessed 10 September 2021].

[3] Adnews (https://adnews.com.br/), Meio&Mensagem (https://www.meioemensagem.com.br/) and Clube de Criação (https://www.clubedecriacao.com.br/).

References

AARP (2019) '2020 Tech and the 50+ Survey', available from: https://doi.org/10.26419/res.00329.001 [accessed 18 April 2022].

Beauvoir, S. (1977) *Old Age*, London: Penguin Classics.

Calasanti, T. (2016) 'How successful is successful aging?', *The Gerontologist*, 56(6): 1093–101.

Calasanti, T. and Slevin, K. (2006) *Age Matters: Re-aligning Feminist Thinking*, New York, NY: Routledge.

Cannes Lions (2021) State of Creativity report, available from: https://www.lionscreativity.com/state-of-creativity-report-2021 [accessed 18 April 2022].

Castro, G.G.S. (2018) *Os Velhos na Propaganda: Atualizando o Debate* [The Elderly in Advertising: Updating the Debate], São Paulo: Pimenta Cultural, available from: https://memorialdoconsumo.espm.edu.br/os-velhos-na-propaganda/ [accessed 18 April 2022].

Cetic.Br. (2020) 'ICT Household Survey' (COVID-19 Edition - Adapted Methodology), available from: https://cetic.br/en/pesquisa/domicilios/ [accessed 10 September 2021].

Dardot, P. and Laval, C. (2016) *A Nova Razão do Mundo: Ensaio Sobre a Sociedade Neoliberal* [The World's New Reason: An Essay on Neoliberal Society], São Paulo: Boitempo.

Davis, A. (2013) *Promotional Cultures: The Rise and Spread of Advertising, Public Relations, Marketing and Branding*, Cambridge, UK: Polity.

Debert, G.G. (2003) 'Os velhos na propaganda' [The elderly in advertising], *Cadernos Pagu*, 21: 133–55.

Debert, G.G. (2018) 'A reprivatização do envelhecimento nas imagens da mídia' [Re-privatizing ageing in media images], in G.G.S. Castro and T. Hoff (eds) *Comunicação, Consumo e Envelhecimento no Contemporâneo: Perspectivas Multidisciplinares* [Communications, Consumption and Ageing in Contemporary Times: Multidisciplinary Perspectives], Porto Alegre: Sulina, pp 75–93.

Gullette, M.M. (2017) *Ending Ageism: Or How Not to Shoot Old People*, New Brunswick: Rutgers University Press.

Ha, L. and Hodgson, A. (2020) *Ageing Matters: The Future of Older Populations*, London: Euromonitor International.

Harvard Medical School (2020) 'Supplemental nutrition drinks: help or hype?', *Harvard Health Letter*, Harvard Health Publishing, available from: https://www.health.harvard.edu/staying-healthy/supplemental-nutrition-drinks-help-or-hype [accessed 15 September 2021].

IBGE (Brazilian Institute of Geography and Statistics) (2021a) *Estimates*, Brasilia: IBGE, available from: https://agenciadenoticias.ibge.gov.br/en/agencia-news/2184-news-agency/news/31472-population-estima ted-for-brazil-reaches-213-3-million-inhabitants-in-2021 [accessed 15 September 2021].

IBGE (Brazilian Institute of Geography and Statistics) (2021b) *PNAD Contínua TIC 2019* [Continuous National Household Sample Survey – ICT 2019], Brasilia: IBGE.

Kakulla, B. (2021) *Tech Trends and the 50-Plus: Top 10 Biggest Trends*, Washington, DC: AARP Research, available from: https://doi.org/10.26419/res.00420.001 [accessed 18 April 2022].

Kuschick, C.L.B.R. and Machado, F.V.K. (2016) 'Compre, leia, siga e rejuveneça! Sobre os sentidos movimentados e construídos por *Veja* acerca da velhice ao longo de sua história' (1968–2014) [Buy, read, follow and rejuvenate! On the meanings built and put into motion by *Veja* during its history (1968–2014)], *Galaxia*, 32: 138–50.

Merlin, N. (2017) *Colonización de la Subjetividad: los Medios Masivos de Comunicación en la Época del Biomercado* [Colonizing Subjectivity: Mass Media in the Age of the Biomarket], Buenos Aires: Letra Viva.

Núcleo 60+ (2021) Pesquisa Nacional Bússola 60+ (National field study for the longevity market), São Paulo: Núcleo 60+.

Officer, A., Schneiders, M.L., Wu, D., Nash, P., Thiyagarajan, J.A. and Beard, J.R. (2016) 'Valuing older people: time for a global campaign to combat ageism', *World Health Organization Newsletter*, Geneva: WHO.

Pedrozo, S. (2013) 'New media use in Brazil: digital inclusion or digital divide?', *Online Journal of Communication and Media Technologies*, 3(1): 144–62.

Raisborough, J. (2020) 'Age as trouble: towards alternative narratives of women's ageing', *Psychology of Women and Equalities Section Review*, 2(1): 1–16.

Sesc, S.P. and Fundação Perseu Abramo (2020) *Idosos no Brasil – 2ª Edição* [The elderly in Brazil – 2nd Edition], available from: https://www.sescsp.org.br/online/artigo/14626_PESQUISA+IDOSOS+NO+BRASIL+2+EDICAO+2020 [accessed 15 September 2021].

Silveira, S.A. (2003) *Exclusão Digital* [Digital Exclusion], São Paulo: Fund. Ed. Perseu Abramo.

United Nations (UN) (2002) Press Release. General Assembly. Third Committee. ' "Youth boom", "age quake", emerging as major challenges for both developing, developed countries, third committee told' (GA/SHC/3693), available from: https://www.un.org/press/en/2002/GASHC3693.doc.htm [accessed 15 September 2021].

United Nations (UN), Department of Economic and Social Affairs, Population Division (2020) *World Population Ageing 2019* (ST/ESA/SER.A/444), New York, NY: UN, available from: https://www.un.org/development/desa/pd/news/world-population-ageing-2019 [accessed 15 September 2021].

United Nations (UN), Department of Economic and Social Affairs, Population Division (2021) *World Population Ageing 2020* (ST/ESA/SER.A/451), New York, NY: UN, available from: https://www.un.org/development/desa/pd/news/world-population-ageing-2020-highlights [accessed 15 September 2021].

WHO (World Health Organization) (2021) *Global Report on Ageism*, Geneva: WHO.

Woodward, K. (2006) 'Performing age, performing gender', *NWSA Journal*, 18(1): 162–89.

Ylänne, V. (2012) 'Conclusion', in V. Ylänne (ed) *Representing Ageing: Images and Identities*, Basingstoke: Palgrave Macmillan, pp 226–31.

Ylänne, V. (2018) 'Representações dos velhos e da velhice na propaganda do século XXI' [Representations of older adults and old age in 21st century advertising], in G.G.S. Castro and T. Hoff (eds) *Comunicação, Consumo e Envelhecimento no Contemporâneo: Perspectivas Multidisciplinares* [Communication, Consumption and Ageing in Contemporary Times: Multidisciplinary Perspectives], Porto Alegre: Sulina, pp 95–114.

URLs to the commercials in this chapter (*in order of appearance*):

Nutren Senior (2019) *Uma pergunta que nunca foi feita* [A question that has never been posed], available from: https://www.youtube.com/watch?v=0Ycxc8jXlBI [accessed 10 September 2021].

Prevent Senior (2019) *Acreditamos no empoderamento do adulto+* [We believe in empowering adults+], available from: https://www.youtube.com/watch?v=72bjDfOqB2c [accessed 10 September 2021].

O Boticário (2020) Cuidados faciais é Botik. Botik é O Boticário [Face care is Botik. Botik is O Boticário], available from: https://www.youtube.com/watch?v=FVRLR8R414Q [accessed 18 April 2022].

Itaú (2020) *É hora de ficar em casa: O app Itaú tem tudo para você.* [It's time to stay at home: Itaú App has everything for you], available from: https://www.youtube.com/watch?v=9c2JF76Zk-c [accessed 10 September 2021].

OLX (2015) *Rap do desapega* [The let it go rap], available from: https://www.youtube.com/watch?v=yiGWl_LjT9Q [accessed 10 September 2021].

O Boticário (2019) *Onde tem amor tem beleza* [Where there is love, there is beauty], available from: https://www.youtube.com/watch?v=UZ3qOtiIodw [accessed 10 September 2021].

8

Visual ageism on public organisations' websites

Eugène Loos, Loredana Ivan, Maria Sourbati, Wenqian Xu,
Christa Lykke Christensen and Virpi Ylänne

Introduction

The portrayals of older people as a social group, as well as the type of characteristics in these portrayals, matter in societies that value social justice and power balance. These representations, often visual, can play a role in stereotype formation and reinforce stereotypes. Encountering such stereotypes in the media can negatively impact the self-esteem, health status, physical wellbeing and cognitive performance of older people (Levy et al, 2002a, 2002b). The act of visually under-representing older people in the media or visually representing them in a stigmatised way is not harmless, as it not only reflects societal practices, but also contributes to meaning about these practices (Hall et al, 2013). Empirical studies have been conducted on the visual representation of older adults in the media (see reviews by, for example, Ylänne, 2015; Loos and Ivan, 2018), but only a limited number of studies have focused on the way public organisations visually represent older people in their digital communications. Therefore, this chapter will address the following research questions:

- How do public organisations use visual signs to represent older people in photos on their websites in Denmark, the Netherlands, Sweden and the UK?
- Which connotations of the visual signs predominate in the pictures?
- To what extent is this visual representation characterised by the misrepresentation of older people?

We will first present and discuss insights from the field of the visual representation of older people and the concept of 'visual ageism'. Then, we will analyse how public organisations across a range of European countries use pictures on their websites, presenting information about relevant products and services and representing older people. We do this through the lens of 'visual ageism' – 'the social practice of visually under-representing older people or misrepresenting them in a prejudiced way' (Loos and Ivan, 2018, p 164). If older people cannot identify with the pictures that are supposed to represent them, the probability that they will consult such websites decreases (Loos, 2013, 2018).

The analysis will be conducted by using a semiotic approach (see Loos, 2018; Xu, 2019), focusing on photos from the websites of public organisations in diverse countries: Denmark, Sweden, the Netherlands and the UK. Instead of conducting a classic comparative quantitative study on these countries, we analyse our data per country in a qualitative way. At the end of the chapter, we will present our conclusions and address some limitations of the research and implications for future research.

Visual ageism

Ageism is the process of systematically stereotyping and discriminating against people because of their age (Butler, 1969). Ageism is an umbrella concept (Braithwaite, 2002), consisting of beliefs, attitudes, expectations and behaviours shared by community members often, but not always, towards older people. Although ageism often presents itself and it is experienced at the micro level, for example in interactions between service providers and older people, it encompasses societal practices, recurrently verbalised and pictured in different social contexts.

Ageism in the media has been treated as an asymmetric power structure based on age, a constructed justification of inequalities between different age groups legitimising domination (Angus and Reeve, 2006). By systematically under- or misrepresenting older people, media content legitimises the dominance and reinforces the logic according to which the social construction of ageing is made and maintained (Minichiello et al, 2000). Media content, including visual media, is a continuous reflection of societal practices. It influences everyday interactions, including the way we relate to older people, as well as the way we see ourselves as 'being old'. The past few decades have seen a gradual increase in the presence of older people in the media and a switch towards more positive representations. This change concerns, in particular, younger older people (Ylänne, 2015; Loos and Ivan, 2018). Older people, especially the 'third agers' (Loos, 2013), are more present in the traditional media (television programmes, print press, advertising and film series), represented as active, enjoying life and maintaining a healthy lifestyle. 'Fourth agers' (the oldest old, at the limits of their functional capacity; see, for example, Baltes and Smith, 2003; and see Chapter 2), in contrast, continue to be under-represented. The increased visibility of older people in the media is part of the dominant discourse of 'successful ageing' – an implicit form of ageism whereby people are held responsible for the universal and irreversible ageing process (Katz and Calasanti, 2015; Rowe and Kahn, 2015; and see also

Chapter 7). Also relevant is the notion of 'active ageing', expressing health and activity and a decreased occurrence of frailty and passivity (Moulaert and Biggs, 2013; Van Dyk et al, 2013). This apparently positive trend started in the early 1990s, especially in television and print advertising, when older people were identified by marketing strategists as potentially valuable consumers (see Loos and Ivan, 2018).

Present media convey implicit forms of visual ageism: older people presented as couples, as happy, healthy and enjoying life (see Loos, 2013). There is also a dominance of White older people in the visual media. The different way people make meaning in their lives as they age is often ignored. Katz and Calasanti (2015, p 170) warn that 'what might be considered "positive" attributes in the depiction of old age could in fact be a normative construction which has nothing to do with the real experience of older people in everyday life'.

Visual ageism in public sector organisations' digital communications: four examples

With growing access to and use of the internet, older people are being exposed to and required to access websites that use photos for various reasons (Loos, 2018). It is important that older adults can identify with such photos as the pitfall of visual ageism would thus be avoided. For this reason, we analysed photos from different public organisations' websites in Denmark, the Netherlands, Sweden and the UK. All four countries have seen widespread diffusion of internet access and the take-up of digital/online services among their older population (Eurostat, 2021). We decided to choose Denmark and Sweden as Northern European countries, the Netherlands as a North-West European country and the UK as an Anglo-Saxon country as cases, because they are all rich welfare societies with relatively good public services for older people. Many older adults there (although not all) have the financial means to lead an active life and can easily access health care. It was not the scope of our study to compare the visual representation of older people in such countries with the visual representation of that group in the Global South, for example. But it would be interesting for future studies to focus also on countries across the Global South as, although they are generally not as rich, they are also venturing into digital media solutions in public service reform (Ali and Bhuiyan, 2022). The question would be whether they use similar kinds of pictures about relevant products and services to represent older people on their websites.

Our analysis will be conducted by looking at how signs, composed of signifiers and signifieds, and focusing on connotations (see for example Chandler 2017 for a discussion about these semiotic concepts), are used by organisations to visually represent older people.

Denmark

The DaneAge Association (DAA) is a Danish non-profit membership organisation that lobbies on behalf of the oldest section of the Danish population. The organisation advocates for the inclusion of older people in politics and organisations and works for a society without age barriers and ageism. It proclaims, in particular, to take care of society's weakest groups of senior citizens, and it communicates the social and political agenda on digital platforms, such as on its website and on Facebook, Instagram, Twitter and YouTube. The website, however, is the main communication channel of the organisation, offering text-based information relevant to older people about issues such as pensions, housing and health.

In addition to the text-based information, the organisation makes considerable use of photos of older people. A study of photos on the DAA's website was conducted in 2019 (Christensen, 2019). It demonstrated that photos of older people have a very prominent place. The photos are large, often filling half of the website page, they use bright colours, and most of them imply a positive and happy atmosphere. The study was based on 59 photos circulating on the website at various intervals during the period 2016–18. The website does not make use of stock photos, only photos taken of members and volunteers of the DAA by a hired photographer. Seven of the 59 photos, however, only showed a small part of a person, such as close-ups of the hands of older people. The rest, 52 photos, showed people in front of the camera.

The aim of the study was to investigate who was included on and excluded from the DAA's website, and how we should characterise the older people to whom the DAA gave a visual status, thereby legitimising them as representatives of the organisation. The analysis, thus, looked at visual motifs, such as whether older people appeared alone or with others. Particularly, being aware of the DAA's intention to take care of society's weakest groups of senior citizens, the analysis looked at the characteristics of individuals (for example, signifiers such as grey hair, wrinkles and the bodily constitution of sunken, frail or impaired bodies), the presence of wheelchairs and walking frames, conventionally connoting old age, and whether such characteristics and items were accentuated by the use of image composition and photographical elements, such as close-ups, camera angles and the use of colour (Pauwells, 2012).

The study found that older people with signifiers connoting old age dominated the visual material. Only one child, no younger people and only a few middle-aged people figured in the photos, which points to older people being in focus and the target group of the organisation. Moreover, more than three quarters of the photos represented older people appearing happy, smiling and socially involved with each other. A case in point is Photo 1[1] (see Figure 8.1)[2].

Figure 8.1: Photo 1

At the front of the picture are two women and a man. It seems to be cold, as they are wearing dark winter jackets, but even though black colours dominate as signifiers, their smiling faces provide a connotation of hearty warmth, accompanied by the close proximity of their bodies. The horizontal perspective positions the viewer at eye level with the people in the picture, and they seem to be having fun. They also seem to be mobile and enjoying a walk outdoors. Like most of the pictures on the website, this photo has been photographed in medium close-up, which means that viewers are positioned within the frame and thus have access to the situation and the social space that the people create together but without getting really close to any of them. No individual old person is the focus, but instead the focus is the connoted enjoyable mutual company.

Similar medium close-up photos at eye level with the depicted people show older people sitting down talking to each other. One such photo is Photo 2 (see Figure 8.2).[3] Its focus are three women sitting talking to each other – two older, white-haired women, and a middle-aged woman on the right, probably a voluntary visitor as she wears the logo of the DAA on her t-shirt. Compared to her, the woman in the middle of the photo has a slightly sunken body. On the other hand, her clothes are colourful (pink and turquoise), she has eye contact with the woman to the right, and she appears as a vigorous woman taking part in a joint activity, reading or talking about a magazine. The woman on the left is laughing and seems to be having fun. The photo leads to a connotation of a situation in which the social dynamic and togetherness of the people are important, not the individuals as such.

Just under a quarter of the 52 analysed photos depict older people appearing alone. Most of these pictures, however, show older people as active individuals, exercising, writing shopping lists or using a computer.

Photo 3 (see Figure 8.3)[4] shows a man who seems to be attending a computing class. Rather than giving the impression that using digital media is difficult and that older people sometimes have problems with computers, the smiling face of the man in focus connotes enjoyment and excitement. Other

Figure 8.2: Photo 2

Figure 8.3: Photo 3

photos of older people without the company of others show them outdoors, actively doing physical exercise in nature, or indoors using fitness equipment. Only two photos of the total sample show older people appearing alone, sitting passively by themselves, looking serious and absorbed in thought.

Even though the DAA proclaims to also take care of frail older people, who may be lonely or in poor health, the website visually represents older people in a positive way. Signifiers are used leading to the connotation of older adults being extrovert, engaging with their talk partners. No signifiers such as wheelchairs appear in the photos, and the depicted people do not look frail or impaired, or in need of substantial help from others. On the other hand, signifiers of old age, such as grey hair, wrinkles and sunken bodies are not absent from the website. The depicted people appear as old *and* in good health, and they are often sun-tanned and actively moving around exercising, and the bright colours of all the photos lend them a sense of vitality and freshness. The general impression given is that older people are socially involved with each other. As the DAA is an organisation financed by membership, it probably wants to market an attractive image of what it means to be older. In line with the logic of the Danish welfare society, it underlines the importance – not of staying young and beautiful – but of being part of a social community. The website is, however, a strategic communication tool of the organisation that positively writes up the qualities and gives an idealistic version of being old. That the DAA so unambiguously insists on a visual representation like this, is not consistent with the daily life conditions and experiences of many older people, which could lead to misrepresentation and visual ageism.

Sweden

The municipality of Norrköping is one of the largest municipalities in Sweden with about 143,000 inhabitants in 2019; additionally, the central administration of this municipality has been relatively advanced in social media and visual language use. The municipal administration is responsible for providing public services (for example, social care) and organising cultural activities in the area. According to interviews with communication officers working in the municipal unit of digital communication, they use the Facebook page as a 'window' to present what the municipality does, and as a channel to reach and interact with more citizens living in this area. A study of the photos posted on the municipal Facebook page (@NorrkopingsKommun) was conducted (Xu, 2019). This subsection presents a visual analysis of the Facebook photos of older people (n= 50) posted by the central administration of the municipality in 2018 and 2019, to explore what visual signs are used to portray older people, and what connotations the specific signifiers may carry. Most analysed photos (94 per cent) are of the social care department and could be assumed to generate a Facebook representation of older people receiving care from care services. The photos were analysed in terms of six dimensions: older people's pose, objects, setting, clusters of older people, gaze and viewer positioning. This assemblage of analytical dimensions was built on van Leeuwen's (2008) framework of the ways social actors are visually depicted. This framework was applied to an analysis of the choice of visual signs in depicting older individuals.

The first analytical dimension was the pose of the photographed older people . Twenty-two photos (44 per cent) depict senior care recipients loosely leaning back on a chair, which implies a state of natural relaxation. Seven photos (14 per cent) portray them stretching out their bodies. The signifier of openness and state of the body connotes a calm and relaxing later life.

For the second dimension, the analyst focused on the objects shown in the surroundings. A few recurring objects were identified, including food and drink (36 per cent), artwork (32 per cent) and walking aids (22 per cent). The signifiers of food (such as meals and desserts) and drink (for example, coffee) suggest connotations of a sociable and recreational lifestyle. The presence of artwork (for example, drawings and handicrafts) gives viewers a sense of older people's creative abilities and good cognitive skills in arts activities. Older people in residential care homes are represented as physically challenged only to some extent, as walking aids are marginalised and shown at lower frequencies in the photos. Nowadays in Sweden, only people with extensive care needs are generally entitled a place in residential care (Schön et al, 2016). The absence of older people being ill in the photos could be interpreted as ableist and ageist, as the municipality tends to present care recipients in good health.

The concept of the setting, the third dimension, refers to the circumstances in which older people are placed. In 40 photos (80 per cent), senior care recipients are attached to signifiers such as relaxing indoors and sitting back in chairs, with bright light streaming through the windows. This portrayal may resound and even reinforce the stereotypical views of older people being unproductive and not participating in social life (Schonfield, 1982). Additionally, the presence of signifiers such as windows and shiny surfaces often connotes clarity of vision and modernity (Hansen and Machin, 2013, p 178), which casts a more positive light on older people's life indoors.

For the fourth dimension, 'clusters of older people', the analyst focused on the ways in which the photos visually categorise older people as a homogenous group. On the one hand, many photos (72 per cent) depict older people exclusively without any other age groups. On the other hand, in some photos (32 per cent), senior care recipients are depicted by signifiers such as either performing the same actions (such as drinking coffee) or wearing similar clothes (for example, team suits), allowing viewers to categorise older people as a distinct group through the visual sense. A case in point is Photo 4 (see Figure 8.4).[5] This visual representation may reduce our recognition of heterogeneity among older people and mark the separation of old and young.

The concept of 'gaze', the fifth dimension, refers to the direction in which the older people look at when being photographed. The most common types of senior care recipients' gaze are gazing down and looking at the viewer (26 per cent and 24 per cent, respectively). The photos that portray older people gazing down seemingly give viewers a sense of their being less energetic or more vulnerable. The photos of older people looking at the camera acknowledge the existence of viewers, and establish a relationship

Figure 8.4: Photo 4

between viewers and older people in the photos. This type of photo is a 'demand' image, which invites the involvement of viewers (Kress and van Leeuwen, 1996, pp 127–8). Such photos connote older people's willingness to interact with viewers.

The concept of 'viewer positioning', the sixth dimension, refers to the perspective from which viewers see older people in the photos. In the photos analysed, older people are either on an equal level or at an upper vertical angle (52 per cent and 48 per cent, respectively). The equal level connotes that older people and viewers are on the same level and it builds up the expectation of viewer involvement. The upper vertical angle invites viewers to gaze down at senior care recipients, which creates power asymmetry. A case in point is Photo 5 (see Figure 8.5),[6] which places older people having coffee at a lower position.

Of the 50 photos, six photos (12 per cent) cannot form an explicit representation of older people, given that these pictures either capture a small part of older people's bodies or blur their faces and movements by photographing them out of focus or with a slow shutter speed. An example is Photo 6 (see Figure 8.6).[7] In the photo, viewers cannot recognise and acknowledge certain meanings about older people in a specific context. A lack of photo clarity and insufficient information lead to the under-representation of older people in the media.

Figure 8.5: Photo 5

Figure 8.6: Photo 6

Based on the findings described here, an ambivalent representation of care home residents can be identified in the municipality-managed Facebook pages. The visual analysis illustrates that older people, in subtle ways, are represented as relatively physically incapable and vulnerable care receivers (as part of the notion of the fourth age), in some of the sampled photos. This representation does not seem out of place, as most pictures are of the municipal social care department. It resonates the reality of the care home residents living with impairments. On the other hand, the analysis also shows that senior care recipients are misrepresented by signifiers depicting them as idealistically healthy, and a visually homogenous group (as part of the notion of the third age), in other sampled photos. Communication officers of the municipality argued that they favoured the photos depicting senior care recipients staying in good health and being well cared for by care workers, as they intend to establish a positive image of the administration. They also said that the overly optimistic representation of care recipients may serve to acknowledge co-workers' contributions to the municipality and promote a good image of care workers. However, one officer assumed that this representation may offend care workers as it perhaps leads viewers to underestimate extensive care work. To challenge this misrepresentation (which could lead to visual ageism) and achieve a more realistic image of older people, communication officers are advised to present the actual health conditions of senior care recipients and the richness of later life in municipal settings, such as cultural and volunteering activity, and civil engagement, forming part of the lives of older people.

The Netherlands

To gain insight into the ways the three senior citizens' organisations, Algemene Nederlandse Bond voor Ouderen (ANBO), Unie Katholieke Bond voor Ouderen (Unie KBO) and Protestants Christelijke Ouderenbond (PCOB) in the Netherlands portray their members, Loos (2013) collected 57 images of older people from the websites of the organisations (all downloaded on 6 March 2012). The study focused on the ways a varied group of senior citizens were visually represented on these websites.

The images were examined in terms of sex ('man/woman'), companionship ('alone/together'), health status ('vital'/'frail' [walking, exercising/being dependent on the help of others, for example, in the setting of health institutions or being depicted with wheeled walkers]) and ethnicity (indexed by skin colour).

The depiction of older people alone and older people together appeared to be reasonably balanced on the websites of PCOB and Unie KBO (53.7 per cent and 44.3 per cent, respectively), while images of older people alone were less common on the website of ANBO (30 per cent). The most common category of pictures on the ANBO website was that of 'older woman and man as a couple' (25 per cent); while on the other two sites, this was 'man alone' (27.7 per cent and 25.3 per cent, respectively). Loos (2013, p 33) also states that:

A salient finding was the infrequent occurrence of images of senior citizens with (grand)children: 3x an older man with (grand)child (2x girl, 1x boy) on all 3 websites, while a single picture of an older woman with (grand)child (1x girl) was found on the PCOB website. It would be interesting to study the websites of other organisations to find out whether images of (grand)children occur equally infrequently there, as well, and to ask the creators of the websites why this should be (do they think that a picture of a girl is cuter than a boy?).

On all three websites, the older people were without exception shown as enjoying third age, for example via signifiers such as engaging in sports or taking a leisurely bicycle ride; fourth-age signifiers, such as inactivity due to bad health, or vulnerability, were absent.

Signifiers such as skin colour and exotic objects (such as food) were used to determine the ethnic background of the senior citizens in the pictures used on the websites. It appeared that senior citizens of a Black and minority ethnic background were a rare occurrence on all three websites of the Dutch senior citizens' organisations.

In all, this Dutch study demonstrated that older people gain visibility with the use of signifiers that connote health and vitality, depicting them in the company of others. Visual ageism was present in all three Dutch senior citizens' websites. This is demonstrated, for example, in the fact that the range of photos excluded vulnerable people and older people from minority ethnic backgrounds to a large extent, which is a clear manifestation of under-representation; meanwhile the focus on signifiers related to the third age can be labelled as misrepresentation, only connoting the 'brighter' side of later life. A possible explanation for this is that the organisations are financed by membership and therefore want to market an attractive image of what it means to be older. It was interesting to observe that one of the senior citizens' organisations (ANBO) inserted a bar across the top of the homepage that functions as a photo gallery to represent a greater variety of senior citizens on its website. Acting in this way, it does justice to the diversity within the older population. This is a clear case of putting into practice the principle of 'designing for dynamic diversity' (Gregor et al, 2002, p 152). It would be preferable to use a mix of images that use this concept to make designers of computing systems aware of 'the decline in the cognitive, physical and sensory function [of older people]' (Loos, 2013, p 39).

The UK

In the UK, Sourbati (2015; Sourbati and Loos, 2019) examined how older people are depicted in the websites of the adult social care service. In the UK, social care is a public service provided at local authority level and available to all residents. Sourbati's study was designed to investigate how older people were depicted online at three points during the implementation of the digital transformation of public services, launched by central government in 2012–13 to ensure all public sector information and related service provision happens digitally 'by default' (Cabinet Office, 2013, 2014; 2017). The study examined the homepages of the social care websites maintained by local authorities in the five largest, most ethnically diverse cities where older adults comprise a growing diversity of ethnicities (Simpson, 2013): Birmingham, Bradford, Leicester, Manchester and London, with its 12 inner-city boroughs (Camden, Greenwich, Hackney, Hammersmith and Fulham, Islington, Kensington and Chelsea, Lambeth, Lewisham, Southwark, Tower Hamlets, Wandsworth and Westminster). Visual content analysis was conducted (Bell, 2001) to investigate, first, the visibility of older adults (whether images were used) and, second, their portrayal in the images used. The sample consisted of all images found in archived pages from 2013 and 2016, and in their updated pages, visited in July 2019. The archived pages were retrieved using the Wayback Machine (https://archive.org/web/). Fifty-five pictures were found in the 48 pages examined. Like Loos (2013) – in the case of the Netherlands, discussed earlier – the study used a binary coding of age (same/ different generational group), sex ('woman/man'), health status ('vital'/ 'frail') and ethnicity ('White'/minority Black) for sameness ('homogeneity') or difference ('diversity'). The aim was to examine whether the demographic characteristics and health status of older populations, as made visible in the pictures, were diverse or homogenous. The study defined homogeneity in relation to a lack of diversity (relating to sex, health status, ethnicity and age/ generational category; Sourbati, 2015; Sourbati and Loos, 2019).

Taken together, the images were found to display a mix of cultural approaches to the composition of old age groups, reflecting as well as modifying long-held social and cultural attitudes about the visualities of old age as described in this chapter. In 2013, 11 out of the 16 pages examined included images of older people and five used text- or icon-only navigation. Diverse representations slightly surpassed an equal number of homogenous representations and text-only (no image) websites. Six homepages depicted older people as members of diverse ethnic groups (for example, Westminster), displaying a range of images featuring mixed groups of adult women and men of different generations, with different dis/ability statuses, from a range of ethnic groups (for example, Camden and Westminster). These pages had been recently (at the time) redesigned as part of the 'digital by default' programme. Five homepages depicted older people as members of homogenous groups, in terms of ethnicity and generational membership (for example, Hackney and Lewisham). Five homepages did not use any pictures. During that time, text-only or mixed, text and graphic icon-based page navigation was becoming the standard approach in the design of public sector websites in all e-government services (for example, Islington). By 2016, the overall pattern had been reversed, with five pages displaying images and 11 comprising text- or graphics-only visual interfaces. By 2019, 14 out of the 16 webpages used text and icons only and did not include any

Figure 8.7: Older adult membership and visibility patterns in local authority social service homepages in 2013, 2016 and 2019

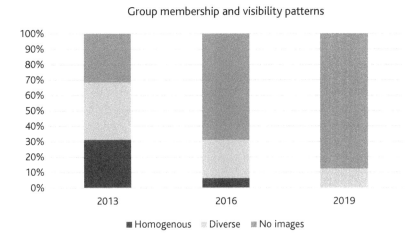

images. The default design choice was by now to not use images, as part of a national digital policy to promote inclusive design and make website content readable (Sourbati and Loos, 2019).

These findings indicate two directions of change in the visualities of old age in the examined public sector websites: first, away from limited and stereotypical depictions of older adults as members of homogenous groups (frail or healthy/active), and towards a more diverse presence, comprising people from different ethnic backgrounds, with a range of fitness, ability and vitality statuses. This was the pattern shown on six council homepages in 2013 and on four in 2016. Second, there is a move towards the opposite direction, the disappearance of images, and therefore the visual disappearance of images of older people, which is a predominant trend since 2016 (see Figure 8.7). Whereas the first direction does not lead to misrepresentation and visual ageism, the second direction risks doing so, by rendering older people visually invisible in these online spaces.

Conclusion

How do public organisations use visual signs to represent older people in photos on their websites?

The photos of public organisations' websites are composed of visual signs often representing older people as healthy and active (in the case of Denmark, the Netherlands and Sweden) or, less often, as relatively physically challenged, and vulnerable care receivers (in the case of Sweden). The visual signs connoting health and activity represent older people as independent third agers, whereas those connoting limited capability and vulnerability represent them as fourth agers, needing care. A possible explanation for this difference in visual representation is that in the former set of cases the public organisations are financed by membership and want to market an attractive image of what it means to be older, while the latter case shows that the municipality intends to present older people in good health and being well taken care of, to the citizens and (potential) care workers in this area. The visual signs in the case of the UK portray older people as a more diverse group, comprising people from different ethnic backgrounds, with a range of fitness, ability and vitality statuses on six council homepages in 2013 and on four in 2016, while the disappearance of images, and therefore the visual disappearance of images of older people, has been a predominant trend since 2016.

Which connotations of the visual signs predominate in the pictures?

Signifiers such as activities outside home connoting health can be seen in the cases of Denmark, the Netherlands and (sometimes) the UK. Signifiers such as grey hair, wrinkles, bodily constitution (sunken, frail or impaired bodies, wheelchairs and walking frames), conventionally connoting old age, accentuated by the use of image composition as well as photographical elements, such as close-ups, camera angles and the use of colours, are predominant in the case of Sweden, Denmark, and sometimes also the UK.

To what extent is this visual representation characterised by the misrepresentation of older people?

The cases we discussed showed that the use of third-age signifiers connoting health and activity on the one hand, and the use of signifiers connoting physical limitations and vulnerability, on the other, enhance the risk of misrepresentation and visual ageism. However, we should add that the specific social situation in which the visual signs produced by the public organisations are embedded, and the way they are distributed to and consumed by the heterogeneous target group of older people, should be taken into account before deciding whether a photo is ageist or not. The analysis of 'visual ageism' is as complex as any analysis of 'ageism'.

Limitations and implications for future research

The studies discussed in this chapter were conducted in a limited number of countries and focused only on the websites and social media of public organisations delivering information about products and services for older people. Future research might involve more countries. Recently, media content, especially digital media, has started to become more visual. However, empirical studies on the presence of ageism in digital media content are only beginning, and we lack systematic literature reviews to reveal trends and patterns.

In stereotypical representations of older people in digital media content, cultural aspects shape the way older people are portrayed. What it means to be old and to age 'successfully' could be understood differently in different countries (Fry et al, 1997; Cruikshank, 2013). Also, examining ageism in the (digital) media should not be restricted to images that other age groups have about older people, but also to images older people hold about themselves. There is a large body of research on internalised stereotypes (Kornadt and Rothermund, 2012; Ayalon and Tesch-Römer, 2017; Kornadt et al, 2017) and how societal practices of (re)presenting old people are adopted by older people themselves – sometimes with negative effects on their performance in different type of activities (that is, visual accuracy and technology appropriation) and on their health and wellbeing (see Levy et al, 2002b; Levy et al, 2020). From this perspective, it is important to study visual ageism in cross-cultural contexts (Loos et al, 2017), and analyse (digital) media content created and distributed by older people, having an older audience in mind.

Future research should also focus on other types of public and private organisations and a variety of digital communication channels and adopt an in-depth visual semiotic approach to analyse the ways organisations produce and distribute visual signs, and how they are consumed by older people. The only way to know whether an image representing senior citizens on a website or on another digital communication channel is appropriate is to ask various groups of senior citizens if they can identify with the image. One way to do this is, for example, by conducting focus groups (see also Chapter 10). The pitfall of misrepresentation and visual ageism, *in the eyes of the older target group*, can thus be avoided. This might well enhance the likelihood that they will consult digital information about relevant products and services presented by public and private organisations.

The presence of signifiers expressing health and activity and the declining occurrence of signifiers expressing frailty and passivity lead to connotations reflecting a dominant discourse of 'active ageing' in Europe (Moulaert and Biggs, 2013; Van Dyk et al, 2013). The signifiers and their connotations being part of the discourse of 'active ageing', together with the notion of 'successful ageing' (Katz and Calasanti, 2015; Rowe and Kahn, 2015), discussed earlier, might lead to visual ageism (see also Chapter 7). Organisations need to keep this in mind when selecting pictures for their website or other media and consider using a variety of images, or avoid using pictures of older people that stigmatise, marginalise or injure. They could look into the cultural situatedness and intersectional character of age relations (for example, related to gender) in our ageing societies.

Notes

1   Permission to use the images in Figures 8.1–8.3 has been granted by the DaneAge Association.
2   Photographer: Claudi Thyrrestrup. Available from: www.aeldresagen.dk [accessed 18 October 2017].
3   Photographer: Claudi Thyrrestrup. Available from: www.aeldresagen.dk [accessed 8 February 2017].
4   Photographer: Claudi Thyrrestrup. Available from: www.aeldresagen.dk [accessed 22 June 2017].
5   Figures 8.4–8.6 are published with permission from Norrköpings kommun/ Norrköping municipality. Available from: https://www.facebook.com/Norrko pingsKommun/photos [accessed 29 February 2020].
6   Available from: https://www.facebook.com/NorrkopingsKommun/photos [accessed 29 February 2020].
7   Available from: https://www.facebook.com/NorrkopingsKommun/photos [accessed 29 February 2020].

References

Ali, H.E. and Bhuiyan S. (2022) 'Institutional reforms, governance, and services delivery in the Global South', in H.E. Ali and S. Bhuiyan (eds) *Institutional Reforms, Governance, and Services Delivery in the Global South: International Series on Public Policy*, London: Palgrave Macmillan, available from: https://doi.org/10.1007/978-3-030-82257-6_1 [accessed 20 April 2022].

Angus, J. and Reeve, P. (2006) 'Ageism: a threat to "aging well" in the 21st century', *Journal of Applied Gerontology*, 25(2): 137–52.

Ayalon, L. and Tesch-Römer, C. (2017) 'Taking a closer look at ageism: self- and other-directed ageist attitudes and discrimination', *European Journal of Ageing*, 14(1): 1–4.

Baltes, P.B. and Smith, J. (2003) 'New frontiers in the future of aging: from successful aging of the young old to the dilemmas of the fourth age', *Gerontology*, 49(2): 123–35.

Bell, P. (2001) 'Content analysis of visual images', in T. Van Leeuwen and C. Jewitt (eds) *Handbook of Visual Analysis*, Los Angeles, CA: Sage, pp 13–33.

Braithwaite, V. (2002) 'Reducing ageism', in T.D. Nelson (ed) *Ageism: Stereotyping and Prejudice Against Older Persons*, Cambridge, MA: MIT Press, pp 311–37.

Butler, R.N. (1969) 'Age-ism: another form of bigotry', *The Gerontologist*, 9(4:1): 243–46.

Cabinet Office (2013) *Government Digital Strategy: December 2013 - GOV. UK*, London: GOV.UK, available from: https://www.gov.uk/government/publications/government-digital-strategy/government-digital-strategy [accessed 25 September 2021].

Cabinet Office (2014) *Government Digital Inclusion Strategy: Updated December 2014 - GOV.UK*. London: GOV.UK, available from: https://www.gov.uk/government/publications/government-digital-inclusion-strategy/government-digital-inclusion-strategy [accessed 25 September 2021].

Cabinet Office (2017) *UK Digital Strategy*: 1 March 2017 - GOV.UK, London: GOV.UK, available from: https://www.gov.uk/government/publications/uk-digital-strategy [accessed 25 September 2021].

Chandler, D. (2017) *Semiotics: The Basics,* London: Routledge.

Christensen, C.L. (2019) 'Visualising old age: photographs of older people on the website of the DaneAge Association', *Nordicom Review*, 40(2): 111–27.

Cruikshank, M. (2013) *Learning to be Old: Gender, Culture, and Aging*, Lanham, MD: Rowman & Littlefield Publishers.

Eurostat (2021) *ICT Usage in Households and by Individuals*, Luxembourg: The Statistical Office of the European Union, available from: http://appsso.eurostat.ec.europa.eu/nui/show.do?dataset=isoc_bdek_di&lang=en [accessed 30 January 2022].

Fry, C.L., Dickerson-Putman, J., Draper, P., Ikels, C., Keith, J., Glascock, A.P. and Harpending, H.C. (1997) 'Culture and the meaning of a good old age', *The Cultural Context of Aging: Worldwide Perspectives*, 3: 99–123.

Gregor, P., Newell, A.F. and Zajicek, M. (2002) 'Designing for dynamic diversity - interfaces for older people', *ASSETS*: 151–6.

Hall, S., Evans, H. and Nixon, S. (eds) (2013) *Representation: Cultural Representations and Signifying Practices*, Thousand Oaks, CA: Sage.

Hansen, A. and Machin, D. (2018) *Media and Communication Research Methods*, London: Macmillan International Higher Education.

Katz, S. and Calasanti, T. (2015) 'Critical perspectives on successful aging: does it "appeal more than it illuminates"?', *The Gerontologist*, 55(1): 26–33.

Kornadt, A.E. and Rothermund, K. (2012) 'Internalization of age stereotypes into the self-concept via future self-views: a general model and domain-specific differences', *Psychology and Aging*, 27(1): 164–72.

Kornadt, A.E., Voss, P. and Rothermund, K. (2017) 'Age stereotypes and self-views revisited: patterns of internalization and projection processes across the life span', *Journals of Gerontology Series B: Psychological Sciences and Social Sciences*, 72(4): 582–92.

Kress, G.R. and van Leeuwen, T. (1996) *Reading Images: The Grammar of Visual Design*, London and New York, NY: Routledge.

Levy, B.R., Slade, M.D. and Kasl, S.V. (2002a) 'Longitudinal benefit of positive self-perceptions of aging on functional health', *The Journals of Gerontology Series B: Psychological Sciences and Social Sciences*, 57(5): 409–17.

Levy, B.R., Slade, M.D., Kunkel, S.R. and Kasl, S.V. (2002b) 'Longevity increased by positive self-perceptions of aging', *Journal of Personality and Social Psychology*, 83(2): 261–70.

Levy, B.R., Slade, M.D., Chang, E., Kannoth, S. and Wang, S.Y. (2020) 'Ageism amplifies cost and prevalence of health conditions', *The Gerontologist*, 60(1): 174–81.

Loos, E.F. (2013) 'Designing for dynamic diversity: representing various senior citizens in digital information sources', *Observatorio*, 7(1): 21–45.

Loos, E.F. (2018) 'The organizational use of online stock photos: the impact of representing senior citizens as eternally youthful', *Human Technology*, 14(3): 366–81.

Loos, E.F. and Ivan, L. (2018) 'Visual ageism in the media', in L. Ayalon and C. Tesch-Römer (eds) *Contemporary Perspectives on Ageism*, Cham: Springer, pp 163–76, available from: https://doi.org/10.1007/978-3-319-73820-8_11. [accessed 20 April 2022].

Loos, E.F., Ivan, L., Fernández-Ardèvol, M., Sourbati, M., Ekström, M., Wilińska, M., Carlo, S. and Schiau, I. (2017) 'Ageing well? A cross-country analysis of the way older people are visually represented on websites of organizations for older people', *Journal of Comparative Research in Anthropology and Sociology*, 8(2): 63–83.

Minichiello, V., Browne, J. and Kendig, H. (2000) 'Perceptions and consequences of ageism: views of older people', *Ageing & Society*, 20(3): 253–78.

Moulaert, T. and Biggs, S. (2013) 'International and European policy on work and retirement: reinventing critical perspectives on active ageing and mature subjectivity', *Human Relations*, 66(1): 23–43.

Pauwells, L. (2012) 'A multimodal framework for analyzing websites as cultural expressions', *Journal of Computer-Mediated Communication*, 17(3): 247–65.

Rowe, J.W. and Kahn, R.L. (2015) 'Successful aging 2.0: conceptual expansions for the 21st century', *The Journals of Gerontology: Series B*, 70(4): 593–6.

Schön, P., Lagergren, M. and Kåreholt, I. (2016) 'Rapid decrease in length of stay in institutional care for older people in Sweden between 2006 and 2012: results from a population-based study', *Health & Social Care in the Community*, 24(5): 631–8.

Schonfield, D. (1982) 'Who is stereotyping whom and why?', *The Gerontologist*, 22(3): 267–72.

Simpson, L. (2013) 'Does Britain have plural cities?', in *The Dynamics of Diversity: Evidence from the 2011 Census*, Manchester: University of Manchester, available from: http://cdn.basw.co.uk/upload/basw_42104-3.pdf [accessed 20 April 2022].

Sourbati M. (2015) 'Age(ism) in digital information provision: the case of online public services for older adults', in J. Zhou J. and G. Salvendy (eds) *Human Aspects of IT for the Aged Population: Design for Aging. ITAP 2015. Lecture Notes in Computer Science*, vol 9193, Cham: Springer, available from: https://doi.org/10.1007/978-3-319-20892-3_37 [accessed 20 April 2022].

Sourbati, M. and Loos, E.F. (2019) 'Interfacing age: diversity and (in)visibility in digital public service', *Journal of Digital Media & Policy*, 10(3): 275–93.

Van Dyk, S., Lessenich, S., Denninger, T. and Richter, A. (2013) 'The many meanings of "active ageing": confronting public discourse with older people's stories', *Recherches Sociologiques et Anthropologiques*, 44–1: 97–115.

Van Leeuwen, T. (2008) *Discourse and Practice: New Tools for Critical Discourse Analysis*, Oxford: Oxford University Press.

Xu, W. (2019) 'Portrayal of life stages on Swedish municipal media: a life course perspective', *n° 4 Cultura Visual, Digital e Mediática: Imagens entre Gerações 2019 editoras do número: Ana Pérez-Escoda*: 93–115.

Ylänne, V. (2015) 'Representations of ageing in the media', in J. Twigg and W. Martin (eds) *Routledge Handbook of Cultural Gerontology*, London: Routledge, pp 369–75.

9

Imag(in)ing ageing futures in comics and graphic novels

Nicole Dalmer and Lucia Cedeira Serantes

Introduction

Despite a steadily increasing number of studies that critically examine representations of older adults in a variety of media formats (for example, Rozanova, 2010; Chivers, 2011; Ylänne, 2012; Low and Dupuis-Blanchard, 2013; Shary and McVittie, 2016; Smith et al, 2017), there are but four existing studies that take up older-age depictions in comics (Palmore, 1971; Hanlon et al, 1997; Miczo, 2015; Neumann, 2015). This dearth of studies is particularly intriguing given the increased visibility and popularity of comics (MacDonald, 2019), coupled with comics' publishers' broadening editorial mandates. Moreover, as comics' readers themselves are ageing, scholars have recently called for further research on older comics fans (Harrington, 2018).

In a recent review of literature dedicated to the portrayal of older adults in different media, Iversen and Wilińska (2016, as cited in Iversen et al, 2017, p 4) concluded that 'the majority focus on either representation in advertising within a variety of media outlets or on film and television fiction'. To diversify the media currently considered for analysis, we propose that although currently underutilised, comics can be a helpful storytelling medium through which to study the representations and portrayals of older adults and later life. Comics scholar Charles Hatfield (2008) highlights the interest that this medium generates among different disciplines and its potential for interdisciplinary work: 'Comics present daunting complexities on many levels – aesthetic, semiotic, historical, cultural, disciplinary, institutional – and so are potentially as challenging to scholars as any cultural form' (p 130). Additionally, comics have a longstanding presence in the media landscape; they 'have been read by a huge audience since the early 1900s' and 'can unintentionally reflect a particular social group's place in society and culture' (Hanlon et al, 1997, p 297), highlighting their potential for examining social status or representation. Specific to this storytelling medium, because of the complementary interplay between text and images, 'neither has to do the work of meaning-making alone' (Myers and Goldenberg, 2018, p 159). This provokes a unique reading experience that warrants further exploration in how it allows for and crafts meaning making and understandings about older characters specifically, and ageing more broadly.

The project under discussion in this chapter takes its start after the authors were awarded an American Library Association Carnegie Whitney Grant, which supports the creation of reading lists and guides that can be of use to a variety of libraries. Given our respective research interests (Lucia focuses generally on teens' and young adults' experiences of reading comics and Nicole examines experiences in later life), we have shared and discussed our mutual interest in representations of age, particularly given that age is often used as a ubiquitous (and problematic) categorising tool (Bytheway, 2005; Rothbauer, 2020). With this shared interest, we bridged our respective research interests through the creation of a reading list (located at comicsandaging.blog)[1] that collects and showcases comics that depict a variety of older adult characters and experiences in later life.

Broadly, this chapter contributes to the slow but steady process of acceptance and visibility of comics, both socially and in academia (Duncan et al, 2019; Woo, 2020). Most importantly, it furthers extant scholarly conversations about comics and ageing, purposefully stepping away from a prevailing focus on either the superhero genre (Miczo, 2015; Neumann, 2015) or American comic strips (Palmore, 1971; Hanlon, et al, 1997), moving instead to a global approach to the form.

This chapter examines five comics, both individually (including themes, characters, settings, plot developments and so on, and their representations visually, textually and narratively), as well as in conversation with emerging ideas about queering ageing futures (couched in a critique of the prevailing and dominant successful ageing discourse[2]), as eloquently proposed by Sandberg and Marshall (2017). In their article, Sandberg and Marshall encourage disability and queer studies to ally to queer ageing in ways that disrupt and reveal alternatives to the dominant narratives of successful ageing as necessarily 'happy ageing futures' that evoke imagery of heterosexual, able bodied, mentally fit, physically fit and affluent older couples. As Sandberg and Marshall (2017) propose, 'successful aging is not just about what one does in the here and now, but contains an imperative for the future – an association of aging with *possible* futures' (p 23).

Through our analysis of the five titles, we argue that these comics, in their exploration of the fullness and the complexities and contradictions of later life, take up a liminal quality, that, when analysing representations of older age in the media, might more realistically understand older characters as simultaneously occupying or weaving through multiple narratives associated with later life (biological decline, an imperative to age successfully and a queering of ageing futures) and thus ultimately, and importantly, recognise a different kind of diversity in ageing futures.

Literature review

Any sort of examination of older adults or ageing in comics or graphic novels is sparse. That our review of relevant literature can report on but four articles is indicative of a pressing need for ongoing study and reflection in this area.

Palmore's (1971) study analysed the interplay between text and images in 264 humorous comics, reporting that over half of the included comic strips reflected a negative view of older adults, with those dealing with physical ability or appearance, age concealment, 'old maids' and cognitive ability as especially negative. Age-concealment comic strips overwhelmingly referred to women, leading Palmore (1971) to note a 'double standard' in the included comic strips, in which ageing among women was portrayed more negatively than ageing among men. This early study spurred and underpinned Hanlon et al's (1997) project, which provides a large-scale overview of representations of older age in comics. In their investigation of *Washington Post* comics strips' portrayals of older adults from the 1970s to the 1990s, older men were more frequently represented than women although both male and female comic characters were far more likely to be portrayed in negative roles than in positive or strong roles, leading the authors to conclude that 'this form of communication supports ageism and has the potential to promote stereotypes of ageing' (Hanlon et al, 1997, pp 302–3).

These two earlier studies approached their examination of representations of older adults in comics from a measured, quantified angle, counting age, gender, ethnicity and positive or weak roles. This approach to measuring or categorising different facets of ageing comics characters mirrors a common approach across investigations of older adult portrayals in the media, including television (Lauzen et al, 2007; Markov and Yoon, 2020), films (Robinson et al, 2007; Zurcher and Robinson, 2018) and children's books (Hollis-Sawyer and Cuevas, 2013). Such investigations tend to draw from Schmidt and Boland's (1986) positive and negative trait clusters, codifying older characters into a single age stereotype, divided along the arbitrary lines of either 'positive' age stereotypes (for example, the sage, the perfect grandparent, the golden ager) or 'negative' age stereotypes (for example, the curmudgeon, the recluse, the vulnerable). These classifications reify a 'binary model of opposing stereotypes of aging' (Low and Dupuis-Blanchard, 2013, p 54), where older adult characters are organised by their appearance of either autonomy and engagement or dependency and decline.

Two recent publications by Neumann (2015) and Miczo (2015) highlight comics as potential spaces of resistance against stereotypical roles in later life. Both authors note that, for the most part, superhero comic characters typically show no appearance of ageing. Despite 'living' in comics for decades, they are not allowed to age, with the understood implication that older age is synonymous with weakness, which superheroes do not or should not possess. Neumann (2015) importantly identifies the added implications of gender on the treatment of older age, noting that superheroines (such as Wonder Girl, Batgirl or Supergirl) 'do not age past youth in the pages of comics, as evident in the larger number of characters named "Girl"' (p 121). Neumann's research draws attention to both the dearth of comics that currently feature older female characters and the dismissal or victimisation of older women when they do appear.

Comics with older adult protagonists: five titles

The five titles that we include in our analysis were purposefully selected from the list of titles that we have gathered, curated and which comprise our larger reading list (available at comicsandaging.blog). Our first criterion was to choose titles that were not considered under the graphic medicine[3] umbrella, a field of scholarly, creative and clinical study and practice that examines the integration of comics as resources for studying, communicating and understanding physical and mental health, medicine, caregiving and disability (Green and Myers, 2010).

Our selection process then moved to the location of titles using WorldCat and the catalogues of large public library systems, including the Toronto Public Library, New York Public Library and Seattle Public Library. Through these searches, an inconsistency emerged: a number of these comics, curiously, had no associated library subject heading that would indicate that the title involved or featured older age, indicating the need to explore how knowledge systems (such as library catalogues) classify and categorise media that are associated with older age or later life. As a result, we then contacted comics' publishers whose assistance was instrumental in helping us identify a wide range of titles from different countries. Our selection process was therefore iterative, starting with over 40 titles, as we sought to include titles from different countries and genres that would portray different representations of ageing. Both authors read the comics, first separately and then in conversation, examining the presence or absence of stereotypes and atypical representations of ageing by documenting visual representations of characters, plot and themes, and relationships (including familial, romantic and intergenerational relationships).

We have selected the following titles (a brief description of each title is to follow) as they each featured an older adult as the main or prominent character, for their ability to depict the fullness, the contradictions and the complexities of later life, and for their ability to grapple with the normalised imperative to age successfully, often stepping outside of or resisting this success/failure binary. In what follows, we provide a citation and a brief summary for each comics' title:

Title 1: Daniels, E.C. (2018) Upgrade Soul: A Graphic Novel, St. Louis: Lion Forge[4]

In this speculative-fiction graphic novel, Molly Nonnar, a Latina scientist, and her husband, Hank Nonnar, an African American media creator and philanthropist, are offered the opportunity to invest and participate in the ground-breaking 'Upgrade Cell' project, an experimental cellular process that promises to enhance their strength and intellect to their fullest potential. When the unexpected occurs, Hank and Molly come face to face with potato-shaped clones of themselves, Henry and Manuela, who have achieved the promised results of superiority in all areas except for their distorted bodies.

Title 2: Franklin, T., St-Onge, J. and San, J. (2018) Bingo Love, Portland: Image Comics

This Kickstarter-funded project introduces the only queer couple in this selection. Unfolding as an everyday life narrative with a fairy-tale quality, in this comic, Hazel Johnson and Mari McCray, both African Americans, reconnect in later life after being denied an earlier romantic relationship in their teens. Hazel narrates this graphic novel, making use of flashbacks that start when the two protagonists, who meet as teenagers at church bingo in 1963, fall in love. Soon separated by their families, the two reunite, now as grandmothers in their mid-60s, and begin to build a new life together.

Title 3: Lupano, W. and Cauuet, P. (2017–) The Old Geezers (5 vols), Europe Comics. Translator: M. Kane[5]

Both a slice of life and an adventure comic of sorts, this series revolves around three lifelong friends: Antoine, granddad to Sophie and a retired union activist; Émile, an ex-rugby player who sailed around the world; and Pierrot, a member of an anarchist group. This series is full of humour and playfulness as well as moments of social commentary and each volume offers readers flashbacks that richly inform the friends' present antics and adventures.

Title 4: Tsurutani, K. (2020) BL Metamorphosis (vol 1 and 2), Los Angeles, LA: Seven Stories. Translators: J. Allen and Y. MacFarlane[6]

Yuki Inchinoi, a 75-year-old Japanese woman and calligraphy tutor, enters a bookstore on a hot day and unwittingly buys a boys' love manga. Captivated with this genre, when Yuki returns to the bookstore for the next volume, Urara Sayama, a high-school girl who works at the store, helps her with this task. The story slowly details the formation of this intergenerational friendship through Ichinoi and Sayama's boys' love fandom.

Title 5: Zidrou and Jongh, A. (2019) Blossoms in Autumn, *Europe Comics. Digital. Translator: M. Madden*[7]

Ulysses, a 59-year-old French widower, is forced into early retirement from his job. Without direction or purpose, the course of his life is changed by a chance encounter with a fellow 'lonely soul', Mediterranea Solenza. Mediterranea, aged 62, has recently lost her mother and runs her late father's cheese shop. A romance blossoms between these two, who are supposedly in the 'autumn' of their lives, and they soon find themselves embarking on a most unexpected odyssey.

Discussion

In this section, we provide a focused analysis on each comic, highlighting the specific aspects that hold significant weight in their questioning of or wrestling with understandings and narratives of ageing. While each comic is deserving of its own close reading, we have elected to venture forward with this overview format as one of our goals is to bring this body of understudied comics' works to the scholarly community for conversation. As a result, however, we unavoidably forgo adequately transmitting the depth and richness within each work.

As we have previously noted, our selection, reading and analysis of the five comics are provoked and informed by our engagement with Sandberg and Marshall's (2017) 'Queering aging futures' article. In this article, the authors both critique and propose alternatives regarding the concept of 'successful ageing'. Successful ageing, solidified by Rowe and Kahn (1987), aligns with related concepts of positive, productive and active ageing. Success here is understood and achieved through three means: the avoidance of disease and disability; the maintenance of high cognitive and physical function; and participation in social activities. Existing critical perspectives on and critiques of successful ageing (see for example Katz and Calasanti, 2015; Martinson and Berridge, 2015; Rubinstein and de Medeiros, 2015) emphasise the dependence of successful ageing on structural opportunities, the assumptions that surround choice and lifestyle, the expectation of individual initiative and the underlying assumption that those who age unsuccessfully are somehow at fault. Furthering these critiques, Sandberg and Marshall (2017) reveal that while successful ageing discourse challenges associations of old age with decline and decrepitude, it, as one consequence, creates a narrow possibility for ageing futures – an active and happy ageing future open chiefly to heterosexual, able bodied, and mentally fit people. Queering ageing futures, then, requires a radical identification and affirmation of 'narratives that provide alternative visions of later-life' (Sandberg and Marshall, 2017, p 7), while concurrently looking to creative, critical ways to problematise those binaries that continue to shape a 'successful' versus 'failed' ageing.

As we read and reread each of the five comics, they each opened up conversations and questions regarding what it means or could mean to age, as understood and critiqued through Sandberg and Marshall's interrogation and queering of successful ageing. Indeed, successful ageing and its critiques emerged as a central (although, importantly, not exclusive) concept in guiding our reading. To be able to fully account for our findings, we drew inspiration from Biggs and Powell (2001) who identified the emergence and establishment of a 'master narrative by which to age' that is composed of two, *co-existing* narratives: 'biological decline on the one hand and consumer agelessness on the other' (p 4) (see also Chapters 2 and 7). Alongside these two narratives by which to age, we append Sandberg and Marshall's (2017) queering of ageing futures as a third, co-existing narrative, where feminist, crip and queer studies help to problematise the narrow binaries (underpinned by heteronormative and ableist assumptions) of success/failure that successful ageing offers and look instead to inviting and acknowledging a multiplicity of ageing futures. We propose that experiences of ageing might simultaneously occupy elements from all three of these narratives, being both 'betwixt and between' (Turner, 1987). As we reveal throughout this analysis and in the concluding remarks, the characters in our analysed comics are most realistically and complexly understood if we acknowledge the liminality of these texts and the presence of these three, co-existing narratives.

Blossoms in Autumn

In *Blossoms in Autumn* (see Figure 9.1), old age is understood as that moment when others (whether society, employers, family members and so on) and older adults themselves perceive a person as being somehow different as a result of their older age. The two main characters are pushed into old age differently; Ulysses through retirement and Mediterranea through chronological and physical signs of ageing (she is described as the oldest sibling [p 12] and laments the wrinkling and sagging of her body [pp 73– 6]). At the beginning of the comic, both characters see their later life as a downward spiral into despair and loneliness. Mediterranea perseverates over her changing physical body; in one particularly haunting panel she compares her ageing body to a rotting apple (p 76). Ulysses notes that the imperfections he accumulated throughout his middle age continue into later life, with the understanding that he, in his 'old age', is not suddenly

Figure 9.1: *Blossoms in Autumn.* The beginning of their first sexual encounter

Source: Europe Comics (p 96)

wise or sweet. The portrayal of older age and its association with successful ageing is complicated in its both realistic (Ulysses pays for sex) and unrealistic (Mediterranea's surprise pregnancy) ways.

The presence of images of soft, wrinkled, naked older bodies and these bodies in sexual acts of intimacy in *Blossoms in Autumn* is, as Twigg (2000) calls it, a 'visual shock' (p 46) and is certainly revelatory. This visual shock is due, in large part, to the scarcity of available images of unclothed ageing bodies. As Twigg (2000) notes, 'we have little sense culturally of aesthetic pleasure in old flesh, or of what a beautiful old body might look like' (p 46). While the visual depictions of naked bodies enjoying intimacy and pleasure with one another is notable, at the same time the heteronormative relationship between Mediterranea and Ulysses does carry an element of 'saving' one another from the loneliness and despair that accompanies older age. Furthermore, Mediterranea's sometimes hostile relationship with her body and her desire for a more youthful, pert body is in keeping with more neoliberal approaches to successful ageing.

Finally, Mediterranea and Ulysses' surprise pregnancy is certainly unexpected and might be included to destabilise the reader in their expectations of ageing bodies. This pregnancy, however, upholds the need for generativity and futurity (dependent on heterosexual reproduction) that is associated with successful ageing, with '(hetero)kinship ... [making] later life meaningful and positive' (Sandberg and Marshall, 2017, p 3). Indeed, Mediterranea indicates profound regret at not marrying and having her own children (p 103). As Sandberg and Marshall (2017) elaborate, 'depictions of older people with children and grandchildren suggest more than their reproductive success in the present – they are a frequent trope in establishing generativity and the extension of life into the future' (p 4). Working from a decolonial and indigenous perspective, Chazan (2020) furthers the critique of an 'imagery of reproductive success' by advancing a different understanding of generativity that includes 'the work of nurturing ancestors seven generations past and working for futures seven generations ahead … or a generativity connected to land, water, and all of creation' (p 114).

Throughout *Blossoms in Autumn*, the 'feeling' of 'being' old emerges both externally, in the case of Ulysses (forced retirement), and internally with Mediterranea (an old body). While the title suggests a liberation of their potential 'oldness' through explicit representations of sex in later life, at the same time, as Marshall (2012) has observed, ' "sexiness" [is] now … an important means of distinguishing oneself as "not old"' (p 340), and the understandings of romantic and sexual intimacy remain entrenched within the auspices of productive and successful ageing.

Bingo Love

In *Bingo Love* (see Figure 9.2), old age, while a smaller part of the overall story, is romanticised as it is what allows Hazel and Mari to become the fullest expression of themselves, both as individuals and as a lesbian couple. Older age, then, is depicted as a helpful interruption to existing societal and familial norms, creating possibilities and opportunities.

A distinguishing characteristic of *Bingo Love* is the intersectionality of the identities of its main characters. Countering studies of older adult representation in media that continue to report that 'typical' characters in media are young-old, male, Caucasian, middle-class, able-bodied and

Figure 9.2: *Bingo Love*. Hazel reflecting on her relationship with Mari

Source: Image Comics (p 80)

straight (Signorielli, 2004; Lee et al, 2007; Markov and Yoon, 2020), this title features older women, older Black women and older Black women in a lesbian relationship. It also represents a rupture in the historical invisibility and 'monstrous' presence of African Americans, Latinos, Asian Americans and Native Americans in mainstream comics (Aldama, 2018, p 303) and a long tradition of queer comics that have primarily focused on White characters. Hazel and Mari's very presence, then, might be 'visually shocking' (Twigg, 2000) given the many diverse intersections on which their lives stand. Their presence, too, challenges the 'whiteness' and colonial normativity discourses through which we come to understand the success/failure binary in successful ageing.

Like *Blossoms in Autumn*, there are scenes of sexual intimacy and pleasure between Mari and Hazel. However, where some elements of the characters and their behaviours, sometimes literally, align to a queering of ageing futures (diverse characters, sexually active older adults), there are still elements in keeping with a more neoliberal understanding of successfully ageing. Sandberg and Marshall (2017), for example, discuss the problematic assimilation of 'others' into current models of successful ageing. In *Bingo Love*, Hazel and Mari's lesbian relationship that dominates the narrative in the comic, while notable as the only homosexual relationship in any of the titles in our larger reading list, might have gained acceptance given that it 'adhere[s] to heteronormative conventions of monogamous coupledom' (Sandberg and Marshall, 2017, p 7).

BL Metamorphosis

In *BL Metamorphosis* (see Figure 9.3), readers are privy to the ordinary and daily life of an older woman in a Japanese city. The simplicity and everyday life focus of this manga title can be linked to the recent trend in manga where older adult characters are becoming increasingly central to the narratives (Kyodo, 2018).

Yuki Inchinoi, the main character, is depicted with stereotypical visual and physical markers of later life: in addition to wrinkles, she has trouble going up stairs (vol 1, p 55) and while at a comic convention for *yaoi* manga, struggles to remain standing in the long, never-ending queues of people (vol 2, p 7). But of note in *BL Metamorphosis* is its association between ageing and new possibilities, looking in particular at the intergenerational (but not familial) friendship as well as a new hobby (reading boys' love manga). Originating in Japan and typically created by women, for women, boys' love (*yaoi*) is fictional media that features homoerotic relationships between male characters. Given the content of the manga that Yuki finds, her discovery and enjoyment of *yaoi* is certainly unexpected and counters prevailing stereotypes of older adults as either asexual, post-sexual or whose sexual expressions are ignored

Figure 9.3: *BL Metamorphosis*. Yuki and Urara part ways after one of their meetings to talk about their favourite boys' love title

Note: Panels are read from right to left
Source: Seven Stories (v 2, p 123)

or conversely ridiculed (Bradway and Beard, 2015). Yuki's engagement with and enjoyment of *yaoi* presents an alternative expression (both in content and in format) of not only sexual function, exploration and pleasure in later life, but also, depending on the type of *yaoi* she is reading, feelings of romance. This engagement with *yaoi* manga as a source of romantic and sexual discovery and pleasure in later life destabilises traditional expectations of continued sexual experiences, functionality and performance that are based on the dominant youthful and heterosexist standards and the hegemony of penetrative sex and that are used as indicators for successful ageing in later life (Katz and Marshall, 2003; Marshall, 2012).

Also of note in *BL Metamorphosis* is the relationship between Yuki and Urara. This title offers a window into the possibilities that an intergenerational friendship creates in the life for *both* characters. *BL Metamorphosis* not only troubles the generational conflict discourse (Bristow, 2019), it also troubles the typical construction of the unidirectionality of the benefits emerging from intergenerational relationships, often from the younger individual to the older individual. Both characters learn from and influence one another; it is a balanced relationship, where Urara is the guide into the *yaoi* universe and fandom, and Yuki is a sounding board for Urara's personal and social insecurities. This narrative could easily have been told as a relationship between a grandmother and a granddaughter, but making it happen outside of familial ties reinforces the possibilities of intergenerational encounters, even if they occur by complete chance.

Old Geezers

Old age is very much at the core of *Old Geezers*' narrative; readers are squarely in Antoine, Émile and Pierrot's lived present, witnessing how they hilariously and, at times, defiantly live in later life in their own ways (see Figure 9.4). Whereas 'processes of social stratification mark some people out by age criteria and institutionalize a set of social positions within which they are required to live out their lives' (Vincent, 2006, p 268), old age in *Old Geezers* serves neither as an interruption nor a vacuum, nor is it used to artificially place boundaries around the characters.

Visually, the trio of main characters feature stereotypical markers (balding, white hair, thick glasses, wrinkles, a hunched stature, trousers pulled up far beyond the waist) that connote old age in men. These stereotypical visual and behavioural markers, however, are often used to emote humour, with the reader brought into the humour, laughing with – not at – the characters. Furthermore, where ageing bodies are often bodies that are immediately associated with risk and vulnerability, the scenarios we find the characters in are startling, prompting readers to perhaps question what assumptions they carry for older adults who 'look' old. Émile, for example, lives in an assisted living facility and is depicted as having some mobility issues and health complaints (vol 1, p 5). At the same time, on a different page, we see Émile, with a large and elaborate chest tattoo, entering a swimming pool (vol 1, p 49).

Like *BL Metamorphosis*, *Old Geezers* is very much about community in later life – not only among the three friends or with Antoine's granddaughter, Sophie, but also with their neighbours and activist community. Notably, this title connects community with intergenerational relationships and political activity. Pierrot, for example, pushes back against the stereotype of older adults as being apolitical or social movements as belonging solely to youth (Sawchuk, 2009; Chazan et al, 2018). Pierrot belongs to an intergenerational anarchist group for those living with vision impairments ('Neither Eyes Nor Master') and while his vision impairment has brought him to be an active participant in his anarchist group, at the same time, he is depicted as a dangerous driver because of his limited eyesight (vol 1, p 6). Curiously, we are left to grapple with older bodies that are simultaneously actively engaged and risky liabilities.

The interaction of intergenerationality and political activism is especially prevalent in the anarchists' headquarters, a building belonging to 'Francine de la Rochebonnefoy, aka Fifi Hot Buns, blessed with the blood of an aristocrat and the heart of an anarchist, who was a zealous sister in our fights yesteryear, and who is now 91, with a spine as twisted as a grapevine' (vol 2, p 13). As an indication of intergenerational solidarity, the Neither Eyes Nor Master headquarters welcomes activists of all ages; it houses struggling students, a resident hacker who trains the 'troops' and a collective of street artists.

Figure 9.4: *Old Geezers*: Émile and Pierrot start a conversation about Pierrot's activism

Source: Europe Comics (v 1, p 22)

Upgrade Soul

In comparison with the previous four titles, *Upgrade Soul* is notably different in its approach to older age. While the other four titles cover representations of everyday life and are best classified as the slice of life genre, as a speculative fiction title, *Upgrade Soul* situates its plot in an alternative reality, resembling ours in most ways, except for the science project that jumpstarts the story.

This work invites its readers to consider what it means to have a 'good old age'. Kaufman et al (2004) note that 'a major effect of biomedicalization today is that the aged body tends to be viewed now as simultaneously a disease entity, a site of restoration and a space for improvement' (p 736). The experimental Upgrade Cell project for which Hank and Molly volunteer as participants is, interestingly, *not* about being younger or more youthful, but it is about being a *better* version of themselves, including an increased lifespan: 'Its purpose is not simply to enrich your life through enhanced strength, endurance and intellect but to allow you to finally achieve your absolute, god-given potential' (p 44). This approach to ageing and ageing bodies creatively troubles the typical biomedicalisation approach or intervention to ageing. In the Upgrade Cell project, ageing is not to be stopped or reversed, but can be transcended in an effort of 'betterment'. As we read *Upgrade Soul*, we questioned whether the Upgrade Cell project might be conceptualised as an extension of existing understandings of successful ageing – one that is not interested in freezing or turning back time but that aims to extend time into the future, ideally to maintain productivity with an increased quality of life after overcoming biological signs of ageing and genetic imperfections. However, the Upgrade Cell project does not completely succeed, and Hank and Molly are not superseded by their new, better selves, but are instead presented with duplicates who fulfil the betterment promise in all areas, save their physical appearance. Hank and Molly meet their 'better' selves, Henry and Manuela, who are drawn as foetus-like blobs and, as the story progresses, disfigured infants. The four characters display frailty through different visual representations; as Hank says to Henry: 'You don't *look* invincible. You look like a potato to me' (p 121, emphasis in original) (see Figure 9.5).

As readers are confronted with the 'original' Hank and Molly (depicted in their older, wrinkled bodies) coexisting in the same world as their clones (disfigured, potato-like blobs), both readers and the book's characters must then struggle with the nature of identity and its intimate relationship with age and ageing. Henry and Manuela are eerie manifestations of an 'other' and through their conversations with Hank and Molly, we witness the strangeness of interacting with an 'other' that is also oneself. Readers and the comic's characters unavoidably grapple with questions about identity. What shapes it? Where does it reside? Is true identity encompassed by our

Figure 9.5: *Upgrade Soul.* Hank and Henry conversing

Source: Oni-Lion Forge Publishing (p 122)

bodies, memories and self-image, or by a version of ourselves that achieves a seemingly full potential in every way except aesthetically? In the case of Hank and Henry, these questions move to the issue of survival and who deserves to keep living, especially when Hank's health is deteriorating (p 231).

While these questions of 'who am I?' are stereotypically relegated to or posed by younger individuals, interestingly, *Upgrade Soul* prompts us to consider them through Hank and Molly and their unappealing, potato-looking clones.

Conclusion

In his discussion of Hillary Chute's *Why Comics?*, Fawaz (2019) concludes that 'comics expand what we can desire from our reading experience, allowing us to explore a range of commonly delegitimized fantasies about how we read, in what direction, and with what outcome' (p 593). This vision of what comics can do naturally connects with an initial finding from our analysis, that the diversity of complex and complicated characters and narratives in our included comics challenges the ageist status that comics as a medium had acquired in previous scholarly projects (Palmore, 1971; Hanlon et al, 1997).

As we read and reread the five comics, complemented by our readings into critical gerontological literature, we began to identify a more nuanced way by which to understand the representations of older characters in the comics. Bytheway (2003) notes that representations of later life have the tendency to lump together and homogenise older people, often exclusively showing those older adults who occupy privileged positions. In her articulation of the politics of visual representations of older bodies, Gullette (2017) similarly asserts that 'visual difference is squeezed out' (p 27), due to socioeconomic pressures related to productivity and desirability. The analysed comics communicate the interrelated contradictions that older adults experience, with characters who embody and exemplify these contradictions; at times, negotiating declining abilities, at other times (or simultaneously), living with the pressures to 'age successfully', and at other times, exemplifying a narrative that provides an alternative vision of later life. In their identification of a 'binary model of opposing stereotypes of aging' in analysed adverts, Low and Dupuis-Blanchard (2013) conclude that 'such a binary model limits the categories through which we understand the ageing body and fails to account for the diversity of seniors' bodies in society' (p 61). However, in the comics analysed in this chapter, it was impossible to classify characters into one of these two stereotypes and no comic never wholly or exclusively occupied a single narrative.

Therefore, we propose that in their representation of older age, these titles act as liminal texts. As we have identified, older characters' bodies, behaviours and relationships occupy and weave through multiple, concurrent narratives associated with later life (biological decline, an imperative to age successfully and our proposed third narrative of the queering of ageing futures). In allowing these three narratives to co-exist, these liminal texts interrogate the narrow binaries of success and failure in dominant successful ageing discourse. This interrogation provides a space to queer ageing futures. Understanding these texts as liminal also aligns with Higgs and Gilleard's (2015, p 128) observation that contemporary ageing experiences '[make] generalisations about old age harder to establish and even harder to sustain'. As an alternative to the linear binary of success/failure that dominates conversations about representations of ageing (see also Chapter 2), we encourage others examining and comparing representations of ageing in comics and other types of media to similarly identify other liminal texts to engender more complex and complicated conversations that are 'informed by the multiplicity of present lived realities' (Hostetler, 2009, p 419) in older adults' lives.

Notes

[1]   A growing list of comics related to this project can be found at: https://comicsandaging.blog/title-list/. With 32 titles currently featured, this list will continue to evolve as we locate and add in new titles.

[2]   Complementing Sandberg and Marshall's (2017) critique, *The Gerontologist* (volume 55, no 1) published a special issue that provides a full and critical commentary regarding successful ageing discourse and related active, productive and healthy ageing discourses.

[3]   A majority of the graphic medicine comic titles that feature an older adult character (notable titles include: *Tangles, a Story of Alzheimer's, my Mother, and Me*, by Sarah Leavitt; Roz Chast's *Can't We Talk About Something More Pleasant? Things to do in a Retirement Home Trailer Park* by Nye Wright; Joyce Farmer's *Special Exits*; or Dana Walrath's *Aliceheimer's: Alzheimer's Through the Looking Glass*) can be further grouped as graphic pathographies, or 'illness narratives in graphic form' (Myers and Goldenberg, 2018, p 158). While these narratives importantly document and depict lived experiences felt by a number of older adults and their families, a majority of these titles focus on the death, decline, dementia and dependency experienced by older people or their families. Being wary of conflating illness with ageing or normalising the medicalisation of older age, where infirmities in older age might receive more attention than everyday life, we have not included these titles in our analysis. Also, graphic medicine scholarship sometimes focuses its attention on the utility of titles in medical education and training (for example, Green and Myers, 2010; Ronan and Czerwiec, 2020). A host of information about graphic medicine (titles, reviews, events and so on) can be accessed at: www.graphicmedicine.org.

[4]   Also available as an Apple app: Daniels, E.C. and Loyer, E. (2018) *Upgrade Soul* (version 2.0.1) [mobile app], available from: https://apps.apple.com/us/app/upgrade-soul/id549051057, accessed 20 April 2022.

⁵ Originally published: Lupano, W. and Cauuet, P. (2014–) *Les Vieux Fourneaux* (5 vols), Brussels: Dargaud Benelux. This title is also available in print: Lupano, W. and Cauuet, P. (2019) *The Old Geezers: 1. Alive and Still Kicking*, Portland: Ablaze.

⁶ Originally published: Tsurutani, K. (2017–) *Metamorphose no Engawa* (5 vols), Tokyo: Kodokawa.

⁷ Originally published: Zidrou et Jongh, A. (2018) *L'obsolescence Programmée de Nos Sentiments*, Brussels: Dargaud Benelux. This title is also available in print: Zidrou and Jongh, A. (2019) *Blossoms in Autumn*, London: Selfmadehero.

References

Aldama, F. (2018) 'US creators of color and the postunderground graphic narrative renaissance', in J. Baetens, H. Frey and S. Tabachnick (eds) *The Cambridge History of the Graphic Novel*, Cambridge: Cambridge University Press, pp 303–19.

Biggs, S. and Powell, J.L. (2001) 'A Foucauldian analysis of old age and the power of social welfare', *Journal of Aging & Social Policy*, 12(2): 93–112.

Bradway, K.E. and Beard, R.L. (2015) '"Don't be trying to box folks in" older women's sexuality', *Affilia*, 30(4): 504–18.

Bristow, J. (2019) *Stop Mugging Grandma*, New Haven, CT: Yale University Press.

Bytheway, B. (2003) 'Visual representations of late life', in C. Faircloth (ed) *Aging Bodies: Images and Everyday Experience*, Walnut Creek, CA: Alta Mira Press, pp 29–53.

Bytheway, B. (2005) 'Ageism and age categorization', *Journal of Social Issues*, 61(2): 361–74.

Chazan, M. (2020) 'Unsettling aging futures: challenging colonial-normativity in social gerontology', *International Journal of Ageing and Later Life*, 14(1): 91–119.

Chazan, M., Baldwin, M. and Evans, P. (eds) (2018) *Unsettling Activisms: Critical Interventions on Aging, Gender, and Social Change*, Toronto: Canadian Scholars' Press.

Chivers, S. (2011) *The Silvering Screen: Old Age and Disability in Cinema*, Toronto: University of Toronto Press.

Duncan, R., Smith, M.J. and Levitz, P. (2019) *The Power of Comics: History, Form, and Culture*, London: Bloomsbury Publishing.

Fawaz, R. (2019) 'A queer sequence: comics as a disruptive medium', *PMLA*, 134(3): 588–94.

Green, M.J. and Myers, K.R. (2010) 'Graphic medicine: use of comics in medical education and patient care', *The British Medical Journal*, 340: 574–7.

Gullette, M.M. (2017) *Ending Ageism, or How Not to Shoot Old People*, New Brunswick, NJ: Rutgers University Press.

Hanlon, H., Farnsworth, J. and Murray, J. (1997) 'Ageing in American comic strips: 1972–1992', *Ageing & Society*, 17(3): 293–304.

Harrington, C.L. (2018) 'Creativity and ageing in fandom', *Celebrity Studies*, 9(2): 231–43.

Hatfield, C. (2008) 'How to read a …', *English Language Notes*, 46(2): 129–50.

Higgs, P. and Gilleard, C. (2015) *Rethinking Old Age: Theorising the Fourth Age*, London: Palgrave.

Hollis-Sawyer, L. and Cuevas, L. (2013) 'Mirror, mirror on the wall: ageist and sexist double jeopardy portrayals in children's picture books', *Educational Gerontology*, 39(12): 902–14.

Hostetler, A.J. (2009) 'Generativity and time in gay men's life stories', in P.J. Hammack and B.J. Cohler (eds) *The Story of Sexual Identity: Narrative Perspectives on the Gay and Lesbian Life Course*, New York, NY: Oxford University Press, pp 397–424.

Iversen, S.M., Blaakilde, A.L., Wilińska, M. and Sandvik, K. (2017) 'Growing old with and via media', *MedieKultur: Journal of Media and Communication Research*, 33(63): 1–8.

Katz, S. and Calasanti, T. (2015) 'Critical perspectives on successful aging: does it "appeal more than it illuminates"?', *The Gerontologist*, 55(1): 26–33.

Katz, S. and Marshall, B. (2003) 'New sex for old: lifestyle, consumerism, and the ethics of aging well', *Journal of Aging Studies*, 17(1): 3–16.

Kaufman, S. R., Shim, J. K. and Russ, A. J. (2004) 'Revisiting the biomedicalization of aging: clinical trends and ethical challenges', *The Gerontologist*, 44(6): 731–8.

Kyodo (2018) 'Manga starting to feature elderly characters', *The Japan Times*, available from: https://www.japantimes.co.jp/news/2018/07/17/natio nal/social-issues/new-genre-manga-casts-elderly-characters-leading-roles/ [accessed 23 August 2021].

Lauzen, M.M., Dozier, D.M. and Reyes, B. (2007) 'From adultescents to zoomers: an examination of age and gender in prime-time television', *Communication Quarterly*, 55(3): 343–57.

Lee, M.M., Carpenter, B. and Meyers, L.S. (2007) 'Representations of older adults in television advertisements', *Journal of Aging Studies*, 21(1): 23–30.

Low, J. and Dupuis-Blanchard, S. (2013) 'From zoomers to geezerade: representations of the aging body in ageist and consumerist society', *Societies*, 3(1): 52–65.

MacDonald, H. (2019) 'Raina Telgemeier's *Guts* is the bestselling book overall in the US this week', *The Beat*, available from: https://www.com icsbeat.com/raina-telgemeiers-guts-is-the-bestselling-book-overall-in-the-us-this-week/ [accessed 23 August 2021].

Markov, Č. and Yoon, Y. (2020) 'Diversity and age stereotypes in portrayals of older adults in popular American primetime television series', *Ageing & Society*, 41(12): 2747–67.

Marshall, B.L. (2012) 'Medicalization and the refashioning of age-related limits on sexuality', *Journal of Sex Research*, 49(4): 337–43.

Martinson, M. and Berridge, C. (2015) 'Successful aging and its discontents: a systematic review of the social gerontology literature', *The Gerontologist*, 55(1): 58–69.

Miczo, N. (2015) 'Aging superheroes: retirement and return in Kingdom Come and Old Man Logan', in N. Jones and B. Batchelor (eds) *Aging Heroes: Growing Old in Popular Culture*, Lanham, MD: Rowman & Littlefield, pp 143–56.

Myers, K.R. and Goldenberg, M.D. (2018) 'Graphic pathographies and the ethical practice of person-centered medicine', *AMA Journal of Ethics*, 20(2): 158–66.

Neumann, C.E. (2015) 'Babes and crones: women growing old in comics', in N. Jones and B. Batchelor (eds) *Aging Heroes: Growing Old in Popular Culture*, Lanham, MD: Rowman & Littlefield, pp 119–28.

Palmore, E. (1971) 'Attitudes toward aging as shown by humor', *The Gerontologist*, 11(3:1): 181–6.

Robinson, T., Callister, M., Magoffin, D. and Moore, J. (2007) 'The portrayal of older characters in Disney animated films', *Journal of Aging Studies*, 21(3): 203–13.

Ronan, L.K. and Czerwiec, M.K. (2020) 'A novel graphic medicine curriculum for resident physicians: boosting empathy and communication through comics', *Journal of Medical Humanities*, 41(4): 573–8.

Rothbauer, P. (2020) 'Imagining today's young adults in LIS: moving forward with critical youth studies', in A. Bernier (ed) *Transforming Young Adult Services: A Reader for Our Age* (2nd edn), New York, NY: Neal-Schuman Publishers, pp 151–62.

Rowe, J.W. and Kahn, R.L. (1987) 'Human aging: usual and successful', *Science*, 237(4811): 143–9.

Rozanova, J. (2010) 'Discourse of successful ageing in The Globe & Mail: insights from critical gerontology', *Journal of Ageing Studies*, 24(4): 213–22.

Rubinstein, R.L. and de Medeiros, K. (2015) '"Successful aging," gerontological theory and neoliberalism: a qualitative critique', *The Gerontologist*, 55(1): 34–42.

Sandberg, L.J. and Marshall, B.L. (2017) 'Queering aging futures', *Societies*, 7(3): 21.

Sawchuk, D. (2009) 'The raging grannies: defying stereotypes and embracing aging through activism', *Journal of Women & Aging*, 21(3): 171–85.

Schmidt, D.F. and Boland, S.M. (1986) 'Structure of perceptions of older adults: evidence for multiple stereotypes', *Psychology and Aging*, 1(3): 255–60.

Shary, T. and McVittie, N. (2016) *Fade to Gray: Aging in American Cinema*, Austin, TX: University of Texas Press.

Signorielli, N. (2004) 'Aging on television: messages relating to gender, race, and occupation in prime time', *Journal of Broadcasting & Electronic Media*, 48(2): 279–301.

Smith, S.L., Pieper, K., Choueiti, M., Tofan, A., Depauw, A.-M. and Case, A. (2017) *Seniors on the Small screen: Aging in Popular Television Content*, Los Angeles: USC Annenberg Press, available from: http://assets.uscannenberg. org/docs/Seniors_on_the_Small_Screen-Dr_Stacy_L_Smith_9-12-17.pdf [accessed 23 August 2021].

Turner, V. (1987) 'Betwixt and between: the liminal period in rites of passage', in L.C. Mahdi, S. Foster and M. Little (eds) *Betwixt & Between: Patterns of Masculine and Feminine Initiation*, La Salle, IL: Open Court, pp 3–19.

Twigg, J. (2000) *Bathing: The Body and Community Care*, London: Psychology Press.

Vincent, J.A. (2006) 'Ageing contested: anti-ageing science and the cultural construction of old age', *Sociology*, 40(4): 681–98.

Woo, B. (2020) 'What kind of studies is comics studies?', in L. Aldama (ed) *The Oxford Handbook of Comic Book Studies,* New York, NY: Oxford University Press, pp 1–16.

Ylänne, V. (ed) (2012) *Representing Ageing: Images and Identities*, Basingstoke: Palgrave Macmillan.

Zurcher, J.D. and Robinson, T. (2018) 'From "Bibbid-Bobbidi-Boo" to Scrooge: an update and comparative analysis of the portrayal of older characters in recent Disney animated films', *Journal of Children and Media*, 12(1): 1–15.

PART III

Older adults' interaction with the media and media technologies

10

Advertising old men: Swedish old men reflect on 'seeing themselves'

Karin Lövgren, Linn Sandberg and Jeff Hearn

Introduction

Two elderly men sit on a bench. They are dressed in beige, wearing a cardigan, waistcoat and a cap. One is leaning on his walking stick. The men are absentmindedly observing the goings-on around them, their gaze vacant, one is chewing gum. The connotation is of locals in a warm country. Footsteps approach.

She swaggers. Walks full of confidence. She is a young woman; her dress is short, a halter cut, leaving her shoulders bare, hair tied up in an effortless knot. She seems to be on holiday, judging from the environment. On seeing the men, she stops short, leans over the man chewing gum, straddles his lap and demonstratively kisses him. He is left gaping open-mouthed, and in a later sequence has a befuddled look; the man beside him looks astonished, though not alarmed. We see her smiling contently, as she walks on, chewing gum.

A voice-over pronounces: *Some people are willing to do anything to quit smoking. Nicorette chewing gum.* The camera is back on the two men, where the kissed man vacantly searches for the gum in his mouth, while the other sneakily reaches over and takes the packet of nicotine chewing gum from his pocket.

This advert tells a story, using the short timeframe of commercials of approximately 30–45 seconds to set the stage for a young, assured woman, certain of her ability to get what she wants, using the old man to get the gum, to quit smoking.

Could this commercial have featured two older women, and a young man giving one of them a long sexual kiss? Try substituting the characters with others of different age categories, gender, skin colour – and it is soon evident that the advertising agency would have realised it would be sexist or racist, and impossible to air. But the 'post-feminist' message of women able to get what they want is used to circumvent the blatant ageism of comparing kissing an old man to a readiness to do anything.

In this chapter, building on interviews in focus groups with old men, commercial adverts featuring old men are used as visual prompts to explore men, masculinity and ageing. The analysis focuses on adverts that depict old men, and how old men themselves talk about these. We ask what reflections on being men and old are invoked by the adverts; whether the interviewed men feel hailed by the images and their appeal to consumption; and how these responses can in turn be understood as old men's ways of identifying with, negotiating and resisting different cultural scripts on old age, ageing, men and masculinities.

Studies of old men and masculinities that explicitly discuss men as gendered and aged still constitute a relatively marginal area of scholarship. Studies of representations of masculinities are well established (Wernick, 1987; Craig, 1992; Edwards, 2004), and indeed in recent years there have been further signs of growing interest in such representations (Röber, 2020). However, that body of research has typically not dealt with images of old(er) men and masculinities in mass media and advertising to any notable extent.

Discussions of gender in gerontology have predominantly focused on women, while most studies of men and masculinities have focused on youth and midlife (Thompson, 1994, 2019; Spector-Mersel, 2006; Sandberg, 2007, 2011). This has sometimes led to assertions of old men as invisible or marginalised, both academically and socially (Fleming, 1999; Fennell and Davidson, 2003; Thompson, 2019). However, claims of this relative 'invisibility' of old men also warrant more nuanced analysis.

Although invisibility may reflect exclusion and marginalisation, it may also point to relative privilege, where men's normative position goes unnoticed. The invisibility of old men is thus complex. Old men are invisible and marginalised by ageism and by being positioned further away from hegemonic forms of masculinity, especially as defined by activity, work and being able-bodied. Still, old age and masculinity may continue to be a source of power and privilege, not least through the accumulation of capital and resources. Invisibility can, then, be understood as a reflection of a dominant unmarked gendered position (Hearn, 1995; Sandberg, 2007; Hearn and Sandberg, 2009).

Spector-Mersel (2006) has argued that the relatively few established cultural scripts on becoming an old man have been rather limited and one-dimensional, but arguably are now in the process of becoming more diverse and elaborated. In contrast to many other cultural representations in films or literature that are consumed by particular groups of men, advertising may be understood as images that old men encounter in their everyday lives, and which provide popular scripts on ageing, masculinity and desirable or undesirable old men. Advertising is an arena where old men and old masculinities are both visible and invisible. Adverts as cultural scripts are actively interpreted, negotiated, resisted and challenged by old men themselves (Richardson and Wearing, 2014). For this reason, this chapter focuses primarily on old men's own understandings of advertising and depictions of old men therein.

Representations of gender and old age in advertising

In much mainstream commercial advertising, whether directed at women, men or both, 'youth' is presented or invoked as positive. It is also mainly young adults who are represented in advertising, as well as in other media (Ylänne et al, 2009; Ylänne, 2015; Edström, 2018). Compared to the proportion in the population of the age category represented, there is a clear pattern of gender and age discrimination in media representations. While old women are especially under-represented and invisible in all media, old men are also often excluded from the mass media, with some notable exceptions, for example around reporting on certain 'world leaders'. There is furthermore a gendered pattern in terms of which topics men and women are represented in relation to. For example, men are made visible as experts and associated with so-called hard topics such as mainstream politics, whereas women are made visible as representatives of ordinary people and in relation to topics such as relationships, fashion, home and lifestyle (Richardson and Wearing, 2014; Edström, 2018).

One may, thus, in the words of Tuchman (1978), speak of a *symbolic annihilation*, the omission, trivialisation and condemnation of old people in media representations overall and adverts in general. If women are made invisible earlier in the lifecourse, with markers of ageing already when in their 50s and 60s, men's ageing is invisible in the sense that there are fewer cultural scripts about men and ageing.

Depending on the kind of media outlet, the target audience and the purpose of the advert, images of old age can be used to connote longevity, endurance or long-durability (including of products), as well as to promote health aids (Williams et al, 2010; Ylänne, 2012; Ylänne, 2015). But more often, old people are reduced to subsidiary figures or portrayed in reductive ways as grumpy, outdated, figures of fun or ignorant of IT (Ylänne, 2015). Many adverts are for consumer products such as cosmetics and fashion, which further enforces the skewed age representation (Lövgren, 2009).

Images of old men in advertising seem complex, however. In his analysis of old men in mass media and advertising from the early 1990s, Thompson (1994) argued that old men were primarily portrayed as passive, plump grandfathers, lacking virility and positioned away from hegemonic spheres of work. A decade later, Calasanti and King (2005) claimed that new images were emerging, with old men as successful third agers who were continuously 'playing hard', engaging in activities such as sport and travel, and 'staying hard', by displaying continued virility and sexual function. In a similar vein, Hurd Clarke et al (2014), in their analysis of old men in men's magazines, showed that they were primarily depicted as 'experienced and powerful' and 'happy and healthy'.

The advertising shown to the men in our study reflects both negative and overtly ageist images, such as the passive undesirable old men in the *Nicorette* commercial quoted at the beginning of this chapter, and images of the so-called successfully ageing old man. We also discuss what Röber (2020) terms the 'laughable old man' – old men in absurd humorous narratives. The laughable old man is not unambiguously positioned in terms of negative/ positive or decline/success. These images could be seen as both paving the way for visibility and greater variability in representations of old men and ageing masculinity, while at the same time positioning the old man as ridiculous (see Ylänne, 2015; Röber, 2020).

Research project on ageing masculinities

The material discussed in this chapter emerged from a study within a wider research project, 'MASCAGE: Gendering age – representations of ageing masculinities in contemporary European literature and film'.[1] The aim of this project is to analyse representations of ageing and masculinities, using cultural representations in fictional material and popular culture. The research also examines how old men themselves understand and perceive representations of age and ageing, men and masculinities. Accordingly, focus group interviews have been carried out with men in different European contexts, inviting them to discuss being in this phase of life, as well as how they themselves understand such representations. Different media examples, as well as works of fiction, have been used as a point of departure to initiate and invite reflections on being an old(er) man in contemporary society.

The focus groups we discuss here were conducted in Sweden. Sweden is a relatively egalitarian society, by class and gender, compared to, say, the US or UK, with a long history of a welfare state, from 'cradle to grave'. On the other hand, the welfare society has been subject to major neoliberal changes in recent years, along with some increases in inequality, significant immigration and societal changes across generations. Age, class, ethnicity, gender and generational relations all need to be contextualised accordingly.

Participants in the study

This chapter draws on the Swedish part of the project and interviews with three focus groups, during which a corpus of adverts featuring old men that were aired/shown in Sweden was shown and discussed. The focus group interviews lasted around two hours and were conducted jointly by researchers Lövgren and Sandberg. The participants – with three to five men in each group – first met with one of the researchers for an ethics briefing and to provide informed consent, as well as for an individual biographical background interview. Thereafter during a focus group meeting, the men discussed being in their current phase of life and reflected on ageing and masculinity. They were shown different adverts, both print and videos, that featured old men, and were invited to share their thoughts on these.

Recruitment for the three focus groups varied. One was recruited through a Swedish municipal library on the outskirts of a middle-sized Swedish city. Another focus group was recruited through an activity centre for retirees in suburban Stockholm. The third group consisted of five men, recruited using a snowball method, by having one interviewee invite the others. This group convened online due to the ongoing COVID-19 pandemic. All in all, 12 men participated in the focus groups discussed here.

The men were between the ages of 65 and 92, with the majority being over 75. There were great differences in the meaning that old age had for the men, depending on their chronological age, their sense of generational belonging and – judging from what the informants themselves emphasised – their embodied ageing and health. The men generally assessed their health as fair, stating that some ailments were a natural part of growing old. Several of the interviewees came from a working-class background, and started out in working-class manual jobs, later having had careers as foremen or works managers, or running their own business. Several had a university degree and had worked in well-paid positions. Whatever their earlier background, they could now reasonably be described as middle-class.

The men described heterosexual relationships in the past and present, with most of the men living with a female partner. Several were divorced and had remarried, and several had children and grandchildren. Some of the participants in their 60s and early 70s had living parents. All the men were White with a Swedish ethnic background. Overall, the participants were very socially active.

Focus group interviews

Interviews are in themselves sites of identity construction in which desirable selves are presented and managed, including gendered and aged selves. This was reflected in the background interviews where most men spoke extensively of careers and work trajectories, whereas relationships and family had to be probed for by the researchers. These self-presentations testify to how masculinities are often bonded with performances and achievements, and thereby also with the loss of identity some men experience when retiring and are no longer able to identify with a profession (Pietilä et al, 2020).

Focus groups are a method of data collection for studying 'the co-construction of realities between people, the dynamic negotiation of meaning in context' (Wilkinson, 1998, p 112). While most existing studies on old men and masculinities have been based on individual interviews, the focus groups were useful in understanding how men discussed their experiences and negotiated masculinity and age in a group context. This allowed contrasting interpretations of the adverts to emerge, allowing for a diversity of responses.

Several of the men knew each other beforehand, which allowed for more spontaneous and relaxed conversations, often characterised by joking and a humorous tone. This suggests their attempts to get along, particularly in cases where the men did not know each other beforehand, in tandem with the fact that two of the commercials employ humour as a narrative strategy. But it could also reflect how the focus groups were sites for homosociality where the men constructed masculinity in group interactions (see Allen, 2005).

Cognitive and bodily ageing is of importance when discussing media representations and responses thereof. In particular, we learned that the very tempo of the multimodal commercials excluded some of the men. For example, for those with hearing impairments, the narration in the adverts was too rapid for them to process. Also, media literacy and belonging, in terms of different media generations, seemed to impact on the reception to, knowledge of and familiarity with the genre and format of the advertising.

Selection of adverts

One significant theme of the MASCAGE project has been the exploration of ageist gender stereotypes, including men's perceptions thereof. This builds on previous research on stereotypes used when portraying old people – both negative and positive ones, such as the 'golden ager', the 'perfect grandparent' or the 'grumpy old man' (Hummert et al, 1994; Williams et al, 2010). As advertising can be a significant social sphere for the production and reinforcement of ageist and gendered stereotypes, the overall project chose to include advertising that reflected various stereotypes of old men in order to prompt discussion. This included both negative stereotypes, as in the commercial described at the beginning of the chapter, and what might arguably be more positive stereotypes, such as that of the successfully ageing old man (Calasanti and King, 2005). Such an example is the holiday company TUI's print adverts, showing a group of people, both men and women, gathered on a beach, in some images surrounding a surfboard. Their body posture, as well as signs of ageing, such as white hair and a greying beard, connote belonging to an older age category. The grouping in the photographs suggests couples travelling together. Of importance is also what is absent from the images: people in other age categories, such as children. This implies adults in the so-called third age.

The third visual prompt was a commercial from a long-running award-winning docu-soap series of adverts, where several characters working at a Swedish chain of grocery stores are followed. The storyline is often humorous, commenting on current issues. The commercial works through strengthening the brand of the grocery chain, portraying the characters as fun, and seeking to form a relationship between the brand and the consumer. In the commercial, Stig, the boss, is concerned about his wrinkles, asking a male colleague for advice on "an ointment" to help. Jokingly the younger man holds the hand scanner to his face, saying "if this shows results, then we can talk about wrinkles". Both men react with astonishment when the scanner shows the price for sun-dried tomatoes.

Analysis of interviews

All interviews were transcribed verbatim. The transcripts were then read through several times and coded in accordance with the guidelines advocated in Braun and Clarke (2006) and Rennstam and Wästerfors (2015). This entails a first general, broad, inclusive coding, where both patterns and recurrences, as well as nuances and deviations, are considered, together with coding on wording, choice of expressions and narrative form. This open coding was followed by a second coding. Codes were discussed and compared between the researchers who conducted the focus group interviews. This chapter is built on a selection of these latter codes. The interviewees have been anonymised and the quotations in this chapter are presented with pseudonyms. All quotes have been translated from Swedish.

Masculinity/ies and old age

In this section we focus on the informants' talk that centred on the theme of masculinity and ageing.

"Old people pretending to be young": resisting images of youthful old men

While the TUI advertising could be interpreted as a positive image of old men and men's ageing, emphasising a healthy, active and socially engaged later life, the focus group participants in most cases clearly expressed not feeling hailed by the images. The 90-year-old Frank, for example, expressed how it made him feel "really old" and that it "was a really long time since he was like that": the images rather underlined what he was no longer able to do. These sentiments were reiterated by several of the men, in particular the oldest of the participants.

Sixty-six-year-old Peter was one interviewee who explicitly spoke of the campaign as excluding old people:

> 'So they [the producer of the advert] claim that age isn't a factor for adventure. Seventy is the new 50 like we spoke of before. That's what they visualise here. But what they won't take into account is that I would never be able to get on a surfboard, right? My ailments won't allow me. So we're excluded, some of us, right?'

In this quotation Peter refers back to conversations earlier in the interview, where the participants discussed new third-age scripts on ageing available to their generation. But Peter also challenges the images of healthy active older people in the advert as incongruent with his ageing embodiment. This experience resonated with several other interviewees. In particular, those in their late 70s and older associated, to a great extent, growing old with the ageing of one's body, such as reduced mobility and nimbleness, pain, impaired hearing or eyesight and in some cases more serious illnesses. These were experiences they found largely absent in commercials but also generally in cultural representations and fiction. The men were critical of what they thought of as an exclusion.

That the advert for the travel agency did not concur with their own reflection on their embodiment and as such did not appeal to them also meant they rejected it as "meaningless" and something they would simply ignore. As expressed by Lars, aged 75: "If I'd seen that in the metro, I wouldn't even be looking, I wouldn't have noticed that it contained old people, I would have thought that it was 20-year-olds, 'cause I wouldn't even look at that shit." Lars' opinion that he would not even see these people as old, reflected a theme in the focus groups overall; there were recurring discussions of whether the men and women featuring in the adverts were, in fact, old. Although grey hair and a greying beard suggested being old, body shape, slimness, posture and props such as a surfboard indicated youth, according to the interviewees. But the people featuring in the TUI advert were also discussed as masquerading as young "old people pretending to be young ... he is dressed like a teenager". While feminist cultural gerontologists have discussed how old women not acting their age and not dressing age-appropriately are being labelled as grotesque or failed in terms of gender performance (Twigg, 2013; Lövgren, 2016), this is rarely discussed when it comes to old men. However, that the men in the TUI advertising were described as pretending to be young could be understood as a form of resistance to the imagery of youthful ageing as pathetic and undesirable. This was also reflected in the words of 80-year-old Edvard who said: "They're trying to reflect through their dress and looks that 'We're young, we are healthy and well'", and then pointed to his head and added: "But there is nothing in here." Edvard could be understood as resisting the youthful ageing man as a cultural script, positioning himself and his old peers as smarter and more authentic than the men in the image, distancing himself and his peers from the media images.

Not all men resisted the portrayals of the old men in the TUI commercial, however. Several of the men in the focus group who were under 75 understood the images as positive and expressed identification with the images: "But if they styled us a bit, and gave us some trendy clothes. ... We'd all fit in that image too." They expressed feeling included by the campaign as they themselves were travelling in retirement, although they claimed to have more interest in other forms of travel than going to the beach. They could see themselves in the photos, as people who enjoyed the freedom after retirement to travel with friends and who had both the financial resources and the time to do so. As such, they themselves identified as the "gold in grey", so-called third agers, appealed to in commercial contexts.

The discussions that emerged around the TUI commercial suggest that new scripts on ageing masculinity, which emphasise health, activity and a lack of disabilities, are not necessarily experienced as positive by old men. Although the participants were in many ways following dominant cultural scripts of positive ageing by being socially active, they did not feel hailed by the advertising since it made embodied ageing invisible, something which they experienced as central to growing old. The men's resistance to the images could also be understood as a way of resisting not only the ideals of youthful ageing but also the ideals of youthful masculinities, characterised by strength, stamina, health and vigour. As 81-year-old Nisse laughingly said: "These are work-out fanatics – far from who I am." While the men sometimes expressed their resistance using scornful words, the commercial was also negotiated through humour and laughter. This is, for example, seen in a witty conversation between Peter and Roger.

Peter: 'I seriously doubt I would fit into that image.' [laughs]
Roger: 'You could always hide behind the surfboard.'
               [group laughter]
Peter: 'I think I would be visible still.' [laughs]

In terms of the visibility and invisibility of old men, the focus group discussions suggest that although the adverts may contribute to a new visibility of old men in the media, they may still contribute to a sense of invisibility among old men themselves, since embodied ageing is overlooked.

"I don't think men in our generation use skin care products" – "well, I do!": negotiations of gender and ageing appearance

Overall, most of the participants expressed a dislike for the adverts and commercials, but the commercial for a chain of grocery stores was noted by several as the kind of commercial they appreciated and would enjoy watching: "One stays in the room instead of sneaking out for a cigarette or coffee." The commercial featuring Stig, the manager of a supermarket, who is concerned about his wrinkles, was one that brought both laughter and appreciation. In the focus group with the youngest old – aged 65 to 72 – it spurred a lively discussion on the use of skin cream, which revealed negotiations of cultural scripts of ageing and the gendered appearance of old men.

Peter started sharing his interpretation of the commercial saying that the humour partly lay in the reversed roles and the absurdity of an old man being concerned with his looks, since it is generally women who, in his opinion, are more anxious about their ageing appearance and therefore use anti-ageing creams. Per-Erik, aged 65, responded and pointed to how expectations about old men have changed in their lifetime. Signs of ageing are increasingly understood as a concern also for men:

'It's totally different from ten years ago. And if you go even further back it was even more unusual that a man used any kind of skin cream. But now it's soon 50/50 I suspect. Not that there is anything wrong with it, that's not what I mean, but it's become that men's ageing is somehow more talked about than it was before. Earlier I think that [being] an old man was associated with authority.'

The others in the group concurred, and Peter added that the old saying used to be that "men age with dignity". Nils in turn said: "Men are like red wine of the better vintage, they mature with age." These quotations point to the identification of a shift in the cultural scripts of the old man where he, according to the interviewees, previously gained status from his age. Looks have become increasingly significant for men as they age and in the shaping of contemporary masculinity. Notably, by interjecting, "Not that there is anything wrong with it" when discussing an increasing focus on appearance among old men, Per-Erik positioned himself as in favour of these changing cultural scripts, and as open-minded.

The reasons for the changes in attitude towards bodily appearance work were discussed as having to do with advertising: "Perhaps because we [men] have been persuaded by all these commercials." But the changes were mainly linked to changing cultural scripts on masculinity and towards increasing gender equality among men and women. To exemplify the change, Per-Erik compared old men today to his father and said that for him it was "mostly about working", while men today think more about the signs of ageing.

Changing masculinities and changing gendered practices among men are clearly presented as positive and signs of progress. Rather than considering an old man's concern with his looks as something unmanly or ridiculous, the interviewees linked it with a wider gender equality discourse and progressive changes in masculinity. It is significant also that men's increasing concern for their appearance is described with the term "brave", often connoted with men and masculinity. A similar feeling was raised in another focus group where the men discussed household chores, claiming the gendered contract had changed and that it was no longer frowned upon if men and women shared the load – whereas earlier, one would have risked being seen as 'henpecked'. Instead, the men came across as rather proud when saying they in fact did most of the work around the home.

These articulations must be understood and analysed in relation to the Swedish context where alignment with gender equality discourses may be considered central to shaping one's self as a desirable/good man, and perhaps even a contextually specific hegemonic masculinity (Gottzén and Jonsson, 2012; Hearn et al, 2012). These kinds of arguments in turn become a form of identity work, which enable the old men to position themselves, not as backward old men, but as a new generation of old men who are different from previous generations.

However, although the men in this focus group showed their support for new and more gender equal forms of masculinity, which included a greater focus on appearance, there were some disagreements on the actual use of facial creams among men their age.

Peter:	'Well, still I don't think men in our generation use skin care products, I don't have a cream that I put on. But among younger generations. … But I don't think among us, I don't know if any of you use any moisturisers or things like that.'
Nils:	'Well, I do.'
Per-Erik:	'Me too, occasionally.'

The men who used skin care products talked of it mainly in terms of comfort and feeling, not in terms of looks, suggesting that discussing one's ageing appearance was not uncomplicated, and that there were subtle limits to the kind of interest one may show in skin care. The discussion seemed to suggest that there are several cultural scripts on gender and ageing appearance at work in old men's lives, where it is both unthinkable and possible for an old man to use, and admit using, skin care products.

The character Stig in one of the commercials is a clear example of the laughable old man character, as discussed by Ylänne (2015) and Röber (2020), a figure that could potentially function to subvert social norms, while reinstating the old man as a source of ridicule. The very fact that old men's appearance and concern with wrinkles can be joked about in a commercial could be interpreted as a sign of the topic not being sensitive, in contrast to adverts targeting women where ageing skin and looks are represented as a serious topic requiring both disciplining work and products (Lövgren, 2009; see also Chapter 7). The fact that this topic is joked about in the data may also provide possibilities for contestation and negotiations of cultural scripts.

"A young woman molesting a man who looks so old": resisting and negotiating images of the sexually undesirable old man

In the focus group discussions, there was not one but many different interpretations of the adverts shown, which point to the polysemic nature of media texts. This was most visible in the discussions of the Nicorette commercial presented at the beginning of this chapter. This was understood as both ageist and inappropriate, and, by some, as funny. Moreover, in one of the focus groups, it stimulated quite a discussion on the double standards around sexuality depending on age and gender.

Erland, Ivar and Östen took turns to express their dislike and repudiation of the Nicorette advert, and how it presented what they understood as an assault on an old man, with the age-inappropriate sexual encounter between a younger woman and an old man.

Erland:	'It's vulgar.'
Ivar:	[chuckles]
Erland:	'I would be shocked.'
Ivar:	'Yes … extremely odd.' [laughter]
Östen:	'A young woman molesting a man who looks so old.'
Ivar:	'An 80-year-old chap.'
Östen:	'… and frail looking too. Yes, it is somewhat aggressive.'
Erland:	'It should have been a young guy. A young guy should have been sitting there, that would have been more normal.'

The rejection of the commercial is not explicitly done based on its ageism, yet the words used in the dialogue presented here clearly suggest that the men understood the commercial as negative and an offensive portrayal of an old man (see Robinson and Popovich, 2003). The discussion pointed to how the participants reacted to the kiss of the man as derogatory, but also to gendered aspects of appropriate age differences in sexual encounters. Peter, in another focus group, was explicitly critical towards the message and how it degraded the old man: "So what she wanted was the chewing gum, not you. So it's kind of funny, but still it's sort of degrading ageing also."

Whereas Peter pointed out the ageist use of humour to conceal the humiliating dimension of the event, some interviewees did not pick up on the ageism in the commercial. Instead, they considered it only as funny and positive (although a not very credible) commercial: "there is no suffering in this image" and that receiving a kiss must have been "pleasant for the old man too". Perhaps the different interpretations about whether the man was assaulted or received an enjoyable kiss depend on whether the focus of the viewers was on age or masculinity. Whereas some saw an asymmetrical relationship in terms of age, others saw a heterosexual encounter – a man receiving a kiss by a woman. Since constructions of masculinity are closely intertwined with sexuality, and men are assumed to always desire sexual contact, this may allow for the latter reading (Sandberg, 2011). The cultural script at play here seems to be that an old man can never be a victim of sexual assault, since he is always willing.

However, a humorous discussion emerged in one group on sexual harassment and double standards regarding gender and sexuality. It started with Karl stating that the episode in the advert could be seen as a case of sexual harassment.

Karl: 'Well. I'm thinking in terms of #MeToo, if one should report her [the woman in the commercial] [everyone laughs]. If this was a guy doing what she's doing, he'd been in real trouble. But now he surely approved.'

The men seemed to negotiate the double standards where an old man's sexual approaches are viewed negatively as either offensive or ridiculous, in contrast with those of younger women. The figure of 'the dirty old man', inappropriately sexual for his age, seems to linger here as a stereotype that the old man must relate to and resist (Sandberg, 2011). The resistance to the double standards and the negative associations of old men's sexualities led to subsequent discussions of #MeToo, why there had been no calls from men on sexual harassment, and that they had not witnessed sexual harassment against women in their working life. In contrast to the earlier discussion, where men actively sided with gender equality discourses and positioned themselves as a new and more gender equal generation, the discussions on #MeToo rather called this movement into question, with the men disassociating themselves from feminist claims. That the discussion and challenge of #MeToo followed the watching of the Nicorette commercial could be interpreted as a form of resistance to the negative portrayal of the old man and a wider negative depiction of men's sexualities.

Conclusion: masculinity and ageing, mirrors and cultural scripts

Although old people are very frequently absent in the media and old men rarely figure in advertising, in contrast to younger men, there is some variability in how old men are depicted, both in negative terms as passive, sexually undesirable and ridiculous, and more positively as healthy, happy third agers. In this chapter, we have explored how old men themselves respond to advertising that displays different stereotypes of old men. Using advertising in focus group discussions is a creative method to prompt, discuss and elucidate, in this case, old men's understandings, and cultural scripts of age and ageing.

The method employed in this study provides a platform to discuss various commonplace ways in which age, ageing and old men are represented, eliciting different forms of data, compared with, say, one-to-one interviews or extended social surveys. This method is visual, oral and social, involving debate and negotiation between participants. There were discussions of different interpretations of the adverts, and the relaying of other experiences pertaining to ageing, sharing thoughts and reflections – often with a tentative and exploratory attitude. Several said they had not previously reflected on being male, and even less on ageing. The interviews thus provided an opportunity to explore different aspects of this, together with others, and with two interested researchers, providing a means of access to cultural scripts of ageing, old men and masculinities that are not always self-evident.

The relative lack of representations of being an old man means an absence of representations in relation to or against which old men, and others, can reflect themselves. Some interpretations by the men involved resisting the limited images that do exist, along with what the images and narratives convey, in that they did not capture how they experience their own situation. This mirrors the research literature on men doing masculinity by resistance, by *not* being something, rather than embracing something willingly and positively (Wetherell and Edley, 1999). Such rather less than positive narratives may also be steps towards new, incipient or emerging ways (see Inhorn, 2012) of being old men and doing ageing masculinities.

The absence of depictions through which to mirror oneself, compare with, renounce, dissociate from or recognise oneself in, means a loss of a potentially powerful cultural resource. Media and fictional depictions can be understood as a metaphorical cultural 'larder' with narratives and discourses that contribute to understanding oneself and one's life situation, but also to understanding others. They also provide visibility and intelligibility on a wider societal level. What is it like to age? What is it like to be in one's 80s? What is old age like? And for a man? The men testified to feeling at a loss here. There were few, if any, narratives that *centred* on old men – other than as a person to be made fun of. This absence can also entail being more alone, and perhaps lonely, with a lack of cultural resources for understanding and reflecting on oneself. The oldest men struggled with talking about being old, which was at times described as quite awful. Talking about the negative aspects of ageing and being afraid of coming across as negative or bitter seemed taboo to communicate. Perhaps the men also felt there was an indifference and lack of concern from those around them.

Another way of understanding the absence of depictions of ageing as a man can be to see this as a certain freedom – freedom of movement and liberty of action. Men's ageing is not co-constructed with fertility and reproduction, unlike for women, assigned to an older age category already in their 50s, with menopause as a transitional marker. Signs of ageing are not made hypervisible, or even as problematic or stigmatising for men. Importantly, the cultural interpretations of putative ageing signs, in the focus groups, were made from a point of status and privilege. Men are the unmarked, privileged gender. Men's ageing is invisible in mediated representations, both freeing men from being disregarded as belonging to an old age category, but also depriving old men from a resource in doing age.

Note
[1]   The primary objective of this project is to analyse social constructions of ageing masculinities and/through their cultural representations in contemporary European literatures and cinemas (see https://www.mascage.eu).

References

Allen, L. (2005) 'Managing masculinity: young men's identity work in focus groups', *Qualitative Research*, 5(1): 35–57.

Braun, V. and Clarke, V. (2006) 'Using thematic analysis in psychology', *Qualitative Research in Psychology*, 3(2): 77–101.

Calasanti, T. and King, N. (2005) 'Firming the floppy penis: age, class, and gender relations in the lives of old men', *Men and Masculinities*, 8(1): 3–23.

Craig, S. (ed) (1992) *Men, Masculinity and the Media*, Newbury Park, CA: Sage.

Edström, M. (2018) 'Visibility patterns of gendered ageism in the media buzz: a study of the representation of gender and age over three decades', *Feminist Media Studies*, 18(1): 77–93.

Edwards, T. (2004) *Cultures of Masculinity*, London: Routledge.

Fennell, G. and Davidson, K. (2003) 'The invisible man? Older men in modern society', *Ageing International*, 28(4): 315–25.

Fleming, A.A. (1999) 'Older men in contemporary discourses on ageing: absent bodies and invisible lives', *Nursing Inquiry*, 6(1): 3–8.

Gottzén, L. and Jonsson, R. (2012) *Andra Män: Maskulinitet, Normskapande och Jämställdhet* [Other Men: Masculinity, Normativity and Gender Equality], Malmö: Gleerups.

Hearn, J. (1995) 'Imaging the aging of men', in M. Featherstone and A. Wernick (eds) *Images of Aging: Cultural Representations of Later Life*, London: Routledge, pp 97–115.

Hearn, J., Nordberg, M., Andersson, K., Balkmar, D., Gottzén, L., Klinth, R., Pringle, K. and Sandberg, L. (2012) 'Hegemonic masculinity and beyond: 40 years of research in Sweden', *Men and Masculinities*, 15(1): 31–55.

Hearn, J. and Sandberg, L. (2009) 'Older men, ageing and power: masculinities theory and alternative spatialised theoretical perspectives', *Sextant: Revue du Groupe Interdisciplinaire D'Etudes sur les Femmes et le Genre* [Sextant: Review of interdisciplinary studies on women and gender], 27: 147–63.

Hummert, M.L., Garstka, T., Shaner, J.L. and Strahm, S. (1994) 'Stereotypes of the elderly held by young, middle-aged and elderly adults', *Journal of Gerontology: Psychological Sciences*, 49(5): 240–9.

Hurd Clarke, L., Bennett, E.V. and Liu, C. (2014) 'Aging and masculinity: portrayals in men's magazines', *Journal of Aging Studies*, 31: 26–33.

Inhorn, M. (2012) *The New Arab Man: Emergent Masculinities, Technologies, and Islam in the Middle East*, Princeton, NJ: Princeton University Press.

Lövgren, K. (2009) '"Se Lika Ung ut som Du Känner Dig": Kulturella Föreställningar om Ålder och Åldrande i Populärpress för Kvinnor över 40' ["Look as Young as You Feel": Cultural Conceptions of Age and Ageing in Popular Press Aimed at Women over 40'], PhD Thesis, Linköping University.

Lövgren, K. (ed) (2016) *Att Konstruera en Kvinna: Berättelser om Normer, Flickor och Tanter* [Constructing a Woman: Narratives on Norms, Girls and Little Old Ladies], Lund: Nordic Academic Press.

Pietilä, I., Calasanti, T., Ojala, H. and King, N. (2020) 'Is retirement a crisis for men? Class and adjustment to retirement', *Men and Masculinities*, 23(2): 306–25.

Rennstam, J. and Wästerfors, D. (2015/2018) *Analyze! Crafting Your Data in Qualitative Research*, Lund: Studentlitteratur.

Richardson, N. and Wearing, S. (2014) *Gender in the Media*, Basingstoke: Palgrave Macmillan.

Röber, F. (2020) 'Laughable old men: conceptions of ageing masculinities in the Britcom', *Anglistik: International Journal of English Studies*, 31(2): 153–69.

Robinson, T. and Popovich, M. (2003) 'Older adults' perceptions of offensive senior stereotypes in magazine advertisements: results of a Q method analysis', *Educational Gerontology*, 29(6): 503–19.

Sandberg, L. (2007) 'Ancient monuments, mature men and those popping amphetamine: researching the lives of older men', *NORMA: Nordic Journal of Masculinity Studies*, 2(2): 86–108.

Sandberg, L. (2011) *Getting Intimate: A Feminist Analysis of Old Age, Masculinity and Sexuality,* Linköping: Linköping University Electronic Press.

Spector-Mersel, G. (2006) 'Never-aging stories: Western hegemonic masculinity scripts', *Journal of Gender Studies*, 15(1): 67–82.

Thompson, E.H. (ed) (1994) *Older Men's Lives*, Thousand Oaks, CA: Sage.

Thompson, E.H. (2019) *Men, Masculinities, and Aging: The Gendered Lives of Older Men*, Lanham, MD: Rowman & Littlefield.

Tuchman, G. (1978) 'Introduction: the symbolic annihilation of women in the mass media', in G. Tuchman, A.K. Daniels and J. Benet (eds) *Hearth and Home: Images of Women in the Mass Media*, New York, NY: Oxford University Press, pp 3–38.

Twigg, J. (2013) *Fashion and Age: Dress, the Body and Later Life*, London: Bloomsbury Academic.

Wernick, A. (1987) 'From voyeur to narcissist: imagining men in contemporary advertising', in M. Kaufman (ed) *Beyond Patriarchy*, Toronto: Oxford University Press, pp 277–97.

Wetherell, M. and Edley, N. (1999) 'Negotiating hegemonic masculinity: imaginary positions and psycho-discursive practices', *Feminism & Psychology*, 9(3): 335–56.

Wilkinson, S. (1998) 'Focus groups in feminist research: power, interaction, and the co-construction of meaning', *Women's Studies International Forum*, 21(1): 111–25.

Williams, A.M., Wadleigh, P.M. and Ylänne, V. (2010) 'Images of older people in UK magazine advertising: toward a typology', *International Journal of Aging and Human Development*, 71(2): 83–114.

Ylänne, V. (ed) (2012) *Representing Ageing: Images and Identities*, Basingstoke: Palgrave Macmillan.

Ylänne, V. (2015) 'Representations of ageing in the media', in J. Twigg and W. Martin (eds) *Routledge Handbook of Cultural Gerontology*, London: Routledge, pp 369–76.

Ylänne, V., Williams, A. and Wadleigh, P.M. (2009) 'Ageing well? Older people's health and well-being as portrayed in UK magazine advertisements', *International Journal of Ageing and Later Life*, 4(2): 33–62.

11

Older women and women's magazines: audience, agency and the lifecourse

Dana Sawchuk

Introduction

Women's magazines are closely targeted to specific age groups, whether this fact is publicly disclosed by magazine publishers or not (Twigg, 2013; Jenkins, 2020). Fashion and beauty 'glossies' tend to be directed to women in their 20s and 30s, whereas the more traditional women's lifestyle or homemaking magazines are targeted to women up to their mid-50s (Mahrt, 2012). In some countries, such as Sweden, older age is used as a selling point for certain women's magazines (Lövgren, 2012).

In Canada, there is no such magazine for older women, even though the country's older population is disproportionately female (Hudon and Milan, 2016), magazines are very popular in the country overall (Vividata, 2020) and print magazine readership is highest among adults over the age of 55 (Vividata, 2021). There, the only widely circulating magazine explicitly targeted to an older demographic is *Zoomer* magazine, which is aimed at both women and men. Much more popular than *Zoomer*, however, are the Canadian-published women's titles *Chatelaine* and *Canadian Living*, which rank among the top ten in print readership of all magazines in the country (Vividata, 2021). Advertising guides indicate that *Chatelaine*'s audience is women aged '18+' (Rogers Publishing, 2020), while *Canadian Living* represents its readers as women over the age of 35 (Québecor, 2021). Consistent with nationwide data on print magazine readership, however, the actual readers of these two publications are somewhat older: nearly half are over the age of 55 and over a quarter are over the age of 65 (Vividata, 2021). Beyond these publications, US titles such as *Cosmopolitan*, *Women's World* and *O (The Oprah Magazine)* are also widely read (Magazines Canada, 2016).

Within this context, this chapter discusses the reading of women's magazines in general among a sample of 21 Canadian women over the age of 55. Using an audience-centred approach, this study explores how these participants cast themselves as part of the readership of such magazines, which by the women's own assertion appear to exclude them from their target audience. As we shall see, the women negotiate the apparent tensions inherent in enjoying magazines that are not 'meant for' them by emphasising their selective and creative consumption of magazine material. They further ascribe value to ostensibly irrelevant magazine content by offering a lifecourse-based rationale for its deeper meaning to them. By exercising their agency as readers and revealing how a broader understanding of their lives is the basis for judging the relevance of magazine material, the participants demonstrate their control over defining whether and how women's magazines are suitable for them to read. In doing so, they challenge narrow age-based conceptions of target audience in the publications and prompt us to reconsider other elements of the relationship between women, ageing and magazines.

Theoretical orientation and previous research

In broad terms, the analysis in this chapter is inspired by and aims to contribute to what is known as audience (or audience reception) research in popular media studies (for a concise history see Livingstone, 1998). In relation to women's magazines, this approach differs from those of analysts who primarily shed light on the producers (publishers, editors, advertisers) of these periodicals (for example, Gough-Yates, 2003) and from those who conduct content analyses of their pages (for example, Brown and Knight, 2015). Instead, here readers and *their* interpretations of women's magazines are foregrounded. The pioneering work of Hermes (1995) in this vein most radically asserted that women's magazines 'become meaningful exclusively through the perception of their readers' (p 6) as they employ interpretive repertoires that facilitate fantasies of their ideal selves. However, this chapter more closely follows in the footsteps of Ytre-Arne (2014), who underscores the agency of readers as they reflect, often critically, on magazine content in relation to their identities and daily realities. In addition, Ytre-Arne's (2011) and Aronson's (2010) acknowledgement that the textual structures of the magazines themselves can facilitate and interact with certain reading strategies also becomes relevant in the exploration of reader agency.

In terms of women's magazines and ageing, one could apply this audience-centred approach by asking older women themselves how they use such magazines and what they think of representations of ageing in the publications, a topic explored elsewhere in relation to the larger study on which this chapter is based (Sawchuk and Ly, 2020). Here, however, the focus is on older readers' interpretation of the 'target audience' of women's magazines. Indeed, the topic of to whom women's magazines are targeted has been broached before and predominantly from the production side by Lövgren (2012) and Twigg (2012, 2013). In Twigg's work, the important concept of 'age slippage' in women's magazines is introduced. This is the notion that magazine professionals frequently describe the target audience as younger than the age profile of the actual readership. Twigg explains that such slippage, which reflects and reinforces an ageist cultural context, often manifests in the younger visual world depicted in magazines aimed at older women, which in turn allows the reader 'to identify with a younger, generally more successful self' (Twigg, 2013, p 106). The question from the perspective of the audience – and the one with which this chapter is centrally concerned – then becomes whether readers recognise age slippage in the more general women's magazines they read and, if so, how they negotiate the apparent mismatch between what they see and read and how old or who they are.

In exploring readers' positions on these questions, this chapter draws on a set of assumptions commonly associated with lifecourse theory, which encourages us to take a broader and deeper view of older women's lives in relation to the magazines they read. Instead of concentrating on static points or isolated stages in individuals' lives, lifecourse theorists try to understand the contextualised span of such lives, with their constituent trajectories, transitions and turning points (Elder et al, 2003). Hence, lifecourse theorists acknowledge not only the present but also the past, along with the potential variability of life journeys in between (Fry, 2003). This perspective further incorporates the notion of 'linked lives', which emphasises that 'human lives are typically embedded in social relationships with kin and friends across the life span' (Elder, 1994, p 6). Significantly, lifecourse principles can be fruitfully applied to media studies as well (for example, Harrington and Bielby, 2010). As we shall see, the assertion of Policarpo (2013) that it is the family lifecourse that gives women 'specific interpretive frameworks to face the media product' (p 26) becomes particularly salient.

Methods

This chapter is based on a larger research project on older Canadian women and ageing-related themes in women's magazines. Participant recruitment took place in mid-sized cities and smaller towns in a southwestern region in the province of Ontario, Canada. After university research ethics board approval was secured, fliers advertising the study were circulated to members of a retired women's social club and were placed in a variety of libraries, community centres, bookstores, cafes and senior centres. Adverts were also placed in local newspapers and on the email listserv of a local service organisation for older adults. A small number of women were also referred to the study by friends who had participated. The starting point for participation was set at age 55, the approximate age of the youngest post-war 'baby boomers' in Canada at the time of the study.

A total of 21 women (all White), ranging in age from 57 to 78, were interviewed. Most participants were retired, but their occupational and educational profiles indicated generally middle-class backgrounds, with some working-class participants as well. Slightly fewer than half of the women were married, with most others being widowed, separated or divorced. One woman had never married, and information on sexual orientation was not collected nor directly disclosed. All the women consented in writing to participate in the study, received a coffee shop gift card in exchange for their time and input, and were asked to choose their own pseudonyms. These pseudonyms are used in this chapter, except in the cases of inadvertent conflict with another participant's actual name (in which case other pseudonyms are adopted).

The semi-structured interviews were digitally recorded, with most lasting between 60 and 80 minutes. The women were interviewed in public spaces, such as cafes or libraries, in the author's university office or in their own homes. The sessions began with preliminary demographic questions and an attempt to generate a list of women's magazines each woman read. In order, the most commonly mentioned titles were *Chatelaine*, *Canadian Living*, *Woman's Day*, *O, The Oprah Magazine*, *Redbook* and *Good Housekeeping*. The remaining interview questions were grouped into two categories: general questions about the role(s) that women's magazines played in participants' lives (questions probing when, how and why they read these publications); and more specific questions about the ageing-related content of such magazines. The material in this chapter draws primarily on the women's answers to the questions in this latter category, which included queries about the age or age range to which the participants felt the magazines they read were targeted, and whether or how this perceived age range affected their willingness to read the publications. A research assistant and the author analysed the transcribed interviews in line with Braun and Clarke's (2006) thematic content analysis approach, to arrive at the three themes discussed next: identifying age slippage as exclusion; picking, choosing and changing content; and lifecourse relevance.

Findings

Identifying age slippage as exclusion

Most participants interviewed were keenly aware of the age slippage (Twigg, 2012, 2013) in the women's magazines they read. They based such assessments on the ages, life stages and lifestyles that were featured – or not – in the publications. Given this content, they concluded that they were largely excluded from the magazines' intended target audience.

When asked to comment on the age of women to which they felt the magazines were targeted, almost all the participants indicated that the magazines were meant for younger – and frequently much younger – women. While sometimes interviewees made distinctions between magazines, overall they cited an age range for the magazines anywhere from ten years to several decades younger than they were themselves. Interview participants frequently referred to the content of adverts or the style of fashion, hair or make-up worn by young models to support their assertions. Tanya (aged 65), for example, corroborated her assessment that most women's magazines were targeted to women in their 20s and 30s by explaining: "A lot of it is visual. The models are all 18-year-olds who weigh a hundred pounds. All the cosmetic ads. Basically, every woman's face in the magazine is under 40. It is just really obvious." Sometimes participants could not or did not want to pinpoint exact ages when asked. In response, however, and unprompted during other points in the interviews, they would frequently refer to the magazines as being oriented to the "younger generation" or a "younger age group".

The participants' interpretation that they were not included in the age range targeted by the women's magazines was reinforced by their observations that women of their own age were under-represented in the publications. Several participants noted that older women were "invisible" or "lost" in the pages of the magazines, but Connie (aged 61) was more blunt when she said that "it's like [older women] drop off the edge of the world". When older women were depicted in photos or featured in stories, the representation was still characterised as inadequate. As Beyoncé (aged 64) explained:

'Let's put it that way: if they're older adults, like they're never as old as my age group. Now when they're saying older adults, at maximum they're probably 55 or something like that. I would say that's probably the oldest they show, and they say this is for older people. In that way they would not, I would think, feature a 70-year-old model or 75.'

Reader (aged 68) also alluded to inadequate tokenism when she declared that "they are zeroing in and they are targeting [a younger age group] and then they are saying 'okay, if an old girl picks up this magazine, what would she like to read, and so we'll give her something that might appeal to her, but we're really targeting this [other] particular age group'". Finally, other women talked about individuals' erasure through the problematic "lumping" of older women into overly broad categories, noting that younger women were discussed in terms of decades (being in their "20s" or "30s") but everyone over the age of 50 or 60 was treated the same, with indistinguishable beauty, fashion or health concerns (compare Twigg, 2012, p 137).

Interestingly, the sense of not being the focus of attention was linked to broader historical trends by Laura (aged 62). She reflected that, for women of the baby-boom generation like herself, such marginalisation was a relatively new and jolting experience. She explained how she had grown accustomed, as part of this large and influential generation, to being the centre of popular culture attention for so long. Now, in these magazines, that was no longer the case as she felt that the concerns of her generation were largely pushed to the periphery.

In fact, participants frequently noted that the magazines' content often did not address their current life stages or lifestyles at all. They observed, for example, that the magazines appeared to be geared to working women with children still at home. As Pokey (aged 67) summarised: "They're women who are ... producing children, being mothers, being career women, being married, being single, being divorced, having more disposable income than a senior woman would". Some women complained that the typical recipes featured were not useful to them because they emphasised cooking the quantity or style of food more suited to a family with young children, as opposed to one or two older adults living alone. Along with the emphasis on younger families, some noted that grandparents were not depicted. As Kaydee (aged 62) explained:

'They'll talk about families. ... You know, people that are in their 40s or 30s, married with children. Ok, they're not talking about grandparents. ... You don't see this whole family with the grandparents and it focusing on the grandparents and the things that they're going through with their kids and the grandkids.'

In terms of other relationships, a couple of women mentioned that the concerns of older single women, including widows, were not addressed or that the articles on sex in the magazines were also not intended for older readers such as themselves. As Tanya reiterated: "It's younger women, and their love life, sex ... some parenting, career issues, money managing issues. It seems all geared to younger women."

In all these ways, age slippage was identified in women's magazines and lamented or criticised as exclusionary. Nonetheless, the participants' recognition of their marginalisation in the magazines did not seem to dampen their enthusiasm for reading the publications, as in other parts of their interviews the women frequently spoke of how entertaining or useful they were. Sometimes women even commented on the apparent contradiction between their critique of this exclusion and their enjoyment of the magazines. The next two subsections below therefore explore the ways in which the women appeared to reconcile these potentially contradictory opinions. They demonstrate how the matter of inclusion or exclusion from a magazine's audience rests not in the content of such magazines but rather in the readers' practices and perspectives in relation to that content.

Picking, choosing and changing content

Although they stated that the magazines they read appeared to exclude women of their own age or life stage, participants were adamant about the fact that they, as readers, were in control of the reading experience. Here, there was a sense of defiance and agency in the way several women addressed such ostensible contradictions and emphasised that they were the ones who defined whether and how they fit into the magazines' audience.

Some participants stressed that it was their choice whether to read the magazines in the first place. Virago (aged 70), for example, labelled the mismatch between her own age and what she interpreted as the targeted age of fashion magazines a "dissonance." As she reflected:

'See, I don't mind the dissonance. That's my privilege. In fact, that is what I should be doing, is having a dissonance. And continuous dissonance. And I didn't have it back in the 70s and 80s because I saw myself on the pages ... and then I disappear[ed] off the pages.'

When asked to elaborate on the notion of privilege, she replied: "I have the privilege of not reading that magazine if I don't want to." Indeed, other participants pointed out that, while they generally enjoyed women's magazines, they no longer read or refused to read those titles (such as *Cosmopolitan*) they saw as targeted to much younger women.

In reference to the women's magazines they did read, however, participants frequently referred to their selective reading practices. As Matilda (aged 68) declared, after reflecting on the practices of age categorisation that "lump together" all women over the age of 50 in magazines, "I don't take offence. I don't really care because I think I'm not their target market anyway. I think the target market is, say, 30 to 50 and I'm okay with that." When asked if that age-specific character of the magazines detracted from her enjoyment of the publications, she clarified: "Not really. Yeah, I dip in and get what I want out of it." This sense of 'dipping in' and extracting what they considered to be appropriate material was common among the women, who frequently talked about how they would "pick and choose" appropriate content while reading, even if, as Pokey commented, finding material explicitly geared to their age group was akin to "mining for gold".

To be clear, and as is discussed later in this chapter, much of the women's conversation about what they found useful in the women's magazines was not framed in terms of their current age. Indeed, they generally did not cite the magazines as sources of information on how to age 'well' and were often critical of how ageing-related matters were treated in the publications (for a fuller discussion, see Sawchuk and Ly, 2020). Thus, while some women searched keenly for the few models of a similar age when seeking inspiration for how to dress, other women ignored or explicitly rejected the publications' ostensibly age-appropriate advice, indicating they did not want to be told what to do. In contrast to those participants who appeared to navigate the magazines by 'mining' for material in an age-conscious way, other women portrayed their reading as more age neutral. As Sparkles (aged 64) explained: "When I pick up a magazine, I'm just looking for ideas and I don't think of, 'I'm looking for 63-year-old ideas'." Finally, and in contrast to the women who did not read *Cosmopolitan* because it was perceived as targeted to much younger women, Connie commented that she read *Teen Vogue*, particularly zeroing in on its political content. Hence, whether seeking out information on the basis of age, or wilfully ignoring the magazine's age-related prescriptions, most participants emphasised their selective reading practices.

Finally, some women went beyond selective reading to interpret or even physically modify magazine contents. Virago, for example, explained how she consciously ignored the faces of models in magazines and focused on the fashion, which she then interpreted for her "70-year-old self" by putting "her own spin on it". As she said: "So yeah, I'm choosy, I'm picky, yeah. And right now, I am happy with my [magazine] selections because I can interpret them." Lady Di (aged 60) had even manually edited the headline of one article we came across while sorting through her clippings collection during her interview. The article was originally entitled: '10 easy tips to keep you looking young forever'. However, she had crossed out 'looking young' and written in 'healthy' instead, in effect distancing herself from the age-related framing of the material. Overall, then, participants stressed that what the women's magazines were doing was less important than what *they themselves* were doing with the magazines. In the words of Reader, who was 68 years old but who estimated that the magazines she read were targeted to women in their 30s and 40s:

'I think that [age range is] what they're targeting but that's not why I read them. ... I'm going to take from the magazine what I want. I mean, who they're targeting or what they're doing is immaterial for me. I mean, I just know I like magazines, so, you know, these magazines fulfil my needs.'

In these passages, the sense of exclusion previously reported by the women when asked to describe the magazines' target audiences is countered by the agency revealed in their selective reading and interpretive practices. Indeed, the eclectic nature of the magazines' content itself facilitates such selectivity. As Aronson (2010) argues, women's magazines are an inherently mixed and polyphonous form, and this polyvocality itself opens up possibilities for women's creative agency to 'navigate media texts actively and in ways that serve their own needs, interests and pleasures' (p 36). Clearly, and whether they do so in an age-conscious or age-agnostic way, several participants do leverage the polyvocality of the text to meet their needs. Through such agentic practices, they are challenging the target age implied (and identified by the women themselves) by the magazines' tendency to focus on younger ages and earlier life stages than the participants themselves currently inhabit.

Lifecourse relevance

In the previous subsection, it was shown that participants emphasised their agency in choosing to read (or not) magazine material based on whether they saw it as including them (or not). Such connections to magazine content, however, were made in relatively narrow relation to their current and individual selves. In this final subsection of the findings, participants advance a broader lifecourse-based rationale as the means for asserting or judging the relevance of women's magazines to their lives.

Most often, the women referred to their own family-based lifecourse to make the point that women's magazines did remain relevant to them despite ostensibly skewing younger in target audience. Janet (aged 69), for example, took particular interest in content on domestic violence and divorce, because she too had lived through those scenarios. She liked biographical stories in magazines, even if they featured younger women, because "so many things I read have happened to me and I can relate to it, or like it makes me feel not alone because this has happened to me in the past". In some cases, participants with children commented on a connection to content featuring younger mothers. At age 78, Louise reported relating to stories that focus on women with young families, because they reminded her of things she used to do when her own children were young. Matilda also commented on how she could identify with such material because of the common "bond of motherhood" that women with children share. Finally, some participants took an even wider perspective on what they considered relevant in women's magazines. Lady Di, for example, found magazine articles covering everything from childhood through to grandparenthood attractive "because I was a kid once, and I'm going to be a grandmother in a couple of months. So all the stuff in between is, you know, familiar. And I think familiar is good." In this sense, as Sparkles expressed, these participants were making connections to magazine content pertaining to all stages in "the cycle of life", and not simply the stages they currently inhabited.

Such connections did not only pertain to readers' reminiscences of their past lives; several participants drew on their current roles as mothers or grandmothers to cast magazine material on children as relevant to their 'linked lives' (Elder, 1994). Lucy (aged 69), for example, surmised that women's magazines were primarily meant for women in their 30s, "with children that are still at home". When asked, in light of the fact that this was not her particular age group, if that affected her willingness to read the magazines, she responded: "Well, I still need them for my daughters, my grandchildren. So, it's all right. But it's not targeted at me, no. I still find them useful." Lucy was one of several participants who emphasised what they could learn from magazines. These participants reported that part of their motivation for reading women's magazines was so that they could pass on information, helpful articles and advice to their own children, particularly in relation to parenting. As Kaydee reported, she pays attention to magazine material on "children's issues, you know, raising children. I find those articles interesting because then I gain knowledge and then I can sort of support my daughter with her child." In some cases, participants talked about how the magazines helped inform them about contemporary trends or social issues, which in turn helped them better relate to the younger generations of their families. Moreover, some participants reported passing on or sharing the physical issues of women's magazines with their daughters, a final way in which the women used the publications to enhance intergenerational bonds. In all these ways, the women referred to their own family-based lifecourses and past and present linked lives to assert themselves as legitimately part of the audience for women's magazines.

Finally, and in contrast to participants' identification of age slippage and the framing of women's magazines as excluding older women by failing to represent them or address their interests, participants sometimes spoke as if *they* were the ones leaving the magazines behind as they aged. This assertion was often based on how they had changed over the course of their lifespan. Recall Laura (mentioned earlier), who observed that as a member of the baby-boom generation she was unaccustomed to being marginalised in popular culture. Interestingly, while on the one hand she felt excluded from the youth-focused content of the magazines, on the other she judged the contents as irrelevant when viewed from her own vantage point in life. As she commented, in women's magazines "there's a very heavy focus on certain stages of life, and I'm past those stages". Similarly, Connie explained that readers of her age "grow past" the magazines: "at a certain point you are not raising small children anymore, you got your cooking system down, you have different interests ... women change". Here, the magazines are criticised for not ageing, as Connie said, "along with their readership". Some participants went further and emphasised that the magazines' contents were unoriginal. Hence Pokey dismissively asserted that much of the content in magazines was not interesting because there was "nothing further [for her] to be learned about fashion, men, or make-up". Bunny (aged 76) similarly commented:

'So many of the women's magazines now, things that young women think they have discovered, we in my age group forgot! You know, like when everybody really got into composting it was like yeah, so what? I was composting when we were kids. So this is nothing new. Why are you bragging or trying to sell people on this?'

Seen through the lifecourse lens reflected in the participants' comments, the youth centredness of women's magazines is not as exclusionary of older women as it first appears. In some cases, material that appears unrelated to older female readers, when viewed from a fixed or narrow point of age or life stage, is rendered relevant when readers themselves view it from the perspective of their linked lives or broader lifespans. Moreover, the references to past lives are not always – or at least not simply – a matter of nostalgic identification with their younger selves. When participants judge the magazines for either not keeping up with them or for containing little that is new to them, they are also, as Twigg (2012) suggests, asserting their memories and experiences 'in the face of the cultural erosions of age' (p 140). By noting that they have already learned to cook, raise children or compost (first), they are underscoring that they are more in a position to discount the magazines' relevance to them than to be discounted as readers themselves.

Conclusion

The older readers of women's magazines in this study were aware that they were excluded from the target audience implied by the ages, life stages and lifestyles typically depicted in the publications. Nonetheless, they demonstrated how, through picking, dismissing or interpreting certain material, they still made the magazines serve their own needs. Such practices reinforce Ytre-Arne's (2014) finding that women consistently interpret and evaluate magazine content in relation to their own identities and personal experiences. In this case, too, the magazines were assessed as relevant or irrelevant to the readers *by* the readers through their own understanding of their lives. Further, they conceived of such lives not as individuals living alone in some sort of static present but rather as women linked to others, and often to their children, over the dynamic course of a lifespan.

Through their agentic reading and reinterpretation of magazine content, the women in this study cast themselves as legitimately included in the audience of ostensibly younger-focused magazines. The older readers themselves make the magazines relevant to their lives, in ways greater than the invisibility and exclusion of such women in their pages might suggest. To a certain extent, the readers are also reclaiming the power to exclude, by reassigning it to themselves as they choose to ignore certain content or portray themselves as having grown past it. Overall, the participants push back against overly narrow understandings of target audience, and of magazine audiences as conceptualised without considering the practices and opinions of the readers themselves.

A reader-centred approach to defining magazine audiences counterbalances the chronologist (Kohli, 1986) tendency to overemphasise specific age segments or cut-off points that Iversen and Wilińska (2020) argue is problematically reinforced in much media and ageing scholarship. Even the interview script of the current study asked participants to pinpoint a specific target age range for the magazines they read – one they readily identified but then proceeded to challenge. This reader-centred approach also contrasts with that of others in the broader magazine industry, including advertisers and the producers of market data reports, who operate largely on the basis of assumed differences between individuals inhabiting precisely defined chronological strata (Lövgren, 2012). As Bolin and Skogerbø (2013) argue, and the participants in this study confirm, age in media consumption is 'blurred' by a variety of social, familial and other interlinked background characteristics, which themselves may be in flux over the phases of the lifecourse (p 6). Of course, the recognition of how little of people's lives, interests or needs are determined by chronological age has long been one of the hallmarks of 'thinking like a gerontologist' (de Medeiros, 2018). But demonstrating the way in which this principle is expressed by older female magazine readers themselves, thereby broadening our understanding of the 'multiple audience' property (Moeran, 2006) of women's magazines, is one of the contributions of this chapter.

Still, reader age is not meaningless, particularly if we understand age as something other than a set point offering indelible clues as to what a reader is like – or what she will like in a magazine. The participants' insights invite us to reconsider other elements of the relationship between women, ageing and magazines. The women in this study, for example, suggest that evaluations of ageing-related material in women's magazines should not be restricted to focusing on aspirational portrayals of, or prescriptions for, ageing 'successfully' at the end of the lifecourse. Taking a broader and deeper view of women's lives also means that while age slippage and its associated ageism in women's magazines may be worthy of critique, they also do not eliminate the magazines as a cultural form that holds value for the older women who read them. Certainly, it can also be argued that all readers, regardless of age, leverage the polyvocality of women's magazines to serve themselves (Aronson, 2010). Nonetheless, the fact remains that the older women interviewed, most of whom were lifelong readers of such magazines, have had many years of practice to develop the reading and interpretive skills needed to engage with the magazines in such a way.

The emphasis on the readers' role in defining the audience membership, however, should not be interpreted to mean that their agency is completely unfettered. As Aronson (2010) notes, there are always hegemonic limits, often related to race or sexuality, to readers' interpretations. In terms of race, women's magazines in general are notorious for being relatively racially homogeneous (that is, White; see Hirsch and Cherubini, 2018), and the homogeneity of the participant sample for this study precludes commentary on ethnically or racially diverse readers' perspectives. In terms of the intersections of sexuality and age, the observations of Sandberg and Marshall (2017) on 'hetero-happiness' and generativity appear salient in relation to at least one study participant. Sandberg and Marshall assert that magazines privilege portrayals of 'coupledom', 'reproductive success' and 'happy intimacies with grandchildren,' as hallmark representations of successful ageing (p 3) (see also Chapter 9). While they argue that such normative representations limit the range of possible 'good' futures, I would argue that such portrayals similarly restrict the degree to which some readers can relate to the magazines based on their pasts. Hence, while many study participants underscored the relevance of women's magazines in their lives by referring to connections to past mothering (and present-day children and grandchildren), Susan (aged 66) simply could not forge such links. She referred more than once to how, having never married or had children, so much material in women's magazines was not geared to her. Certainly, like other participants, she exercised her agency in terms of which and how much of the magazines she chose to read. But, given her lifelong single and childless status, this particular family lifecourse-based rationale for the magazines' relevance to her life was less available to her than to others.

Further to the point on hegemonic limits, the deeply engrained ageism that particularly affects women in Western culture (Hatch, 2005) may also be at play in the participants' engagement with the magazines. Given a societal context in which youth is prized and privileged and old age is denigrated and devalued, it is certainly possible that the women are subject to internalised ageism – their critique and negotiation of the youth-centredness of women's magazines notwithstanding (Hurd Clarke, 2011). In this sense, declining to seek out ideas for oneself as a 63-year-old or wilfully ignoring advice for older women may not (only) be an expression of resistance to publishers' age framing. Such selective reading, instead of showing how the women are age neutral, may actually reveal how they are age *sensitive* and, as such, attempt to distance themselves from a culturally devalued status. More generally, simply reading (and saying that one reads) magazines recognised to be for younger women may be one way for the women to counter being seen or addressed as old (compare Twigg, 2012, pp 143–4). While this possibility was not probed directly during the interviews, in an ageist society there is certainly a strong motivation to associate oneself with a younger age category and reading women's magazines may be a means to do so.

Finally, there is another dimension of older women's magazine reading in such a sociocultural milieu. It was mentioned earlier how participants reported using magazines to learn about current fashions, social trends and parenting advice, and how staying 'in touch' in this way could be one way to strengthen bonds with younger family members. Elsewhere, the author has explored the participants' broader uses of women's magazines for information seeking (along with relaxation and enjoyment; Sawchuk and Ly, 2020). On one level, the readers' connections with women's magazine content, regardless of immediate individual or familial relevance, make sense given that they are still women, only older. But, accompanying magazine reading for personal purposes is often participants' leveraging of the information gleaned in order to position themselves as informed and knowledgeable, positioning all the more necessary *because* they are older (Sawchuk and Ly, 2020). When ageism means that their opinions and expertise are often dismissed, citing women's magazine content is one more way for older women to claim legitimacy in conversations and contexts from which they might otherwise be excluded.

This chapter began with the implication that, in light of the Canadian mediascape that lacks magazines specifically targeted to an older female demographic, older Canadian women read general women's magazines in the absence of magazines 'of their own'. The readers interviewed here, however, remind us that we should not assume older women are reading such magazines simply because they have no other choice. On the contrary, the women in this study show the extent to which they as readers do exercise their choices and, in so doing, ask us to reconsider for whom such magazines might be 'meant' after all.

Acknowledgements

I am grateful for the time and contributions of all study participants and for the research assistance of Mina Ly and Jasreen Pannu. For their insightful comments on an earlier draft of this chapter, I thank Virpi Ylänne, Karin Lövgren and Jo VanEvery. This research was supported by the Social Sciences and Humanities Research Council of Canada (file no. 430-2018-00150).

References

Aronson, A. (2010) 'Still reading women's magazines: reconsidering the tradition a half century after The Feminine Mystique', *American Journalism*, 27(4): 31–61.

Bolin, G. and Skogerbø, E. (2013) 'Age, generation and the media', *Northern Lights*, 11(1): 3–14.

Braun, V. and Clarke, V. (2006) 'Using thematic analysis in psychology', *Qualitative Research in Psychology*, 3(2): 77–101.

Brown, A. and Knight, T. (2015) 'Shifts in media images of women's appearance and social status from 1960 to 2010: a content analysis of beauty advertisements in two Australian magazines', *Journal of Aging Studies*, 35: 74–83.

De Medeiros, K. (2018) 'What can thinking like a gerontologist bring to bioethics?', *Hastings Center Report*, 48(S3): S10–S14.

Elder, G.H. Jr. (1994) 'Time, human agency, and social change: perspectives on the life course', *Social Psychology Quarterly*, 57(1): 4–15.

Elder, G.H. Jr., Johnson, M.K. and Crosnoe, R. (2003) 'The emergence and development of life course theory', in J.T. Mortimer and M.J. Shanahan (eds) *Handbook of the Life Course*, New York, NY: Kluwer Academic/ Plenum Publishers, pp 3–19.

Fry, C.L. (2003) 'The life course as a cultural construct', in R.A. Settersen Jr (ed) *Invitation to the Life Course: Toward New Understandings of Later Life*, Amityville, NY: Baywood, pp 269–94.

Gough-Yates, A. (2003) *Understanding Women's Magazines: Publishing, Markets and Readerships*, London and New York, NY: Routledge.

Harrington, C.L. and Bielby, D.D. (2010) 'A life course perspective on fandom', *International Journal of Cultural Studies*, 13(5): 429–50.

Hatch, L.R. (2005) 'Gender and ageism', *Generations*, 29(3): 19–24.

Hermes, J. (1995) *Reading Women's Magazines: An Analysis of Everyday Media Use*, Cambridge, MA: Polity Press.

Hirsch, A. and Cherubini, E. (2018) 'Glossies so white: the data that reveals the problem with British magazine covers', *The Guardian*, 1 April, available from: https://www.theguardian.com/media/2018/apr/10/glossy-magazine-covers-too-white-models-black-ethnic-minority [accessed 24 January 2021].

Hudon, T. and Milan, A. (2016) 'Senior women', *Statistics Canada*, 30 March, available from: http://www.statcan.gc.ca/pub/89-503-x/2015001/article/14316-eng.htm [accessed 24 January 2021].

Hurd Clarke, L. (2011) *Facing Age: Women Growing Older in Anti-Aging Culture*, Lanham, MD: Rowman & Littlefield Publishers.

Iversen, S.M. and Wilińska, M. (2020) 'Ageing, old age and media: critical appraisal of knowledge practices in academic research', *International Journal of Ageing and Later Life*, 14(1): 121–49.

Jenkins, J. (2020) 'Magazines' construction of life markers', in M. Sternadori and T. Holmes (eds) *The Handbook of Magazine Studies*, Hoboken, NJ: Wiley-Blackwell, pp 226–40.

Kohli, M. (1986) 'The world we forgot: a historical review of the life course', in V.W. Marshall (ed) *Later Life: The Social Psychology of Aging*, Beverly Hills, CA: Sage, pp 271–303.

Livingstone, S. (1998) 'Relationships between media and audiences: prospects for future audience reception studies', in T. Liebes and J. Curran (eds) *Media, Ritual and Identity: Essays in Honor of Elihu Katz*, London: Routledge, pp 237–55.

Lövgren K. (2012) '"They see themselves as young": the market addressing the older consumer', in V. Ylänne (ed) *Representing Ageing: Images and Identities*, Basingstoke: Palgrave Macmillan, pp 53–67.

Magazines Canada (2016) 'Magazines: a comparison of Canada & U.S.', *Magazines Canada*, available from: https://magazinescanada.ca/wp-content/uploads/2016/12/USCanComparison2016English_FINAL.pdf [accessed 4 January 2021].

Mahrt, M. (2012) 'The attractiveness of magazines as "open" and "closed" texts: values of women's magazines and their readers', *Mass Communication and Society*, 15(6): 852–74.

Moeran, B. (2006) 'More than just a fashion magazine', *Current Sociology*, 54(5): 725–44.

Policarpo, V. (2013) 'Media, audiences and the life-course', in J.R. Carvalheiro (ed) *Media, Gender and the Past: Qualitative Approaches to Broadcast Audiences and Memories*, Covilhã: Livros LabCom, pp 25–60.

Québecor (2021) *Canadian Living Media Kit 2021*, available from: https://quebecorexpertisemedia.com/wp content/uploads/2021/04/Canadian_Living_mediakit_2021_FR.pdf [accessed 28 June 2021].

Rogers Publishing (2020) *2020 Media Kit*, available from: https://www.readkong.com/page/rogers-publishing-2020-media-kit-9379273 [accessed 28 June 2021].

Sandberg, L.J. and Marshall, B.L. (2017) 'Queering aging futures', *Societies*, 7(3): 21.

Sawchuk, D. and Ly, M. (2020) 'Older women using women's magazines: the construction of knowledgeable selves', *Ageing & Society*, 42(4): 765–85.

Twigg, J. (2012) 'Fashion and age: the role of women's magazines in the constitution of aged identities', in V. Ylänne (ed) *Representing Ageing: Images and Identities*, Basingstoke: Palgrave Macmillan, pp 132–46.

Twigg, J. (2013) *Fashion and Age: Dress, the Body and Later Life*, London: Bloomsbury.

Vividata (2020) 'Overview of results: winter 2020 study', *Vividata Winter 2020 Study*, Toronto: Vividata, February, available from: https://vividata.ca/wp-content/uploads/2020/02/Vividata-Winter-2020-Overview-of-Results-Eng.pdf [accessed 4 January 2021].

Vividata (2021) *Vividata's Survey of the Canadian Consumer, Spring 2021*, Toronto: Vividata.

Ytre-Arne B. (2011) 'Women's magazines and their readers: the relationship between textual features and practices of reading', *European Journal of Cultural Studies*, 14(2): 213–28.

Ytre-Arne, B. (2014) 'Positioning the self: identity and women's magazine reading', *Feminist Media Studies*, 14(2): 237–52.

12

The double logic of care: age, gender and media technologies in Austria

Barbara Ratzenböck

Introduction

Evident in the growing number of studies exploring older adults' use of information and communication technologies (ICTs), the topic of age, gender and media practice has become a central concern for both researchers and policy makers. Studies in the social sciences have documented the multifaceted and complex media use of older adults, such as their use of digital devices and technologies for staying in touch with family (Gales and Loos, 2020), pursuing leisure activities (Gallistl and Nimrod, 2019), following specific interests such as genealogy (Quan-Haase et al, 2016), tracking their fitness levels (Marshall, 2018), looking up information (Hilt and Lipschultz, 2004) and engaging in activism (Aging Activisms, 2016). Influencing this engagement are individual biographies, former work environments, specific skill levels and interests, as well as collective and structural factors (Ratzenböck, 2016). Despite the common stereotype that older people are simply not interested in 'new' ICTs, studies have shown that sociostructural factors, such as income, education and related literacy levels, access to technological infrastructure, generational positioning, lifecourse stages and gender, are most relevant to older adults' use of ICTs.

In the context of gender, it is notable that although early studies have indicated differences in older men's and women's engagement with ICTs, to date relatively few studies on older people's ICT use have focused explicitly on older women. Exceptions include recent investigations by Ivan and Hebblethwaite (2016), Fernández-Ardèvol (2019), Gales and Loos (2020) and Ivan and Nimrod (2021), as well as pioneering studies by Campbell (2004), Kurniawan (2006), Buse (2009), Loe (2010) and Sawchuk and Crow (2012). Many studies discussing older women's ICT use have either focused on specific purposes of use, such as improving health care and wellbeing (Campbell, 2004; Loe, 2010), or on aspects of use, such as the appropriation and usability of a device (Kurniawan, 2006). Studies that consider older women's everyday engagement with ICTs in a broad fashion are less common. In a similar vein, studies often examine older women's use of a particular device or technology, such as a mobile phone (Kurniawan, 2006; Sawchuk and Crow, 2012; Fernández-Ardèvol, 2019), the internet (Campbell, 2004) or a specific online platform (Ivan and Hebblethwaite, 2016), rather than considering a range of ICTs simultaneously.

Research on older women's ICT use has shown that they use technologies to express their lived experiences of age and gender identities (Loe, 2010). As Fernández-Ardévol (2019, p 98) puts it in her study on older women's mobile phone use, 'gendered pattern[s] of use' matter when considering ICT engagement in everyday life. Traditional gender and family roles influence ICT use and vice versa. Kurniawan (2006), in her UK study on older women's appropriation and use of mobile phones, notes that her participants predominantly used their phones to communicate with family. The older women in Buse's (2009) study, also conducted in the UK, used 'old' ICTs, such as radio and the television, as a backdrop for housework, while only few of the men interviewed did so. It is noteworthy that studies have repeatedly found that a familial understanding of ICTs is prevalent among older women. Sawchuk and Crow (2012) discovered that for Canadian women aged 65 and older, talking about mobile phones frequently meant talking about their own children and grandchildren, as well as their grandparents. Similarly, Ivan and Hebblewaithe (2016, p 19), who interviewed Canadian and Romanian grandmothers about their use of Facebook, state that '[a]s a relational identity, being a grandmother impacted the experience of ICTs, particularly social media'. In Peru, Fernàndez-Ardévol (2019) observed that the mobile phone is key for older women's support of relatives. In Gales and Loos's (2020) study, conducted with older women from Germany, relationship and family status were found to decisively influence older women's ICT engagement in everyday life.

Research also points towards a practical understanding of ICTs by older women. Conducting internet training sessions with older people in the US, Campbell (2004) found that the women's most common motivation for participation was to be able to locate health information online. For Kurniawan's (2006) participants, safety concerns were an important reason to engage with mobile phones. Similar observations were made by Loe (2010) with regard to older women's phone use. Finally, the literature review highlights older women's capability and interest in ICTs. In Campbell's (2004) study, it was mostly older women who volunteered to take part in a series of internet training sessions. Kurniawan (2006) notes that her participants were already well informed about the intricacies of mobile phone networks and were eager to learn more. Loe (2010) emphasises that older women are agentic and creative in their appropriation of technologies. Fernández-Ardévol (2019) found in her Peruvian study that older women were sometimes more proficient mobile phone users than men, which she attributes to their leading role in family communications.

Contributing to this growing body of critical scholarly literature, this chapter reports on a mixed-methods study that has explored how older women in Austria use ICTs in their everyday lives, including both 'old' ICTs (radio, television and a landline phone) as well as 'new' ICTs (a mobile phone, computers such as PCs, laptops and tablets, and the internet) (Ratzenböck, 2020). This topic is of high societal relevance. In Austria, considerably fewer older women than men are online, with 62.8 per cent of Austrian women and 77 per cent of men aged 55 to 74 years using the internet (Statistik Austria, 2019), implying women's increased risk of exclusion from participation in a 'digital society'. To contribute to preventing such exclusion, the chapter offers insights into older women's understanding of ICTs and critically discusses cultural beliefs, social norms and life situations that facilitate the use and non-use of ICTs in everyday life.

Older women are diverse and thus have diverse experiences with ICTs. Still, the study identified important commonalities in how older Austrian women make sense of media technologies in their lives. Most notably, their engagement with new ICTs is informed by a *double logic of care*: either they use new ICTs to care for others (particularly their families) or, on the contrary, report being too busy caring for others to engage with them.

Methodology

Consisting of a main qualitative strand and a supplementary quantitative component, this study employed a variation of an 'embedded design' (Creswell and Plano Clark, 2011). For the main qualitative strand, 12 women between 60 and 69 years of age participated in life graph discussions, guided interviews and walking interviews through their homes, sharing their experiences with various media technologies. Recruiting relied on referrals through personal and professional contacts, an information session at a computer course for older people offered by the city of Graz, an advert at a University of Graz event on ageing and ultimately snowballing. The interviews took place between December 2014 and February 2016, including three distinct phases of data collection, resulting in almost 30 hours of audio recordings. All interviews were conducted in German and excerpts were translated into English by the author. For contextualisation of the qualitative material, statistical data from the Austrian dataset of the first wave (2016) of the ACT Cross-National Longitudinal Study: Older Audiences in the Digital Media Environment (ACT Project, 2021) has been analysed.

The reason for limiting the chronological age range of participants was the need to create a comparable group of informants in terms of media generation as well as social age. At the time of the interviews, none of the participants of the main qualitative investigation were engaged in formal full-time work. Some had retired fully from work, others continued to work part-time in retirement, and one interviewee had been a homemaker and family caregiver for most of her life not pursuing formal employment for any considerable stretch of time. In addition, all shared a 'generation location' (Mannheim, 1952) regarding ICTs. All of them had grown up with radio, witnessed the more common popularity of television during adolescence and experienced the spread of mobile phones, computers and the internet in adulthood and/or during the late phase of their careers. Apart from these commonalities, however, the interviewees were diverse. In terms of residential area (urban versus rural), family status (living alone, with a partner or in a multigenerational household), levels of education (general, vocational or academic), occupation (manual, social or clerical), as well as levels of skill and engagement with ICTs, informants represented a heterogeneous group.

For the supplementary quantitative component of the study, responses of 1,281 Austrian internet users aged 60 to 70 (both men and women) were analysed. It is important to note that the quantitative survey was conducted online, thus only including older adults who were active users of the internet at the time of participation. As a group, the quantitative sample of women who participated in the online survey was proportionately well educated and urban, compared to Austrian women aged 60 to 70 in the general population (Statistik Austria, 2017; STATcube, 2018). For the analysis of the qualitative material, a three-part strategy was used, integrating elements of grounded theory (Glaser and Strauss, 2009; Corbin and Strauss, 2015), content-structuring qualitative content analysis (Kuckartz, 2018) and typification (Kelle and Kluge, 2010). This implied a combination of deductive and inductive coding and a circular approach to interpretation with numerous rounds of analysis to develop compact but nuanced categories (themes) from the qualitative material. The statistical data were used for descriptive analyses to contextualise the qualitative results.

Findings

In the overall study, the analysis of the qualitative material included three dimensions of older women's media engagement: (a) factors in their biographies that have had a major contribution to their media engagement; (b) evaluation of ICTs; and (c) ICT use in everyday life. This chapter focuses on the third category, on how and why older women use ICTs in their current day-to-day lives. Notably, much of older women's everyday engagement with media technologies can be characterised as *ICT use in service of others*. This includes family-centred as well as professional and community-oriented use. In the conversations, the women often foregrounded how they use ICTs to help others and to provide services to their families, friends and communities. Although the interviewees did mention more self-oriented and individually fulfilling ICT use, such as the pursuit of personal interests, education or 'casual leisure' (Stebbins, 1997, 2011), they usually focused on how they use ICTs in a manner that is beneficial to *others* and not primarily themselves.

As a central theme, ICT use in the service of others is an integral element of what has been termed in this study the *double logic of care*. This logic refers to both the purpose and extent of older women's engagement with ICTs. Frequently, either the women interviewed used new ICTs to care for others or, on the contrary, explained that they were too busy caring for others to engage with new media technologies. However, regardless of whether they were using new ICTs extensively in retirement or not, their understanding of media technologies most often revolved around the topic of caring for others. An illustrative example for this logic is the case of interviewee 7 (I7, aged 62). As a former owner of a grocery store in the countryside, I7 continued to work part-time as a shop assistant in retirement. On the one hand, family care work motivated her ICT use:

> '[B]ecause I look after the kids [referring to grandchildren], the small ones and everything. It already happened twice that while [my daughter-in-law] was at work and the school calls ... [to inform us] that [my grandson] is unwell, he has to be picked up. And I mean, fortunately, I have *always been available right away and able to pick him up and these are* the things in the back of my mind, where I think, well, if I have the mobile phone with me, I am available and then nothing can happen in that sense. Well, ... in some way I am a bit dependent.'

On the other hand, family care work had prevented I7 from expanding her ICT knowledge and participating in a computer class:

> 'I have always wanted to participate [in a computer class] at some point ... because there are students offering courses for seniors. But I never managed timewise with the kids [referring to grandchildren] because at the beginning I had to watch [my grandson] and there was always something, so ... I never managed timewise.'

Similar to I7, interviewee 9 (I9, aged 62), a high-school graduate working part-time as an accountant, emphasised the importance of the mobile phone for caring for her family. Although I9 used a variety of ICTs to support her grown-up children – such as the internet to do taxes online for one of her sons – the mobile phone was of utmost importance:

> 'Well, the mobile phone is like an umbilical cord. Without the mobile phone, I have to say, that might sound strange, but then [without the

phone] I feel [that] something is missing, that I am not connected with the world. You see, it is even in the bedroom. At night, I put it on silent mode, but I am always worried [about] the two sons, and I don't know why, but I am always worried if they would call, and I am not available. I always have to be available for them.'

These examples are representative of the interview material. As such, they highlight the vital role ICTs play for participants' daily family care work (Ratzenböck, 2017). The overall list of mediated care activities shared by the interviewees is impressive and includes using the internet to entertain grandchildren, looking up recipes for multigenerational household meals, making mobile phone calls to arrange grandchildren's doctors' appointments or helping their grown-up children with administrative issues. 'Old' ICTs also play a role in care work. The interviewees used both television and radio as a backdrop to make domestic labour more enjoyable.

In some instances, ICT use in service for others involved creative practices. Interviewee 4 (I4, aged 62), a commercial school graduate and former accountant, used her personal computer for family history writing, keeping a digital family chronicle in Word to stay on top of her extensive and continuously growing family and as a memory aid to avoid awkward situations:

'Sounds weird, but … we have a big family and at some point, I have noted down everybody with their siblings and their kids and there I note down certain things … because you cannot remember all of this . … [laughs] [If] we did not get there [to her relative's place] for a long time, I take a look [at the file], what was his name, what was the kid's name, how old is the kid, that helps a lot and prevents embarrassments [laughs] when visiting.'

ICT use with others in mind was often extended to colleagues and clients (for those women still working part-time in retirement) as well as to local communities, clubs and volunteer organisations. Interviewee 11 (I11, aged 66), for example, a former secretary and later small-town mayor, emphasised her volunteer work in terms of online communication:

'Well, with my children, with my friends, now with you [refers to interviewer], about the [non-profit network], where we do everything via the internet, well the mailing list, well, anything, if somebody has a PC [personal computer] and got me on their list, that is included. Also, all the associations, … that works via the internet, there is no letter being sent anywhere anymore and it works that way. Also, with the municipality, if I need something from there, I write an email … instead of calling.'

Almost half of the interviewees were active members of a club or association. In addition to the internet and email, participants also used computer programs such as Excel and their mobile phones for their activism and volunteer work. The older women also contributed to their local communities in informal ways. For example, interviewee 12 (I12, aged 67), a former accountant, now living alone in a small village, and her friend watch out for each other through regular 'check-up calls'. Calling each other daily, they make sure that the other one is well, particularly in winter when the weather is harsh.

It is key to note that it is not only the frequent users of new ICTs who referred to the topic of caring, but also those interviewees who explicitly identified as limited users. Interviewee 5 (I5, aged 62), for example, who completed an apprenticeship as a seamstress and then became a homemaker, explained her non-use of the internet by stating that the family dog prevented her from going online: "Internet isn't applicable ... because we have a dog, right." As the main caregiver in a multigenerational household, internet use and family care work were deemed incompatible (also see Bakardjieva, 2005), with both the dog and the internet merely assessed in terms of care. I5 underpinned this belief by explaining the frequent internet use of a friend by mentioning that this friend only had a small apartment and no grandchildren.

As noted, most interviewees who engaged with new media technologies on a regular basis foregrounded ICT use in the service for others. However, there were instances of countering the dominant narratives. When interviewee 12 (I12) emphasised ICT use for personal reasons, such as travelling, foreign languages and nature, she explicitly distanced herself from a traditional grandmother role:

'Most of my generation, ... they think they are indispensable, because they have to watch the grandkids ... There are no grandkids and I have to say, I don't care how this might sound, I am also very grateful that there are none, because I might not be able to take care of children as one imagines that because generally this is simply a part of it.'

The absence of major family care responsibilities was juxtaposed with the use of ICTs. Watching webcams of different cities as a daily morning ritual was described by I12 as unrelated to others' interests or needs, as being "for [her]self only". Despite her opposition to a traditional female role, she nevertheless made explicit references to gendered norms of caring. Thus, it is a key finding of this study that older women's sense-making in relation to ICTs includes notions of care. Regardless of what ICTs are being used for, *discursively* they are always linked to the notion of care.

The importance of relationships and caring for older women's ICT use is supported by findings from the supplementary quantitative component of the study. For example, in the online survey, both older men (n=692) and women (n=589) were asked to imagine that they had a few hours of free time and asked to choose their preferred pastimes from a list of various media activities. While only about a quarter of the men aged 60 to 70 said they would use their free time to call friends or family, more than a third of the older women expressed this intention. In a similar vein, while more than a quarter of the men would visit a website in their free time, only an eighth of the older women said they would. This is indicative of many older women's *relational* understanding of new ICTs, in particular as tools for care work and not primarily for leisure.

This resonates with results of previous studies. Talking to 240 Canadian older people, Sawchuk and Crow (2012) found that many older women used their mobile phones to be in touch with their grandchildren, while this was not the case for any of the male participants. Similar observations have been made by Fernández-Ardèvol (2019), who interviewed 37 older adults aged 61+ in Peru in 2013. This study showed that mobile phones were an important tool for older women to care for close and extended family, while this was not the case for married older men of the sample. Both investigations focused on older adults' mobile phone use and exemplify the relevance of gender norms for older adults' ICT use for a broader range of media technologies. Importantly, comparing studies from different regional contexts shows that gendered norms and expectations surrounding media use are critical to consider when investigating older adults' engagement with ICTs, as they seem to transcend geographical contexts.

Discussion

Looking at the empirical evidence, it is key to reflect on *why* caring is so prominent in older women's reported and actual use of ICTs. There seems to be several influential factors. As has been found in previous studies, such as by Suopajärvi (2015), older interviewees generally emphasised their busyness to comply with societal ideals of productivity. Such activity norms, Cruikshank (2013, p 207) argues, put pressure on older women to continue performing a 'service role'. Media biographies equally matter. The interviewees of this study, for example, shared a wealth of stories on how they had used media collectively throughout their lives. They reported on how they had watched television with others from the neighbourhood during adolescence, or how they had worked with large-frame computers together with multiple colleagues. Throughout the course of their lives, they had acquired an understanding of ICTs as collective objects. This concept also influenced their use of media technologies in retirement.

However, repeated analysis of the material, as well as comparison of the results with other previous studies, indicate that *general gendered norms of caring* as well as the *social desirability of the grandmother role* as part of a positive self-presentation are of special relevance for older women's ICT use in service for others. As a practice, caring for others involves two interrelated processes: perceiving others' needs; and taking actions to meet those needs in a responsible manner. As Cancian and Oliker (2000, p 2) note, the first of these in particular requires considerable emotional engagement: 'Care includes feelings of concern, responsibility, and affection.' Offering and receiving care is inherent to the human condition and a prerequisite for our wellbeing (Bozalek and Hooyman, 2012). Culturally and socially, caring and the work it implies is strongly gendered. Women have been and, in many instances, still are expected to provide care in various social settings. Living up to these expectations, women perform most of the care work in families and communities over their lifecourse (Backes and Wolfinger, 2009). The social norms stipulating women's considerable engagement in everyday care work are steeped in underlying traditional beliefs that caring comes 'naturally' to women in general and to mothers in particular (Albertson Fineman, 2017). Although caring as a cultural concept and social practice is also mediated by other factors, such as class (Conlon et al, 2014), gender is salient for its understanding. These strong general gender norms and deeply entrenched beliefs are likely to contribute to older women's service-oriented ICT use.

It is equally key to consider the *intersections* of age and gender to understand older women's frequent references to ICT use in the service of others. As international research has unequivocally demonstrated, age, like gender, is culturally and socially constructed (Woodward, 1999; Maierhofer, 2012; Cruikshank, 2013). Consequently, the lived lives of older men and women differ in important regards, such as income (Auth and Leitner, 2019) and the opportunities for social participation (Iller and Wienberg, 2012), for example in terms of leisure (Avital, 2017). Another crucial difference between older men and women, which is consequential for ICT use, is that older women usually do not retire from domestic labour or family care responsibilities (Calasanti and Selvin, 2001). This means that often, instead of retirement, other milestones are paramount for older women's personal identity and social perception. As Timonen (2008, p 158) highlights, '[f]or many women, widowhood and other family events (grandparenthood or the youngest child moving away from home) are more important as markers of old age than retirement from work'.

In addition to personal significance, the social role of grandmother attains high social acceptance and cultural legitimacy (Seidler, 2007), thus creating a grandmother type. This is exemplified by the gendered expectation that older women should primarily contribute to society through prolonged care work, while older men are called on to pass on their professional knowledge (Auth and Leitner, 2019). Therefore, grandmotherhood as a social role is 'cultural' rather than 'biological', as Soden (2012, p 99) has highlighted. To date, the cultural dimension of grandmotherhood involves rather restrictive ideals of behaviour (Maierhofer, 2003) as well as constant availability (Markhánková, 2019). In their discussion of ICT use, the women interviewed for this study clearly built on this normative cultural knowledge.

Nevertheless, it is important to note that grandmotherhood was not only important to the interviewees because of its social prestige and the behavioural guidelines implied a social role. Grandmotherhood also mattered to many interviewees in practical terms. Older women are high performers in the context of intergenerational care (Zajicek et al, 2006). Haddon (2006) has rightly argued that ICT use is not an end in itself, but it is social and people's interest in ICTs is socially motivated. Since older women are expected to, and also in reality do, perform considerable amounts of intergenerational care work, it is plausible that caring is a prominent framework for their discussion and actual use of ICTs.

In addition to social norms and cultural beliefs, however, older women's *agency* is also key for understanding their ICT use. Older women make well-considered decisions regarding their engagement with media technologies. The interviewees were acutely aware of many serious problems and risks related to ICTs. In the conversations, they addressed economic issues, such as the destructive market logic of global digital companies, which threaten the existence of local offline businesses. They were worried about the loss of jobs due to society's increasing digitalisation. The interviewees also observed negative consequences of ICT use on interpersonal relationships, such as more superficial communication. Other issues were security concerns based on in-depth knowledge of potential dangers posed by online fraud as well as violations of privacy through data misuse. In short, the interviewees had an accurate understanding of many serious issues related to ICTs. As older adults often link an awareness of a limited lifetime to their communication preferences (Yuan et al, 2016) and thus carefully evaluate whether a gadget or digital application is worth their time and fit for a distinct purpose, they are critical and conscious ICT users.

Conclusion

Older women's discussion and use of ICTs in everyday life is highly gendered and can best be described as revolving around a double logic of care. Frequently, older women in Austria and elsewhere use ICTs to care for others, particularly their families, or explain that they are too busy caring for others to engage with new media technologies. Older women's focus on caring is a lived reality providing indispensable care work for the community, but also feeds into stereotypical notions of older women as carers, thus limiting older women to narrow social roles in their scope of agency (Maierhofer, 2012). Addressing this perseverance of confining traditional gender and age norms, interviews and data need to be considered that *counter* prominent gendered narratives and patterns. The reporting of empirical results should not only convey the gist of an investigation, but also acknowledge elements that deviate from the common picture. In addition, interdisciplinary research is a promising practice in dealing with stereotypes. In many instances, the 'job' of social science research is to detail 'how things are' or, in other words, to focus on 'empirical facts', as Weber put it (Käsler, 1988, p 193). An interpretation of the interviews not only as data but also as narrated life stories would allow for an interdisciplinary analysis of also 'how things *could* be', offering 'counter world[s]' ('*Gegenwelt*') (Maierhofer, 2007). Future research on older women's ICT use can thus broaden the scope of our imagination.

Note

This project was supported by funds from the Österreichische Nationalbank (Anniversary Fund, project number: 15849), as well as a grant from the Social Sciences and Humanities Research Council of Canada to the 'Ageing + Communication + Technologies' project 895-2013-1018 (actproject.ca).

References

ACT Project (2021) 'Cross-national longitudinal study: older audiences in the digital media environment', *actproject.ca*, available from: http://actproj ect.ca/act/longitudinal-study/ [accessed 12 February 2021].

Aging Activisms (2016) 'Aging activisms media capsules workshop: telling, recording and sharing our activist stories', *Agingactivisms.org*, available from: https://www.agingactivisms.org/media-capsules-workshop-with-act [accessed 12 February 2021].

Albertson Fineman, M. (2017) 'Care and gender', in Y. Ergas, J. Jenson and S. Michel (eds) *Reassembling Motherhood: Procreation and Care in a Globalized World*, New York, NY and Chichester: Columbia University Press, pp 202–22.

Auth, D. and Leitner, S. (2019) 'Alter(n): doing ageing and doing gender', in B. Kortendiek, B. Riegraf and K. Sabisch (eds) *Handbuch Interdisziplinäre Geschlechterforschung*, Wiesbaden: Springer, pp 1185–91.

Avital, D. (2017) 'Gender differences in leisure patterns at age 50 and above: micro and macro aspects', *Ageing and Society*, 37(1): 139–66.

Backes, G.M. and Wolfinger, M. (2009) 'Frauen ab 50 – "andere" Chancen und Risiken des Alter(n)s?', in B. Blättel-Mink, C. Kramer (eds) and Bender, S.-F. (contr) *Doing Aging – Weibliche Perspektiven des Älterwerdens*, Baden-Baden: Nomos, pp 93–104.

Bakardjieva, M. (2005) *Internet Society: The Internet in Everyday Life*, London, Thousand Oaks, CA and New Delhi: Sage.

Bozalek, V. and Hooyman, N.R. (2012) 'Ageing and intergenerational care: critical/political ethics of care and feminist gerontology perspectives', *Agenda*, 26(4): 37–47.

Buse, C.E. (2009) 'When you retire, does everything become leisure? Information and communication technology and the work/leisure boundary in retirement', *New Media & Society*, 11(7): 1143–61.

Calasanti, T.M. and Slevin, K.F. (2001) *Gender, Social Inequalities, and Aging*, Walnut Creek, CA: Rowman & Littlefield.

Campbell, R.J. (2004) 'Older women and the internet', *Journal of Women & Aging*, 16(1–2): 161–74.

Cancian, F.M. and Oliker, S.J. (2000) *Caring and Gender*, Walnut Creek, CA: Alta Mira Press.

Conlon, C., Timonen, V., Carney, G. and Scharf, T. (2014) 'Women (re) negotiating care across family generations: intersections of gender and socioeconomic status', *Gender & Society*, 28(5): 729–51.

Corbin, J. and Strauss, A.L. (2015) *Basics of Qualitative Research: Techniques and Procedures for Developing Grounded Theory* (4th edn), Thousand Oaks, CA: Sage.

Creswell, J.W. and Plano Clark, V.L. (2011) *Designing and Conducting Mixed Methods Research* (2nd edn), Los Angeles, LA, London, New Delhi, Singapore and Washington, DC: Sage.

Cruikshank, M. (2013) *Learning to Be Old: Gender, Culture, and Aging* (3rd edn), Lanham, BO, New York, NY, Toronto and Plymouth, UK: Rowman & Littlefield.

Fernández-Ardèvol, M. (2019) 'One phone, two phones, four phones: older women and mobile telephony in Lima, Peru', in C.W. Larsson and L. Stark (eds) *Gendered Power and Mobile Technology: Intersections in the Global South*, London and New York, NY: Routledge, pp 93–107.

Gales, A. and Loos, E. (2020) 'The impact of the relationship and family status in retirement age on women's incorporation of technical devices in their everyday life', in Q. Gao and J. Zhou (eds) *Human Aspects of IT for the Aged Population: Technology and Society*, Cham: Springer, pp 207–25.

Gallistl, V. and Nimrod, G. (2019) 'Online leisure and wellbeing in later life', in S. Sayago (ed) *Perspectives on Human-Computer Interaction Research with Older People*, Cham: Springer, pp 139–54.

Glaser, B.G. and Strauss, A.L. (2009) *The Discovery of Grounded Theory: Strategies for Qualitative Research* (4th edn), New Brunswick: Aldine.

Haddon, L. (2006) *Information and Communication Technologies in Everyday Life: A Concise Introduction and Research Guide*, Oxford and New York, NY: Berg.

Hilt, M.L. and Lipschultz, J.H. (2004) 'Elderly Americans and the internet: e-mail, TV news, information and entertainment websites', *Educational Gerontology*, 30(1): 57–72.

Iller, C. and Wienberg, J. (2012) 'Altern und Geschlecht: Gesundheit und Wohlbefinden im Alter in einer geschlechterdifferenziellen Perspektive', in V. Moser and B. Rendtorff (eds) *Riskante Leben? Geschlechterordnungen in der Reflexiven Moderne*, Opladen: Barbara Budrich, pp 83–92.

Ivan, L. and Hebblethwaite, S. (2016) 'Grannies on the net: grandmothers' experiences of Facebook in family communication', *Romanian Journal of Communication and Public Relations*, 18(1): 11–25.

Ivan, L. and Nimrod, G. (2021) 'Family conflicts and technology use: the voices of grandmothers', *Family Relations*, 70(1): 104–19.

Käsler, D. (1988) *Max Weber: An Introduction to his Life and Work*, Oxford: Polity Press.

Kelle, U. and Kluge, S. (2010) *Vom Einzelfall zum Typus: Fallvergleich und Fallkontrastierung in der qualitativen Sozialforschung* (2nd edn), Wiesbaden: VS Verlag für Sozialwissenschaften.

Kuckartz, U. (2018) *Qualitative Inhaltsanalyse: Methoden, Praxis, Computerunterstützung* (4th edn), Weinheim and Basel: Beltz Juventa.

Kurniawan, S. (2006) 'An exploratory study of how older women use mobile phones', in P. Dourish and A. Friday (eds) *UbiComp 2006: Ubiquitous Computing* (4206), Berlin and Heidelberg: Springer, pp 105–22.

Loe, M. (2010) 'Doing it my way: old women, technology and wellbeing', *Sociology of Health & Illness*, 32(2): 319–34.

Maierhofer, R. (2003) *Salty Old Women: Frauen, Alter und Identität in der amerikanischen Literatur*, Essen: Die Blaue Eule.

Maierhofer, R. (2007) 'Der gefährliche Aufbruch zum Selbst: Frauen, Altern und Identität in der Amerikanischen Kultur: Eine Anokritische Einführung', in U. Pasero, G.M. Backes and K.R. Schroeter (eds) *Altern in Gesellschaft: Ageing–Diversity–Inclusion*, Wiesbaden: VS Verlag für Sozialwissenschaften, pp 111–27.

Maierhofer, R. (2012) 'Das Leben als narrativer Akt: Altern als Erzählen', in H. Mitterbauer and K. Scherke (eds) *Moderne: Kulturwissenschaftliches Jahrbuch 6 (2010/11). Themenschwerpunkt: Alter(n)*, Innsbruck, Vienna and Bolzano: Studien Verlag, pp 97–111.

Mannheim, K. (1952) 'The problem of generations', in P. Kecskemeti (ed) *Karl Mannheim: Essays*, London: Routledge, pp 276–322.

Markhánková, J.H. (2019) '"I want (to be) an active grandmother"– activity as a new normative framework of subjective meanings and expectations associated with the grandmother role', *Ageing and Society*, 39(8): 1667–90.

Marshall, B.L. (2018) 'Our Fitbits, our (ageing) selves: wearables, self-tracking and ageing embodiment', in S. Katz (ed) *Ageing in Everyday Life: Materialities and Embodiments*, Bristol: Policy Press, pp 197–213.

Quan-Haase, A., Martin, K. and Schreurs, K. (2016) 'Interviews with digital seniors: ICT use in the context of everyday life', *Information, Communication & Society*, 19(5): 691–707.

Ratzenböck, B. (2016) 'Examining the experiences of older women with ICTs: interrelations of generation-specific media practices and individual media biographies', *Nordicom Review*, 37(1): 57–70.

Ratzenböck, B. (2017) 'Everyday life interactions of women 60+ with ICTs: creations of meaning and negotiations of identity', in J. Zhou and G. Salvendy (eds) *Human Aspects of IT for the Aged Population: Aging, Design and User Experience: Conference Proceedings ITAP 2017*, Cham: Springer, pp 25–37.

Ratzenböck, B. (2020) 'Media Relations: How and Why Older Women Care for Information and Communication Technologies', PhD thesis, University of Graz, Austria.

Sawchuk, K. and Crow, B. (2012) '"I'm g-mom on the phone": remote grandmothering, cell phones and inter-generational dis/connections', *Feminist Media Studies*, 12(4): 496–505.

Seidler, M. (2007) 'Zwischen Demenz und Freiheit: Überlegungen zum Verhältnis von Alter und Geschlecht in der Gegenwartsliteratur', in H. Hartung, D. Reinmuth, C. Streubel and A. Uhlmann (eds) *Graue Theorie: Die Kategorien Alter und Geschlecht im kulturellen Diskurs*, Cologne: Böhlau, pp 195–212.

Soden, S. (2012) 'Redefining cultural roles in older age: grandmothering as an extension of motherhood', in V. Ylänne (ed) *Representing Ageing: Images and Identities*, Basingstoke: Palgrave Macmillan, pp 84–99.

STATcube – Statistische Datenbank von Statistik Austria (2018) 'Mikrozensus-Arbeitskräfteerhebung Jahresdaten (Q), Jahr nach Personen in Tausend, Urbanisierungsgrad, Alter in 10-Jahresgruppen und Geschlecht', *Statistik.at*, available from: http://statcube.at/statistik.at/ext/statcube/jsf/tableView/tableView.xhtml [accessed 27 September 2018].

Statistik Austria (2017) 'Bildungsstand der Bevölkerung ab 15 Jahren 2015 nach Altersgruppen und Geschlecht', *Statistik.at*, available from: http://www.statistik.at/web_de/statistiken/menschen _und_gesellschaft/bildung_und_kultur/bildungsstand_der_bevoelkerung/113112.html [accessed 12 June 2018].

Statistik Austria (2019) 'Internetnutzerinnen oder Internetnutzer 2002 Bis 2019', *Statistik.at*, available from: https://www.statistik.at/web_de/statistiken/energie_umwelt_innovation_mobilitaet/informationsgesellschaft/ikt-einsatz_in_haushalten/053946.html [accessed 8 November 2019].

Stebbins, R.A. (1997) 'Casual leisure: a conceptual statement', *Leisure Studies*, 16(1): 7–25.

Stebbins, R.A. (2011) 'The semiotic self and serious leisure', *The American Sociologist*, 42(2): 238–48.

Suopajärvi, T. (2015) 'Past experiences, current practices and future design', *Technological Forecasting and Social Change*, 93: 112–23.

Timonen, V. (2008) *Ageing Societies: A Comparative Introduction*, Maidenhead: Open University Press.

Woodward, K.M. (1999) *Figuring Age: Women, Bodies, Generations*, Bloomington, IN: Indiana University Press.

Yuan, S., Hussain, S.A., Hales, K.D. and Cotton, S.R. (2016) 'What do they like? Communication preferences and patterns of older adults in the United States: the role of technology', *Educational Gerontology*, 42(3): 163–74.

Zajicek, A., Calasanti, T.M., Ginther, C. and Summers, J. (2006) 'Intersectionality and age relations: unpaid care work and Chicanas', in T.M. Calasanti and K.F. Selvin (eds) *Age Matters: Realigning Feminist Thinking*, London: Routledge, pp 175–97.

Conclusion: Reflecting on ageing and the media

Virpi Ylänne

Introduction

In this brief conclusion, we will bring together some of the themes of the preceding chapters about the relationship between the media and ageing/older age. While there has been an increased interest in ageing and the media among cultural gerontologists and some media scholars, the chapters in this collection necessarily offer a select range of such scholarship. But importantly, they offer examples of studies in different cultural contexts and settings to discuss how the media make older age and older people visible, or indeed often invisible, and how older adults, and others, attach meaning to some of the representations therein.

The preceding eleven chapters have, for the majority, looked at how older adults are represented in the media in terms of the content or focus, the medium, geographical region and time. As older age is largely socially constructed, media texts and images contribute to this construction and to our knowledge of old(er) age. In Chapter 1, we noted how ageism intersects with other inequalities, and these have been explored across the collection. We have seen how older age is conceptualised as a problem and a vulnerability in various ways, such as when it is associated with declining health, including mental health, memory and cognition (Chapters 2, 3, 4, 5 and 8). This also links with the association of increased risks with age (Chapters 3, 4 and 5). Invisibility is another theme featured in the studies in this collection (Chapters 6, 10 and 11), rendering groups of older adults marginalised. Invisibility can also be realised in limited, or at times, overly 'positive' representations, as discussed in Chapters 7 and 8, in relation to visual media. We cannot, however, conclude that all media discourses and images are exclusively negative, and each dataset discussed is complex. It is also likely that different cohorts of older adults, and older adults in different socioeconomic groups, will be either more likely or less likely to identify with the models of ageing offered by the media. In fiction, as shown in Chapter 9, conventional ageing scripts are malleable and might offer alternative models of ageing, even though the storylines also rely on readers' recognition of 'default' ageing imaginaries. Chapter 12, in turn, displayed the articulation of societal expectations of 'appropriate' gendered ageing in accounts of everyday mediated practices. We will now revisit the chapters and their salient findings in more detail.

Reflecting on media and ageing

When arguing for the under-representation of older adults in media contexts – which has been a frequent empirical finding in this area of research – scholars might prescribe to a 'reflectionist' perspective in relation to the media (Xu, 2021, p 18). This view sees media discourse and images mirroring a pre-existing 'reality' and society. An expectation would then follow from this, that demographic changes, such as larger cohorts of older adults, would be reflected in their increased media visibility. Yet, arguably, 'reality' is not fixed, and producers of media texts make context-specific choices for specific purposes in representing social groups (Ylänne, 2015). We need to approach media representations critically, while acknowledging that they not only reflect, but also construct social reality, via selective processes. We can then appraise the selections that are made, and hypothesise, or empirically study, how they are received; in other words, what meanings are attached to the representations by the audience, and what are the consequences of this for individual media users themselves and for society more generally.

We started in Chapter 2 with the proposition by Higgs and Gilleard that UK media discourse perpetuates the bifurcation of later life in the contrasting 'third' and 'fourth' ages. These parallel discourses and imaginaries can be seen in the coverage of older age in the Western media more widely, and are alluded to in the subsequent chapters here, too. We should, however, be wary of resorting to a simple binary in the analysis of media discourse and imagery, and several chapters have expanded this binary further in relation to intersections with ageism and other inequalities. In the context of the recent COVID-19 pandemic, the predominant image of later life in the media, discussed in Chapter 2, has conformed to and reinforced the linking of old age with fourth age vulnerability and dependency, while those participating in the third age have resented being categorised as 'old', further contributing to the 'othering' of old age. Othering was a theme empirically demonstrated to characterise UK news discourse about older adults early in the pandemic by Ylänne in Chapter 3. By a close examination of some of the linguistic elements of news articles, including referring expressions, and the composition of headlines, it was shown how the texts used rhetoric about older people that homogenises them as vulnerable and at risk. While this coverage might predispose readers towards compassion and acts of kindness, and feelings of outrage at the treatment of vulnerable groups, the discursive strategies foreground and perpetuate the dependency script of old age, which risks reinforcing, rather than reducing ageism, including in older cohorts themselves. In this context, older adults who perform useful social roles become exceptional 'heroes', itself a marginal category.

A different kind of othering was discussed by Wilińska and Boateng in Chapter 4. An intriguing case regarding women, ageing and the media comprises 'present-day witches' in Ghana. We learned about the role of traditional and new media in exposing the prejudicial treatment of older women with mental health problems, or those who do not fit prescribed ways of being. Here, ageism intersects with gender, health status and possibly class, too. The media can play a role in dispelling long-held myths and superstitions, in this case about old women and witchcraft, and educating citizens about social problems and precarities. However, there is also a danger that stories about the treatment of such women, in this case, function as a resource for fulfilling the news values of surprise and extremity, and therefore result in sensationalising the issues, instead of propelling informed debate. Older adults invariably feature in the mediascape as 'extreme cases', either because of their agedness or, on the other hand, for seemingly 'defying' ageing.

Chapter 5 provided a language-based investigation of ageing and cognition, as presented in Taiwanese newspaper discourse about people living with dementia. Here, discourses of loss and decline predominate, constructing older adults with dementia as vulnerable, at risk and a burden to others, echoing the themes already mentioned. This type of representation contributes to the 'decline narrative' (Gullette, 2011) so frequently found, for example, in the media, reinforcing the fear of ageing. Of note is also a lack of individualisation, erasing the heterogeneity of this population, risking associations of dementia with ageing per se. In Chapter 6, on the other hand, Hurd and Mahal addressed the depiction of another minority social group in Canadian newspapers and magazines, namely older LGBTQ+ identifying individuals. Although many stories there are biographical accounts about named individuals negotiating their sexuality and ageing, a victim perspective was also found. Like in Chapter 4, news discourse can potentially serve a powerful function of exposing discrimination and prejudice, in this case towards those not identifying as heterosexual. This opportunity is not always fully realised, however, when older LGBTQ+ adults are the focus, due to discursive and journalistic practices that result in narrow depictions, often following heteronormative agendas.

We then moved on to examples of Brazilian advertising, discussed by Castro in Chapter 7, which highlights many parallels with previous research in the Global North. Castro critically approached the construction of active, and 'successful', ageing in promotional contexts, while reminding us of the need to take the target audience and the market segment into account in our analysis. Advertisers in Brazil and elsewhere continue the glamourising of 'agelessness', on the one hand, and are slow to let go of the many enduring negative stereotypes of old age, on the other, for example in relation to anti-ageing products, but also elsewhere. The priorities of the advertising industry and its fast-paced culture of production play a role in the end results, and it remains a challenge for age scholars to influence the industry.

A closer focus on the visual and semiotic representation of older adults in promotional contexts was taken in Chapter 8 by Loos, Ivan, Sourbati, Xu, Christensen and Ylänne, who investigated photos on public organisations' websites and social media. Country-specific case studies revealed comparable, but also varying, strategies used by organisations responsible for delivering services and providing information to older adults. Visual ageism in the form of the erasure of age-related limitations was found in the photos, likely motivated by the desire to positively promote the organisation in question and the service sector in general. There was also some evidence of a move to using fewer (or no) images altogether on some sites, therefore resulting in a literal erasure of images of older adults. While it is important to consider the specific context of the website or social media site and the organisation, as well as the predominant user group, the authors called for more evidence from older users themselves of the 'appropriateness' of the images. Some tools for analysing images are presented, so as to uncover the nuances of 'visual ageism', and to avoid simple designations of 'appropriate/ good' versus 'inappropriate/bad' images, and ultimately 'successful' versus 'failed' ageing (Sandberg and Marshall, 2017).

The visual theme continued in Chapter 9, where Dalmer and Cedeira Serantes discussed comics and graphic novels, which is a relatively underexplored area in age and visual scholarship. They offered a critical appraisal on five titles, originally published in different countries, in which the main protagonists were older adults of a range of ethnicities, sexual orientations, lifestyles and life situations. The comics thus enabled readers to explore a range of age-salient themes, such as retirement, reunions with previous romantic partners, intra- and intergenerational friendships, finding new love and even an experimental upgrading of ageing cells in a speculative fiction novel. Via a queering ageing lens (Sandberg and Marshall, 2017), the authors demonstrated how these texts engaged with the many contradictions of later life regarding one's identity and place in society. We can thus, again, problematise the representation of older adults via a reliance on simple binary categories, which has characterised much previous research. Graphic novels offer age scholars a fascinating avenue to contemporary, and possible future, imaginaries and 'realities' of later life, as well as the opportunity to think about ageism from a different perspective and modality.

The last three chapters addressed the reception and interaction of older adults with different media. Lövgren, Sandberg and Hearn, in Chapter 10, discussed how older men interpreted, and to what extent they identified with, print and multimodal adverts depicting old men. This contributes to scholarship on ageing and masculinities, which is a more neglected area of research than ageing femininities, especially in media research (see, for example, Richardson and Wearing, 2014). The focus group discussions in this study prompted shared negotiations of changing masculinities, but also evidenced the participants' relative inexperience in reflecting on their gendered ageing. This supports the proposition that older men's invisibility in the media reflects the privileged position of men in society, as, unlike women, they avoid being marginalised on the basis of age. This is arguably one consequence of gendered ageism. However, old men are thus also denied mediated resources for identity work. This serves to problematise the debates on the in/visibility of older adults and gender in the media. Interestingly, the authors opted for the term 'old' throughout, in preference for 'older', which is a term that age scholars have deemed more neutral, but which also arguably prevents us to reclaim the term 'old'. This practice might inspire others, too.

Chapter 11 also had a gender focus. Here, Sawchuk looked at the meaning and relevance of women's magazines to older women. We saw that many publications that are not explicitly targeting older female readers, nevertheless prove relevant to older audiences. Such readers employ their longstanding media literacy and life experience, and exercise their agency in selecting coverage that 'speaks' to them. Magazines provide resources for gender- and age-identity work and publishing houses should not underestimate the heterogeneity of the readers in terms of their age and other attributes. Interestingly, the women interviewed recognised the prominent age slippage (Twigg, 2013) in the magazines, meaning the content and imagery are incongruent (younger) in age terms with the (target) reader. This at times resulted in feelings of exclusion but was not always seen to dampen the enjoyment of the reading experience. The benefits of a lifecourse perspective were highlighted in understanding audiences with a past and a future and being linked in social networks. This perspective would also benefit the producers of media texts, such as women's magazines, underlining the desirability for a dialogue between cultural gerontologists and editors.

Finally, in Chapter 12, Ratzenböck considered older women's everyday engagement with information and communication technologies (ICTs) in an Austrian context. With the advancement and the increased relevance and necessity of ICTs to older adults' lives, this area is gaining international research momentum. Here, the focus was on older women's accounts of how and why they used ICTs in their daily lives. The main theme of 'ICT use in the service of others' reflects gendered practices in family, community and professional contexts. Caring for others functions as a heuristic and a prominent rationale surrounding the use of, for example, mobile phones. The women in the study also creatively engaged with other technologies to foster familial and communal links and responsibilities. Conversely, family responsibilities can stand in the way of older women's developing expertise in the use of ICTs. Again, we saw that earlier life experiences with the media influenced older adults' orientation to new communication technologies. We were also reminded of the cultural and social basis of roles such as a grandmother, which coloured these women's accounts, but which are also therefore subject to negotiation not only by older women themselves, but potentially also by ICT designers.

Conclusion

We have seen some similar themes cutting across different cultural contexts, perhaps demonstrating enduring concerns with human ageing, but also, at the same time, ageism. A degree of 'othering' has been discussed in Western, Taiwanese and Ghanaian media. Some regional differences emerge when representational strategies are examined at a micro level, such as the terms used to refer to older adults, which in Taiwan incorporate familial terms, reflecting sociocultural practices and age relations there. In the Ghanaian context, religious and superstitious undertones, prevalent in everyday language use, need addressing in media reports, too. Intergenerational tensions and changing gender roles, identities and identifications feature in European and North American media in relation to ageing. Brazilian advertising echoes the marketing strategies previously found in studies in the Global North in presenting 'agelessness' as aspirational imagery and rhetoric in a context of rapidly changing demographics and consumer markets. In various ways, we have seen evidence across the chapters of how ageing and ageism intersect with other social inequalities, be they based on gender, health status, sexual orientation or other social positions and characteristics. These inequalities can be exposed in the media but are typically obscured instead. This can partly be explained by editorial decisions based on media values, which can differ across the globe and across different media. The presumed values of the target audience play a part, too.

Iversen and Wilińska (2020, p 128) argue that some studies on ageing and the media fail to engage reflexively with the age categorisations they inevitably have to make in selecting data for analysis and so risk relying on, rather than challenging, existing stereotypes. It is certainly the case that research on advertising, for example, relies on semiotic and visual cues in order to select adverts depicting older adults for analysis, and the selection criteria vary considerably, using the chronological age of anywhere between 50 and 65 years as a threshold (Ylänne, 2015), although chronological age on its own is of course a problematic index of age. It is therefore crucial that researchers both problematise the strategies that different media use to depict older adults, but also reflect on the categories and descriptions that result from the analyses themselves in theorising older age.

In terms of the frequently found 'othering' of older adults in the media, discussed in many of the chapters in the current volume, it could also be argued that a narrow research focus on 'older adults' itself entails a certain demarcation, and might colour one's predisposition to find differences in the coverage of age groups in the media. As Fletcher (2020, p 7) points out, 'we cannot always develop methodologies sophisticated enough to fully respect the reality of aged heterogeneity, but we should nevertheless always be trying to advance in that direction'. Media discourses that perpetuate age stereotypes and ageist assumptions need to be exposed by age scholars, but we also need to advance the debate constructively by offering empirically grounded alternatives.

Closer interaction and dialogue between cultural gerontologists and media scholars would be a very welcome development (Iversen and Wilińska, 2020, p 137), and we hope to have partly addressed that in this collection. However, there is still work to do to promote a more nuanced understanding by age scholars of the functions and priorities of various media, on the one hand, and by media scholars of the multidimensionality of ageing and the heterogeneity of older adults and how they interact with the media, on the other.

This collection contributes to the growing area of critical research on media representations of older adults and older adults' interaction with the media and media technologies. Various gaps in scholarship remain, especially in research on older adults' use and interaction with the media, including social media (see for example the ACT Project, 2021). Social media afford their users, including older adults, to be part of global networks and communities, fostering connections that might otherwise diminish with age. Older adults as media producers (see for example 'Talking About my Generation' in the UK: https://talkingaboutmygeneration.co.uk/), on the other hand, affords an important counterpoint, offering to display how this diverse section of society wishes to be portrayed and what their priorities might be regarding media content. Research on such projects across the globe would usefully complement studies on media representations that have continued to predominate scholarship to date.

References

ACT Project (2021) 'Cross-national Longitudinal Study: Older Audiences in the Digital Media Environment', available from: http://actproject.ca/act/longitudinal-study/ [accessed 12 July 2021].

Fletcher, J.R. (2020) 'Chronological quarantine and ageism: COVID-19 and gerontology's relationship with age categorisation', *Ageing & Society*, 41(3): 479–92.

Gullette, M.M. (2011) *Agewise: Fighting the New Ageism in America*, Chicago, IL and London: University of Chicago Press.

Iversen, S.M. and Wilińska, M. (2020) 'Ageing, old age and media: critical appraisal of knowledge practices in academic research', *International Journal of Ageing and Later Life*, 14(1): 121–49.

Richardson, N. and Wearing, S. (2014) *Gender in the Media*, Basingstoke: Palgrave Macmillan.

Sandberg, L.J and Marshall, B.L. (2017) 'Queering aging futures', *Societies*, 7(3): 21.

Twigg, J. (2013) *Fashion and Age: Dress, the Body and Later Life*, London: Bloomsbury.

Xu, W. (2021) *Ageism in the Media: Online Representations of Older People*, Linköping, Sweden: Linköping University.

Ylänne, V. (2015) 'Representations of ageing in the media', in J. Twigg and W. Martin (eds) *Routledge Handbook of Cultural Gerontology*, Abingdon: Routledge, pp 369–76.

Index

References to figures and photographs appear in *italic* type.
References to endnotes show both the
page number and the note number (149n3).